HOME HEALTH REDESIGN

A Proactive Approach to Managed Care

Barbara Stover Gingerich, MS, RN
Consultant/Partner
Advantage Health Care Management Resources
Lititz, Pennsylvania
Surveyor
Commission on Accreditation of Rehabilitation Facilities
Tucson, Arizona

Deborah Anne Ondeck, BS, RN
Consultant/Partner
Advantage Health Care Management Resources
Lititz, Pennsylvania
Surveyor
Joint Commission on Accreditation of Healthcare Organizations
Oakbrook Terrace, Illinois

AN ASPEN PUBLICATION®
Aspen Publishers, Inc.
Gaithersburg, Maryland
1996

Library of Congress Cataloging-in-Publication Data

Gingerich, Barbara Stover.
Home health redesign: A proactive approach to managed care / Barbara Stover Gingerich, Deborah Anne Ondeck.
p. cm.
Includes bibliographical references and index.
ISBN 0-8342-0781-8
1. Home care services—Administration. 2. Reengineering (Management). 3. Integrated delivery of health care. I. Ondeck, Deborah Anne. II. Title
[DNLM: 1. Home Care Agencies—organization & administration. 2. Organizational Innovation. 3. Delivery of Health Care, Integrated—organization & administration. WY 115 G492h 1996]
RA645.3.G55 1996
362.1'4—dc20
DNLM/DLC
for Library of Congress 96-19464
CIP

Orders: (800) 638-8437
Customer Service: (800) 234-1660

Editorial Resources: Ruth Bloom
Library of Congress Catalog Card Number: 96-19464
ISBN: 0-8342-0781-8
Printed in the United States of America

1 2 3 4 5

To the memory of my father,
Ellis Roy Stover,
who taught me that you can achieve much
by setting your standards high.

Barbara Stover Gingerich

To **Jane Garwood**,
Editorial Director, Aspen Publishers, Inc.
Her interest and positive encouragement provided the momentum
to continue our pursuit of the completion of this project.
We want to thank her for her friendship and ongoing support.

Barbara Stover Gingerich
Deborah Anne Ondeck

Contents

Acknowledgments

We want to thank the many organizations with whom we have worked for their willingness to open their doors and their minds to us as we developed the core of information necessary for organizational redesign. Their humility, candor, and open-mindedness have provided us with a strong foundation and insight to consult with future organizations as they seek organizational efficiency.

Introduction

In today's health care arena, there is an ever-increasing emphasis on the efficient utilization of resources and the cycle of continuous quality improvement. At the same time, however, it is becoming increasingly obvious that such measures alone are not enough to prepare our home care organizations for the twenty-first century. As we reviewed the top 10 cost reduction strategies presented by the Magellan Management Group (February 1995),[1] it was easy to see that there were strategies with positive undertones and strategies with negative undertones. We asked ourselves, does any health care leader want to choose the strategies of benefit reduction, wage and salary controls, and layoffs? We think not. This book, then, offers the home care leader the opportunity to look at an alternative strategy, one that is more positive and proactive to the achievement of cost reductions. Cost reduction efforts are necessary to meet the impact of managed care as it emerges and spreads within our region and within our local catchment areas.

The buzzwords of values analysis, total quality management (TQM), and continuous quality improvement (CQI) have given way to the concepts of restructuring and reengineering. This book takes a look at the corporate principles of reengineering and applies these to the community home health care service provider. Because each organization is unique there is not one answer to the questions raised throughout the book. But rather like reengineering, where processes are taken apart and realigned for streamlined efficiency, this book takes apart the basic components of home care, such as fiscal, operational, clinical, administrative, and accreditation, and provides examples of how the principles of reengineering might be applied to each of these components.

To further define restructuring, this internal approach to redesigning the organization looks at only one component of reengineering—organizational structure. This approach is often undertaken from a cost containment or profit/loss perspective. It does not take into consideration external and impending forces for change. Usually this approach does not break down tasks as they relate to processes and work flow, but rather looks at the global structure of the organization.

Often, the words *reengineering* and *restructuring* are simply a cover for the distasteful terminology of downsizing. It is important that we, as home health care leaders, do not allow this to occur within our organizations. We must realize that using the facade of reengineering when the real purpose and force behind the process is downsizing does a great disservice to the concepts, principles, and process of reengineering.

What are we in home health to do to remain viable and meet the health care needs of future generations? When we downsize it can be an act of retreat and withdrawal. This is often the case when downsizing is a reaction to the marketplace in which we currently function. The organization that responds only to the now without looking to the future soon begins to live in the past—and at the very best—in the present. We lose sight of the very mission and purpose on which home care has been built—the provision of health care to those in need of services regardless of their ability to pay.

This does not mean we can continue down our current path without changing our delivery methods or our organizational processes. We must change to move forward. It is time that health care providers decide that change be constant, ongoing, and continuous. When we interview potential home care staff we must emphasize this basic premise. In the mission to reengineer for the future, we can ill afford to find ourselves surrounded by a group of dogmatic "we-never-did-it-that-way" staff.

In the past, nurses and managers turned to home care as a career because of the long-term relationships with the patients, the structured caseloads, and the established routines. This home care no longer exists. Today's managed care segment of the home care patient population is often seen for one or two visits and then discharged. The individual case manager's caseload is in constant flux, turnover is high, documentation needs vary from one funding source to another, and there is a general sense of urgency and turmoil. Constantly changing demands and shortened length of service time heighten the need to function efficiently and swiftly in the delivery of care.

With the advent of clinical pathways within the acute care setting, a definitive approach to care developed—a structured path that the patient's care followed. When the care did not follow these established paths an analysis of the variances and deviations from the established norm provided insight into the course of care within the acute care setting.

The home care arena has also spawned several examples of home care clinical/critical pathways, with each system varying slightly in its basic components. The CareMaps® of the Center for Case Management, Natick, Massachusetts, were one of the earlier systems. This system provided a standardized approach to care based on the primary diagnosis. Other systems of home health clinical pathways developed include the VNA FIRST, the Visiting Nurse Association (VNA) of Woonsocket, Rhode Island, and the All Care VNA of Greater Lynn in Massachusetts.

Each system provided a format for documentation and outcome measurements/goals. The clinical pathway system[2] published by Aspen Publishers, Inc., and developed by Gingerich and Ondeck completed the clinical pathway package with a standard of care for each discipline involved in the patient's care and teaching guidelines specific to each diagnosis. This system also included tools necessary to streamline the documentation of the home care organization. As its authors, we perhaps, in retrospect, designed our book on clinical pathways as our introduction to the reengineering process. Having made some minor changes to the documentation system as the organization grew, the clinical pathways approach was actually a reengineering of the documentation process at it existed at that time.

It appears that the development of the home care clinical pathway heralded the beginning of the restructuring/reengineering process for others in the health care arena, such as hospitals. In many hospitals and home care organizations, documentation took on a new streamlined and efficient format. "Best practices" were reviewed and formed the basis of many clinical pathways. The patient's treatment plan and physician's orders formed the core of the clinical pathway documentation system. In this book, we will go beyond the site-specific clinical pathway systems and look at reengineering concepts in relationship to networking with other health care providers.

The reengineering perspective of change is an all-inclusive, radical approach to total organization evaluation. Key organizational processes are identified and analyzed by the reengineering project team. The project team is designated to spearhead the project for the organization. The analysis of processes looks for related tasks, value of tasks, steps in each process, and work flow throughout the organization. All processes are analyzed from a customer, product, cost, and streamlining perspective. Resources that have been identified as necessary to support the new reengineered processes are given careful consideration. Computerization also encourages the restructuring/reengineering process. With the advent of in-field entry of admission data, the business and support service areas are prime candidates for process redesign.

This book will define the principles and concepts of the reengineering process and compare these to restructuring. It has been stated by Simpson that restructuring focuses on internal change and usually is a profit or cost containing force, while reengineering has patient care delivery as its focus.[3] Technology, with its potential to save time and contain or decrease costs, also takes on increasing importance in the reengineered organization.[4]

The emphasis of this book will be on the integration of the home care organization with other prominent health care providers. In order to network and integrate with other providers, we must first gain control of our costs and manage our resources. Human resources are among the most valuable resources an organization has and this book addresses the recruitment and ongoing development needs of our staff in the areas of orientation, competency, and understanding of customer expectations.

When large organizations reengineer, accreditation and regulatory standards and criteria often get lost in the process. This book provides an overview of some of these standards and criteria and suggests ways to apply the reengineering process so it will not negatively affect an organization's ability to meet credentialing standards and criteria. Operational processes are considered and discussed as well, with the aim to enhance the organization's marketability and public image. The key operational process of communication is discussed as it affects all aspects of the reengineering process. There is staff involvement at all junctures of the process and leadership skills necessary to obtain staff participation and to successfully reengineer the organization are also presented.

It is not enough to reengineer for today; rather it is vital that the changes prepare organizations for the future and enable them to maintain their newly streamlined structure. The reengineered organization is prepared to grow in the areas necessary to sustain it into the future. Resources are freed up and made available to develop new programs and services. The reengineered organization is free of the shackles that discourage visionary thinking. Instead of a responsive, reactive organization, the reengineered organization becomes a dynamic force shaping its own destiny and meeting the needs of future generations.

As we developed the concept for this book, we chose to build on the concepts of Hammer and Champy, take their applications from the corporate arena, and mold them to the home care arena—the future of health care. Dr. Michael Hammer is recognized as the leading exponent and originator of the concept of reengineering. He was recognized by *Business Week* as one of the four preeminent management gurus of the 1990s. His coauthor, James Champy, as the founder and chairman of the CSC Index, based in Cambridge, Massachusetts, headed the CSC's consulting group.

This management consulting firm pioneered the development and practice of reengineering within the corporate arena. These men were struck by dramatic performance improvements within corporations that they encountered in their business activities. Hammer and Champy then studied the commonalities of changes within these organizations. They discovered that due to the increasingly competitive climate, these organizations had chosen to look across and beyond functional departments to processes and work flow. This became the central, core concept of Hammer and Champy's reengineering work, i.e., taking a process or group of activities and their results and radically changing or recombining the steps or activities in the process for efficient and cost-efficient operations.[5]

Many times it seemed we were actually weaving a piece of cloth, instead of our final product—this book. Our experiences, our readings, and our conversations with those who had successfully reengineered within the health care arena were the warp threads that provided the foundation for the manuscript (when combined with the concepts and applications of reengineering). As we explored further the application of the strategies to home care, the weft was woven back and forth. Often, as we proceeded in developing each chapter of the book we felt much like someone who sat down at that loom not knowing where the previous weaver had left off in the weaving. Initially we wondered if we would ever complete the weaving, some days we wondered what final use would be made of the cloth we were weaving, and other days the loom awaited us when we had neither time nor inclination to proceed. Our approach to the development of this manuscript, like the weaving of cloth, soon became a reengineering project in its own right, in which we envisioned the end product and then developed the manuscript to that end. We discovered that the reengineering strategies we discussed transcend the chapters in the book, much like the web threads, growing when incorporated with specific examples of reengineering applications within the home care setting. When we address operational considerations, implementation, and evaluation components, these strategies and concepts once again provided the direction for the maintenance and the vision necessary for the expanded role of home care in the future health care world. It is our hope that this book will provide the warp threads, i.e., the foundation to cement the presence of home care in the forefront of health care in the twenty-first century and beyond.

NOTES

1. J. Sherer, Managing Chaos, *Hospital and Health Care Networks* 9, no. 4: 26.

2. B. S. Gingerich and D. Ondeck, *Clinical Pathways for the Multidisciplinary Home Health Care Team* (Gaithersburg, MD: Aspen Publishers, 1995).

3. R. Simpson, Reengineering: Embracing Technology To Improve Patient Care, *Nursing Management* 26, no. 1 (1995): 37.
4. Simpson, Reengineering: Embracing Technology, 37.
5. M. Hammer and J. Champy. *Reengineering the Corporation* (New York: HarperCollins, 1993).

Chapter 1

Reengineering versus Restructuring

CONCEPTS

The first concept in reengineering is the need to go beyond our paradigms and structures and be more open to new and creative thinking. So it is that when first faced with the reengineering/restructuring concept, the initial feeling has been likened to a railroad train bearing full speed ahead down the track.[1] As you begin the reengineering process, you realize that the organization needed to jump on board at the previous station. Then you look at your ticket to determine what stops are ahead and you discover your ticket is blank. That's when you realize that you have no idea where the train started, how you boarded it, or where it is heading. In fact, the train doesn't even follow the tracks!!!! So sit back, take a look out the window, and enjoy the ride. Reengineering is not just a blank ticket, but really is a blank page waiting for the future. As a leader in home care, you have been granted the privilege of being part of the groundbreaking journey. In fact the first step in the reengineering of any organization is to start with that blank ticket, envision the perfect solution, then proceed backward through the process to the beginning. Enough of that for now; we will discuss the strategy of starting with the end result, and other reengineering concepts, in much more detail later.

But you ask yourself what is reengineering and what is restructuring? How can I tell the difference? Reengineering begins with a drastic, radical evaluation of the processes of the organization. It means putting aside those paradigms and preconceived thoughts as to what home care is and isn't. It means being open to less tangible ideas and concepts. It means being willing to totally start over with all aspects of the organization! As the result of reengineering, restructuring often occurs, thus the confusion that restructuring is reengineering. Restructuring the organizational structure is often an end product of the reengineering project, but to restructure is **not** to reengineer.

CORPORATE APPLICATIONS

Corporate reengineering applications were discovered by Hammer and Champy[2] in the early 1990s. They recognized that several corporations that they encountered had achieved dramatic positive results in corporate culture change, cost-efficient streamlined processes, and customer service focus. They studied corporations in their quest for an understanding as to what had occurred and how it had occurred.

At this point you might like to ask, how do the corporate reengineering principles apply to the health care field and how do they specifically apply to home care? Looking at corporate strategies by several leading corporations will provide us with an answer to this question.

AT&T

As recently as September 1995, AT&T announced in a special news release to its stockholders that its strategic restructuring would capture opportunities for the twenty-first century. AT&T stated that its purpose for pursuing restructuring was as follows: to increase corporate value, to increase responsiveness to customers, and to focus on appropriate opportunities for growth.[3]

The restructuring involved the creation of the organization's communication service group, universal card services corporation, a consulting and systems integration organization, a wireless services group, and a dedicated research and laboratory unit. Independent of these would be their leaders of 1994—the AT&T Network Systems Group, Global Business Communication Systems, Consumer Products, Paradyne, and Microelectronics. AT&T also created an AT&T Laboratories unit and several other, smaller, more focused businesses. In addition, AT&T launched AT&T Global Information Systems as an independent company.[4]

All of these structures actually streamlined and decreased the steps in the process to change and allow AT&T to have a smaller, more focused, and more responsive business. Each company will have seasoned management, a productive and experienced work force, and will be customer focused. Each company will be expected to size its operations as efficiently as possible. AT&T's values are a driving force in the offering of job counseling, retraining, and outplacement for affected employees.

Recent quarterly shareholder reports continue to discuss the importance of this reengineering/restructuring effort in terms of remaining competitive in a fast-paced corporate world and being positioned to respond quickly to the customer's expectations. How do these recent actions of AT&T compare with the examples of Hammer and Champy in their book *Reengineering the Corporation?* Let's take a look at one of their examples, Hallmark.

Hallmark

One of the pioneers of corporate reengineering identified in Hammer and Champy's book was Hallmark. In fact, the authors state that Hallmark was the only example of a company that was stable, had a positive bottom line, was recognized as a leader within its competitor group, and was not in dire need of reengineering when the decision to reengineer was made.[5]

As a result of proactive visioning on the part of the Hallmark president, this organization, since renamed PCG, initially looked at the time that went into a printing run and the time from drawing board to sales room, the decreasing quantities of each run, and the increase in "niche" runs.[6] The president and senior management executives realized that everything in the company needed to be examined, from the beliefs and values of Hallmark to its business priorities and the linkages among the elements that affected the organization's performance.[7]

Strong in their belief that all employees need to know about the corporate reengineering, Hallmark's senior executives launched an organizational information campaign. This took the form of one-on-one meetings, group meetings, video- and audiotapes, written articles, and word of mouth. This information dissemination was the keystone in overcoming the employees' inaccurate and negative belief that the company's actions were only a cover for a productivity issue.[8] Gingerich's article, "Home Health Care Reengineered," describes this as the sheep-in-wolves' clothing syndrome.[9]

Some of the examples of the results of the Hallmark reengineering effort included: (1) point-of-sale computerization systems, which monitored inventory levels and provided instantaneous market trending and retail data, (2) decreased downtime in the process from marketplace assessment to new product availability by regrouping and integrating new product development teams, and (3) elimination of a hierarchical review of these teams' work and initiation of a self-review by teams.

Due to the size of the Hallmark organization—22,000-plus employees—this was a top-down process, however, the communication of information, the empowerment of employees, and the utilization of input from all levels of the organization was essential to its success. The Hallmark example is considered a successful reengineering effort.[10]

Summary

Can the above examples be applied to health care? The results that Hallmark achieved from its reengineering: increased customer preference information, decreased inventory, integrated and empowered design teams, decreased hierarchical approach to work, and decreased process completion time, are all applicable to the needs of today's health care organization and to the home care industry.

The citing of Hallmark as a successful reengineering example follows the examples set by Champy and Hammer. But doesn't AT&T's recent announcement of its restructuring—its goals, purpose, and process—also follow similar steps as the Hallmark example? This initial step of AT&T's strategic restructuring is just that—restructuring. But the next series of steps it must take and the ongoing review of tasks, processes, and operations within each of its divisions leads to the reengineering design concept. It would appear that AT&T perhaps has put the cart before the horse and restructured before looking at the processes. In reality, AT&T most likely has looked at processes before making a decision of this nature, and we will continue to receive announcements of ongoing restructuring as a result of the analysis and study conducted within each newly created existing entity of AT&T. They are truly seeking to contain costs and become more customer responsive in the process by restructuring.

To be truly ready for the twenty-first century, an organization must conduct an overall assessment of its operations, structure, and processes. These assessments will identify the strengths and weaknesses of the total organization and of its services, its corporate culture, and its employees. As a result of this total reengineering assessment, the unnecessary accumulation of tasks and processes in the corporation's work flow will be evaluated for continuation, revision, or deletion. This results in an efficient streamlined organization.

HEALTH CARE APPLICATIONS

What does all this mean to health care? Should we simply follow the leader? If not, how can we become the leading edge in restructuring and reengineering home care? How can we create the vision and the structure for health care that will take home care forward?

Acute Care Setting

Health care too has suffered growing pains similar to the Hallmarks and the AT&Ts of the corporate arena. The growing pains are felt not only in the acute care setting but in ambulatory care, outpatient, and community health care settings. In the acute care setting, facility growth occurred across the health care campus in a sprawling spiderlike fashion, scattering new patient care and high-tech care and services throughout the facility. The available space, new regulations, and new technology created obsolescence in facilities and equipment before the finished products and units even became available for use.

When technology advances at such a rapid pace, health care systems find themselves in a whirlwind—needing or wanting the newest in services, technology, and facilities in order to remain competitive, but not necessarily proceeding with a firm direction, complete view of the total picture, or a master strategic plan. As health care resources diminished and an increased emphasis was placed on efficiency and customer services, acute care found itself in the position of needing to take a full panoramic look at itself. Second opinions spawned a decrease in elective surgeries and outpatient surgery centers boomed. In 1983, the diagnosis-related group's (DRGs) reimbursement structure limited Medicare inpatient reimbursable days and in 1993 the ambulatory patient groups (APG) limited outpatient primary and ambulatory care reimbursement. The managed care industry providing health insurance coverage to the working population, limited the funding of traditional inpatient care days for many of the patients who were in this demographic population group.

All of these and many other factors combined to alter the inpatient care setting reimbursement patterns dramatically. Because of the size and relevance of acute care patient beds, reactions to these changes initially were felt within the inpatient settings.

The effects on ambulatory care settings have been slower in coming to fruition. It has become evident that the autocratic hierarchical organizational structure common to most acute care organizations has become a dinosaur destined for extinction within today's health care setting. Because of growing recognition by health care executives of the positive outcomes achieved in the corporate arena through the application of reengineering strategies, reengineering projects began to emerge within the acute health care setting. With increasing numbers of acute care providers utilizing the principles of reengineering for their organizational analysis, reengineering soon became the buzzword of the day.

Reengineering has become the buzzword of the day within the acute care setting. Key concepts that emerge from this setting include:

- continuous quality improvement (CQI)
- patient-focused care
- process teams
- critical pathways
- continuums of care
- on-line computer satellites
- ambulatory treatment units
- centers of excellence
- seamless network development
- flattened organizational structures
- values analysis
- enhanced bottom lines

One group of hospitals on the east coast utilized the concept of business process reengineering, which identifies the core business processes of the acute care facility as access, diagnostic services, care and therapeutics, materials management, hotel services/environment, and cash flow management. This group believed that these core processes intersected and transected nursing, laboratory, radiology, pharmacy, housekeeping, dietary, and the business services of the organization. From these core processes and operational segments of the organization, specific customer-focused and user-friendly goals were developed.[11]

No matter which concept or approach was utilized, dramatic results have been declared and maintained within the acute care arena of health care. These results have a natural outward growth from the acute care organization into the community in the form of integrated care delivery and health system networks. Regionalization of managed care contracts contributes heavily toward these trends and organizations are scrambling to ensure their competitiveness and presence within these systems of care delivery.

Home Care Setting

As these changes are occurring, home health care providers must ready their ships for the voyage. We have seen the results of the reengineering and restructuring process in business and industry and in other health care settings. By scrutinizing the corporate and acute health care arenas' efforts and achievements we have readied ourselves to look internally, as well as externally, to our organization and ask ourselves, "Are we ready to meet the health care delivery needs of the twenty-first century?"

WHY REENGINEER HOME HEALTH CARE?

Many home health care agencies have experienced spiderlike growth similar to that seen within acute care settings. For community-based organizations, such as the VNAs, care was initially funded through benevolent benefactors and the local community. In 1966, when Medicare certification became an alternative to this private funding, many of these organizations sought and obtained Medicare certification. The community-based public health departments were historically funded by state and federal grants and appropriations. These departments also sought and obtained Medicare certification and subsequent reimbursement under the Medicare home health care benefit that was established by the federal government in 1966. Proprietary, freestanding, hospital based, hospital affiliated, and joint ventured are just a few of the organizational variations for the delivery of home health care. Many of these were founded initially for the delivery of Medicare-reimbursed home care services to an elderly population with chronic health care needs.

Intermittent home health care services were the primary focus of delivery of care, but customer demands spawned many outgrowths of services by these organizations seeking to maintain their competitiveness. Today the home care organization might routinely provide private duty services; hospice care; high-tech pediatric care; prenatal, maternal, and newborn services; intravenous/infusion therapy services; rehabilitation services; mental health services; and in many cases, durable medical equipment.

Many home health care agencies also provide meals, transportation services, comprehensive outpatient rehabilitation (COR), adult day care, respite care, preoperative care, and preventive health care services. In reality, there is really no limit to the diversification opportunities available to home health agencies. It is this very diversification that necessitates and supports the reengineering and restructuring process and brings this undertaking to the top of the priority list for home health care organizations.

Even the traditional home health care organization can also benefit from the reengineering/restructuring process. Through this process, the single-focused or the multifocused home care provider can determine additional ways to enhance its market position, decide on appropriate expansion routes, increase its customer responsiveness, maintain its efficiency, and affirm its quality of services.

WHEN IS THE RIGHT TIME?

Because of our belief that it is never too late, we believe that no matter where an organization is in its existence or when it chooses to begin the reengineering process—that is the right time for that individual organization. From an objective outside perspective, the right time might be when specific organizational events are occurring, such as diversification of program services, expansion of service delivery areas, opening of satellite offices, or changes in reimbursement or in the patient population groups.

An organization's recruitment of a new chief executive officer (CEO) is a prime time for the organization to undertake this process. The organization should be identifying and verbalizing its mission, values, philosophy, and purpose so that when it selects the best qualified individual for CEO, it will select the individual who is most compatible with and in support of these goals. A reengineering/restructuring project team can initiate the process, and the new CEO's primary goal can be to carry it forward throughout the entire organization. This means the new CEO must be knowledgeable about and committed to the process of reengineering/restructuring as well as committed to empowering the organization's employees.

An organization can initiate a reengineering/restructuring process when considering the development or acquisition of a new service line or satellite offices. What better time to analyze fully current organizational processes and services, compare them to the developing or expanding service delivery, and revise processes as needed to support this type of expansion?

The right time to reengineer is not necessarily when the organization is making key decisions. The right time can be anytime: when responding to managed care's influence, or when responding to reimbursement changes, or when envisioning the future of the organization within the health care service field. All organizations, regardless of their size or structure, benefit from the process because it keeps employees better informed about the organization, more involved and committed to the organization, and more motivated in their approach to work. Besides the effects on the organization's employees, a reengineering/restructuring project of this magnitude enhances cost efficiencies, increases customer satisfaction with services, and empowers all employees.

REENGINEERING/RESTRUCTURING CONCEPTS AND PRINCIPLES

In order for the home health care executive to move forward in pursuit of reengineering the corporation, an understanding of basic reengineering principles is needed. What then are the basic principles and concepts of reengineering/restructuring? Some of the basic principles discussed at this time include visioning, creative thinking, change, amnesty, and empowerment.

Visioning

The overriding concept of reengineering that appears in all the literature and practical application examples is the principle of visioning. It is important that visioning become part of every organizational process analyzed and that each and every employee be aware of the visioning component of reengineering. Visioning is the process by which we are able to establish our vision. It is imagining and visualizing how things might be and the steps that we must take to achieve the outcome, i.e., the vision or the end result. Visioning entails thinking beyond the day-to-day and not allowing existing barriers to deter you from achieving future success.

Creative Thinking

It is not enough to remake our current organizations into more streamlined versions of our old selves; rather we must recreate our organizations by developing a new organizational mindset. Everyone within the organization must be actively involved and included in the reengineering. Information must be shared on a timely basis throughout all levels and operational divisions of the organization. Creative thinking means thinking outside of the paradigms of our experiences and accepting the unusual as the possible, giving credence to new ideas and potential solutions.

Change

Change is basic to the reengineering project; however, change will be radical, not incremental, and change will become a permanent fixture in the newly reengineered organization. Change is viewed as part of the organization, it is integral to the organization, and it is a positive component in the organization's ongoing success. Without change, the organization becomes stagnant and to be stagnant in today's health care market is to lose ground and competitive advantage. A cautionary word is appropriate here: Change for change's sake only can be detrimental to the organization. The change referred to as part of the reengineering process is planned, focused, and forward moving. We continue the weaving of the change thread in Chapter 6 as it relates to the operational considerations of a reengineering project.

Amnesty

It is important to include the principle of amnesty in reengineering the organization. The concept of amnesty is critical not only to the reengineering organization, but also to the learning organization and to any organization that wants to build trust and team support throughout. Amnesty means there are **no** negative repercussions to the individual as a result of honesty and openness of communications. It also means that information gleaned as a result of the reengineering team's process analysis is not used against individuals. A learning organization uses these findings and information to make process improvements. Situations where amnesty is given only lip service are more detrimental to the organization than the lack of amnesty. Do not purport to support amnesty and then use information gained in a negative fashion; to do so totally destroys the trust of your staff.

When true amnesty prevails throughout the reengineering project then honest and thorough analysis can be conducted of both the formal and informal processes in the organization. This can only be accomplished when blame is not placed and fingers are not pointed. Then processes can be examined and revised according to the needs of the total organization. The subtle difference between fixing the blame and fixing the process is a powerful one. To fix blame sends a negative message and vibrations throughout the organization, whereas fixing the process sends a positive message and vibrations throughout the organization. The reengineering organization knows that there are no sacred cows, no scapegoats, no untouchable positions or programs. Such an organization seeks to effect positive outcomes and influence the organization's processes, but not by punitive measures.

Empowerment

The last concept key to the reengineering process is empowerment. In the reengineering organization, employees do not seek to be empowered, rather they *are* empowered. Each individual is considered integral to the success of the process.

Employees are able to make decisions related to their work area, and with this decision making comes the empowerment. Gone are the tendencies to "Let Joe decide, I just work here." Instead, there is a commitment to process improvement from each individual employee's perspective.

MANAGEMENT ISSUES

In the reengineering project, the old ways of doing things are examined as if under a microscope. Why do we do each step of the process? Why do we do them in this order? Why do we do this step in this department? Who does this step in this process? How long does it take to perform that step in the process? How long does it take to get from this step to the next? Is each step/component of the process necessary? Can some steps be combined or eliminated? Do we need that many copies? Why do we do everything that we do?

Process analysis rethinking makes up the largest component of reengineering and in Champy's book, *Reengineering Management,* there are four management issues involved in process analysis. These are identified as the issues of (1) purpose, (2) culture, (3) performance, and (4) people and caring.[12] We believe each of these issues is an inherent component of each step of the reengineering process and that the organization should examine questions such as those listed below as they relate to each issue. The list suggested here is meant to be built upon by the organization, individualized, fine-tuned, and expanded to include items unique to the organization.

Issues of Purpose

The issue of purpose involves the basic why questions. Why do we do what we do, why do we provide the services that we do, why are we in this business? These questions illicit the mission and purpose of the organization and are the foundation upon which future process analysis is built.

From these global purpose-type questions can be gleaned the more specific process questions. Why do we want to complete this process and/or these tasks? Why do these tasks and steps make up the process? Why do we continue to follow the former structure of the organization? Once we can clearly state the *why* of why we are a home care organization and what services we should provide to support the organization's mission and values, we can further define the purpose of the reengineering project. We also can determine who are the best members of the organization to serve on the project team and how we can assist this team in succeeding. The issue of purpose is the heart of the reengineering process, for only after we clearly define our purpose can we move forward to define the process.

Issues of Culture

An organization's culture includes the written and the unwritten cultural norms, the formal and informal communication channels, and the formal and informal hierarchy or centers of control. How do we examine the effects of the culture on organizational processes? We must honestly seek the answers to the questions about our organizational environment. Is this an open trusting environment? Do we instill security and trust or fear and distrust in our employees? Do our employees have confidence in the leadership of the organization? Are there unwritten rules ("Do not publicly question the decisions made," or "Do not refuse to volunteer for additional work, no matter your current workload.")?

Are there traditions that, if broken, will hinder the forward progress of the organization; or if broken, will enhance the forward progress of the organization? Is there movement between the levels of the organization based upon real achievements and individual professional development? Does a glass ceiling exist for internal promotions? Can current employees only advance so far in the organization before external recruitment is used to fill positions in the upper levels of the management hierarchy?

An organization's culture and tradition can serve as the foundation on which a stable and futuristic organization is built or it can be the chain and anchor that prevents the organization from competing in the marketplace. Unless we thoroughly examine this issue as it relates to the organization's overall structure and to the individual processes and tasks, we will lose the effectiveness of reengineering. It is vital that the culture of the organization be examined closely prior to the implementation of the reengineered processes. If the organization fails to do so, it places itself in a vulnerable position and jeopardizes the chances for success of its reengineering effort.

Issues of Performance and Process

In some organizations performance standards have not yet been established, in other organizations established performance standards have been neither monitored nor met. Which organizations do you think are better off? That is truly an unanswerable question. The performance standards that must be examined as part of the reengineering process are not just those that are a part of evaluation, job descriptions, job responsibilities, and goals and objectives, but also the unwritten performance expectations an organization has set for its employees. The questions paramount to this management issue relate to the existing organizational norms, the traits and behaviors that are fostered and encouraged, and the consistency of the application of the established standards throughout the organization.

When we look at this issue, we need to ask if the employees are encouraged to try new approaches to problem solving? Do we communicate the organization's expectations and our expectations—as managers and leaders—to employees? To a few chosen employees? To all of the employees? Or none of the employees within the organization?

In the area of process, do we have established procedures? Do we communicate to employees how to approach tasks, the job, the customer? Is there consistency in the organization's overall performance with customer groups? Is the organization's performance based on the personalities of our employees? Is there too much structure and constraint to our processes or, on the other hand, are they too unrestricted and unstructured? What is the right mix of structure based on our organization's mission, values, and purpose? As we analyze the issue of performance process, do we find ourselves questioning whether our organization has the right leaders and workers? Do we currently promote people for the most suitable positions? If they do not possess the traits and skills we need, can we develop them?

Issues of People and Caring

The issue of people and caring is the last of Champy's identified management issues. Examining the work environment and the organization's leaders, this issue focuses on the atmosphere within the organization as it exists and as we would envision it for the future. What kind of workplace do we want? What qualities do we seek in the organization's staff and leaders? Can we find and develop these qualities within our current structure? Do we recognize and reward these qualities?

As the organization examines itself and its processes, it becomes better able to enunciate the qualities and traits desired in its workers and leaders. The values identified as important to the organization as a whole take on entirely new meaning when applied to individual workers.

Identifying what qualities and skills we desire and determining our abilities to elicit and develop these qualities or skills from within determines our direction for seeking them. External sources for these skills and qualities can be consultants, future joint ventures, affiliations, preferred provider relationships, networks, and integrated care delivery system relationships.

As stated earlier, these issues were identified as being present within all processes examined and analyzed as part of the reengineering project. Initially we must examine each issue closely as an integral unto itself and then as it relates to each process and to each task. Finally each issue is examined as it relates to the strategies common to the reengineering and restructuring process.

PROCESS ANALYSIS AND TASK BREAKDOWN

Since process analysis and task breakdown is essential to examining the issues discussed above, we will next discuss these components of reengineering. We briefly explained these two components earlier: process analysis being the examination of steps in the completion of a corporate process such as billing, and task breakdown being the listing of each task within each of the identified steps in the process. How do we perform process analysis and task breakdown? As part of a reengineering project team for a mid-sized hospital, we began with a totally clean slate, a blank page—no paradigms, no preconceived solutions, no expectations of how the end product would look.

In order to create a blank page, it is important to discuss the barriers to visioning. These barriers include not only those internal to the task force, but also to the organization. Examples of internal barriers might include the facility design, employee attitudes or paradigms, or the corporate culture. The act of identifying the barriers decreases their effect on the situation. Honest dialogue about barriers further diminishes their effects and frees up the participants to see beyond the horizons of today into the vistas of tomorrow.

Besides the internal barriers to visioning, there are external barriers. These can be within the organization's local community, or they can be regional or national in scope. Examples of external barriers might be the undecided future reimbursement structure for home health care services, the penetration of managed care within the organization's community, and the health care environment of the home health care agency. Here, too, it is important to identify, discuss, and minimize the barriers' impact on the project team's thinking and on the organization as a whole. The project team is the team delegated the responsibility to spearhead the reengineering project for the organization. This team should consist of recognized leaders of the organization as well as employees highly respected by their peers. The project team in turn identifies and assigns employees to task forces that are asked to explore and examine specific organizational processes and tasks.

Once barriers are identified and diminished, the process begins by imagining the perfect end solution—if the organizational work process being analyzed is the patient intake and referral process, the perfect solution might include an on-line up-to-date patient database providing information needed for admitting and processing the patient, developing individualized objectives, providing care, and billing processing. In seeking the perfect end solution, we seek the perfect outcome. This means we should redesign without any limitations placed upon us including our own paradigms.

Having envisioned the perfect end solution and anticipated result, the task force/project team now works backward through each process to the beginning—from the discharge of the patient from home care back through the initial home care admission through the home care referral from the acute care setting or other referral source.

As we reflect upon this process analysis, we find ourselves comparing it to the process of proofreading. True proofreaders, in search of perfection in editing, read printed matter from back to front rather than from beginning to end. This, it is believed, eliminates the mind's response to misspelled words, i.e., automatically correcting the errors in the mind's eye but missing the errors on the page. A similar flow charting approach is described in detail in Chapter 5. This can assist you as you proceed with the application of the reengineering principles.

Once the perfect solution is identified, the process as it exists today is broken apart and moved along the solution continuum, and we determine whether to retrofit or eliminate this process. It is critical to scrutinize each task in a process. Is it essential? Can we objectively support the validity of our reasoning or is this reasoning based on subjective conjecture?

The goal of combining or eliminating components of a task and of each process is to increase organizational efficiency and customer satisfaction. These reengineering concepts and principles as discussed today parallel several reengineering strategies utilized by a diverse cross section of organizations. Examples of commonly utilized reengineering strategies include decentralization, patient-focused care, cross training, elimination of duplicative efforts, and organizational redesign. These and other examples are discussed either at this time or can be found throughout the remaining chapters of this book.

REENGINEERING STRATEGIES

What can we learn from observing the reengineering efforts of other health care organizations, industries, and corporations? As we look at these service provider arenas, we see that reengineering projects can be grouped into several strategic categories, designed to achieve the following strategic objectives:

1. decentralization
2. patient-focused care
3. multiskilled workers, cross-trained staff
4. work redesign/simplification
5. customer-focused service
6. establishment and monitoring of standards
7. technological support

Decentralization

The reengineering strategy of decentralization has several purposes. When initiated, the locus of autonomy moves from the center of the organization to the individual program and department areas. This eliminates bureaucratic delays and enhances the front-line service provider's autonomy and empowerment. The home health agency's divisions will operate under a shared governance model. The decentralized operations result in an individualized approach to customer service and service provision.

This strategy is particularly relevant when the organization already has or is establishing branch or satellite offices and services. The branch and satellite offices can operate under varying community and geographic customs and norms, thus necessitating different standard operating procedures and structures.

Patient-Focused Care

The patient-focused model of health care delivery has emerged as a byproduct of reengineering within acute care settings. This care concept has always been integral to the home health care arena. Due to the distance between a patient's home and the provider's office and the required homebound status of the Medicare home health recipient, health care was delivered to the patient at home rather than transporting the patient from the home to the laboratory, to radiology, to the pharmacy, to the therapy gym, or to the mental health counselor. These services were historically brought to the patient rather than the reverse. This has now become the model of care delivery throughout many acute health care settings as a result of reengineering and is regarded as a reengineering strategy.

Multiskilled Worker/Cross-Trained Staff

With patient-focused care and reengineering in the acute health care setting, we find that the days of specialized job classifications are long gone. It becomes increasingly important to concentrate more work time on actual patient care, thus, the staff on inpatient units are expected to learn additional and more diverse work skills. Today, each staff member working bedside provides more services than in the past and possesses a greater diversity of skills. The newly established patient care job classifications within the acute health care setting include titles such as multiskilled worker or multiskilled technician. These individuals are all-purpose workers who provide housekeeping, personal care, dietary, and transportation (when necessary) services to patients. The care associate or care technician also is multiskilled, who as a cross-trained caregiver now provides not only basic and advanced nursing care, but intravenous therapy, phlebotomy, electrocardiology, and respiratory care and services to the acute care patient.

In the home care setting, cross-trained field workers are already on staff in the form of the home health care aide, who, in addition to providing personal care, provides light housekeeping, meal preparation, food shopping, feeding, and transportation when appropriate, according to agency policy. The home care case manager is trained in phlebotomy and intravenous therapy skills, as well as in rehabilitation nursing, and provides teaching in the areas of community resources, diet and disease treatment, and preventive health care.

These concepts are not new to home care providers; the efficiency gained by cross-training of field staff has long been considered standard operating procedure. In the reengineering process, however, the cross-training goes beyond the boundaries of the field staff arena and applies to job classifications of management and support staff positions. Staffing is paramount to the success of the reengineering project and is the keystone of the restructuring process. For that reason, Chapter 5 focuses on the topic of staffing in relationship to the standards of applicable accrediting and regulatory bodies. In Chapter 3, examples of our paradigms as they relate to interpretation of these standards and staffing requirements prepares us to examine staffing in a new way, without some of the traditional interpretation restrictions perceived to exist within these standards. (See Appendix 1–A.) Within Appendix 1–A can be found an example of a multiskilled job description and its corresponding performance appraisal. The development of these two examples took into consideration the accrediting and regulatory requirements present within home health care today. This appendix is provided as a resource to the organization for application when revising its existing performance appraisal/job description system.

Work Redesign/Simplification

Years of adding layers upon layers of actions, steps, and processes in response to the organization's interpretation of professional standards and regulatory changes have often yielded unwieldy tasks, processes, and systems of operations. For example, we still recall the time we first read the published *Federal Register* regulations in 1989 regarding home health aide certification and training revisions. This was regulation 484.4, in which the personnel qualifications for home health aides was specified as to the number of hours and content of training and the clinical competency testing requirements. We questioned the state department of health regarding the language of training or competency testing and were told absolutely that home health aides must complete the mandatory 75 hours of in-class training prior to certification and that only those aides "grandfathered" in could become certified by the competency testing process. We were convinced that what the lawmakers may have thought they had put in the regulations and what the verbiage actually mandated were two different things. We were correct in our interpretation of the new regulations and, by analyzing the regulations before implementing a 75-hour training program for all newly hired home health aides, we saved steps, money, and time in the recruitment and hiring of home health care aides. Being concerned with quality of staff, we made the training program available for applicants who truly needed the course work, but spared the organization from implementing a training process for all applicants that was neither necessary nor mandated.

The reengineering process analysis and task breakdown has as one of its primary strategies and one of its ultimate goals, the elimination of unnecessary tasks and duplication of work. The focus is on value-added work—work that adds value to the product and/or service, not just work for work's sake. The process identifies work that is deemed necessary and value added and focuses on enhancing this work. Where possible, tasks are simplified and kept together in one program or work area. This decreases the "travel" time between offices, and/or locations and between decision making and/or actions. The wait time from one location's schedule and the next location's schedule and from one person's priority list to another's is eliminated. As a result, the turnaround time for completing a work process is shortened, increasing efficiency and enhancing customer satisfaction.

The reengineering project team must take an "out of the box" view of professional standards and regulations to determine if the organization can take a streamlined approach to their interpretation. The interpretation of accreditation body and regulatory agency standards and criteria that results in streamlining of processes while still meeting quality expectations must be basic to the reengineering of home health care.

For that reason, this process—in itself a key to the success of reengineering within the home health care setting—is woven more elaborately into Chapter 3. This chapter discusses the application of this strategy with specific examples such as the one provided above.

Customer-Focused Service

Another reengineering strategy is to focus service goals to exceed customer expectations. In the home health care field, there are multiple customer groups and within each group one can find diverse expectations.

The first step in the process analysis of customer service performance is to review the existing and readily available data about the organization's customer groups. If the organization has not gathered these data, then a retrospective and concurrent survey must be completed to determine which customer groups contribute to the bulk of the referrals and what the reimbursement sources are for those referrals. In the process of identifying primary referral sources and customer groups, it should become evident that the organization's customers are both internal and external to the organization. This means our customer service expectations come from our referral groups, our patients, other community agencies, our funding bodies, our health care institutions, and our staff. The most commonly identified customer groups for home health care organizations often include those listed in Exhibit 1–1.

The focus of the reengineering efforts in the area of customer service is to exceed the expectations of all identified and unidentified customer groups. When considering external customers, many organizations have focused initially on admission, referral, and billing processes and systems of the organization. Much can be accomplished in these areas when an assigned task force or the project team work creatively and "outside of the box."

Autonomous decision making is a behavior that needs to be encouraged among staff and management so that the organization is more responsive to the customer and exceeds customer expectations. Other attributes that need to be developed among all staff are the abilities to be flexible and to individualize care and services. Listening and strong communication skills

Exhibit 1–1 Home Health Care Customer Groups

Referral Sources:	Collaborative Sources:	Internal Sources:
Physicians	Primary care centers	Staff
Acute care facilities	Community agencies	Peers
Long-term care facilities	Physicians	Other:
Community agencies	Insurer groups	Departments
Case managers	Health care facilities:	Program areas
Families/significant others	Acute care	Divisions
Patients	Long-term care	
Rehabilitation facilities	Rehabilitation	
Emergency departments	Mental health	

should be encouraged in all staff and staff should understand that they might find themselves in situations where the customer is not satisfied with the services. In these instances, listening to and reflecting on customer concerns and promptly resolving them is important. Customer satisfaction is everyone's responsibility, whether the staff member works in the office or in the field. Marketing is everyone's job and our staff our are best marketers.

Establishment and Monitoring of Standards

In order for their reengineering or restructuring to be successful, skill level expectations and efficiency of functioning must become the organization's culture and norm. Standards should be established not only by and for the staff, but staff should be evaluated consistently against these standards and expectations. These standards should provide measurable objective goals that are clearly understood by both the staff member and the evaluator.

Consistent, reasonable standards for every job classification and ongoing monitoring of staff achievement of these standards is conducted on an ongoing basis within the reengineered organization. All staff positions must contain customer service responsibilities and productivity standards.

Ongoing development of professional skills should be included in the performance appraisal system based upon the individual needs of employees within the positions.

Technological Support

Technological support is another paramount prerequisite for reengineering for integration. Technology provides access to and the ability to disseminate information across the continuum of care. Through state-of-the-art technology in the form of computerization and Internet capabilities instantaneous access is here. Laptop and handheld computers that can be used to document care are just one example of technology that can streamline tasks and care.

Besides computerization, other technological advances that support the cross training and efficient use of home care staff include enhanced communication technology such as cellular and mobile telephones. Ready access to office and physician staff and the ability to respond immediately to calls greatly improves these customer satisfaction areas. Chapter 10 provides more detailed information about other telemetry and telemonitoring capabilities available within the home health care setting.

Another example of ready access equipment is the tracking systems that provide continuous feedback to the office on the location of field staff at any given time. This technology can decrease the amount of downtime for both the office and field staff. Decreased telephone search time and decreased scheduling time results when this type of technology is in place within the organization.

The advances in communication technology provide the organization with the ability to respond promptly to inquiries for patient status updates and enhances the safety of the staff within the community. This communication technology will also provide support for networking with health care systems and for the integration of care.

TOOLS AND RESOURCES

As we discuss technology, we see that a basic component critical to the success of the reengineering/restructuring process is the availability of the tools and resources needed to implement the reengineering/restructuring outcomes and strategies.

We already have named some of the equipment and types of technological resources above: laptop or handheld computers, mobile or cellular telephones, and tracking and scheduling systems. Other resources vital to the success of the project are the human resources. This includes the availability of the key staff to participate on the project team and the task forces that analyze the organization's tasks, processes, and credentialing standards. Time is a major resource necessary to complete the project. Other resources crucial to the project's success include: team and employee involvement, good communication flow, employee participation, and adequate facility work space and support.

Team/Employee Involvement

Employees and teams must be kept well informed of the reengineering process and involved in the project early on. This involvement should begin with an employee envisioning questionnaire. Employees should be given the opportunity to contribute their input to the mission, philosophy, values, and vision of the organization and not be handed organizational statements that are already written in stone. Nothing is more frustrating and detrimental to employee morale than when key organizational statements are distributed and input sought, when in fact the employees have received the final product. If their suggestions are not given real consideration, employees will not believe in their worth to the organization. Employees are a valuable resource to the organization and when their input is sought it must be with sincere interest. Insincerity is easily recognized by employees.

Besides sharing these important statements, it is also important to interpret them to the employees in meaningful terms and examples. Examples of how they affect the organization's mission and demonstrate the organization's values on a daily basis will bring these statements alive to them.

Communication Flow

Crucial to the success of the reengineering process is communication. Resources need to be committed to maintain the communication flow throughout the organization at every step in the process. Newsletters and hot lines are examples of communication tools that the organization can use to keep employees informed of the project's progress.

Newsletters

Suggested strategies for maintaining employee involvement and communication include the development and distribution of a regular news update in the form of a newsletter. It is suggested that this newsletter be disseminated to the employees with paychecks on a biweekly basis and be a one-page, easy-to-read, and fun update on the project's status. The content of the newsletter should include a listing of the members of the project team and the task force, the processes being studied, current findings, and whom to contact regarding the process. It should also include planned completion dates for various stages of the task force's and project team's work. See Appendix 1–A for a sample newsletter format.

Hot Line Numbers

An innovative way to encourage two-way communication throughout the organization is to designate an on-line computer email location (REE.PROJECT@__HHC.COM) or a telephone hot line extension (REN-7336) that employees can use to make suggestions for process/system operations improvement, to volunteer to participate, or to seek information about the project.

Employee Participation

Communication strategies such as those suggested above promote discussion and shared information throughout the organization, but we must also encourage employee participation and motivation for the project to be truly successful. Communication within the large group setting as suggested above is one avenue for obtaining employee input into the scope and purpose of the project, but employee involvement must go even farther. The organization needs to encourage employees to develop their creative thinking skills. This process is examined more thoroughly in Chapter 9. For the purpose of gaining employee participation, it is sometimes necessary to use gimmicks such as a contest or game show approach. Several examples of these that can help your organization initiate a brainstorming session on employee involvement are included in Appendix 1–A. (See Tool 1–A–4.) These contests can be run throughout the reengineering project and the answers and winners published in special employee newsletters, such as *Reengineering Times.*

Facility Workspace and Support

It is important that the reengineering project team be provided with a workspace with sufficient room for posting of brainstorming ideas, process designs, and continuum of care models. The space should be designated and secured so that work redesign materials can be left in place and team members can work in the area individually as well as in team project meetings.

Facility redesign and support to meet the newly created processes is essential to the project success. These designs should be considered based upon the start-up costs and renovation estimates and should be an integral part of the outcome costing analysis completed for each reengineered/restructured process. The integration of care delivery and networking with health care systems will lend direction to the facility and space usage questions faced by the project team. Resources are needed to analyze and determine which facility redesign to implement.

CONCLUSION

When embarking on the reengineering/restructuring project, it is important to remember that not every nook and cranny can be analyzed at once, nor do all processes of the organization need to be analyzed initially. Through the course of the project, however, most processes will be considered, reviewed, implemented, and evaluated for efficiency. The cost of resources needed to analyze some processes far outweighs any benefits to be gained, so consider the costs versus the benefits before proceeding. Look to the projects that are far-reaching throughout the organization, feasible, and realistic to scrutinize and those that have the greatest impact on operational excellence and customer satisfaction. Choosing wisely in the beginning can save anguish in the results.

The tools provided in Appendix 1–A are intended for use by the organization in its redesign efforts. Tool 1–A–1 is the multiskilled job description and Tool 1–A–2 is the multiskilled performance appraisal, both of which were discussed earlier within this chapter. They are intended to be a resource to the organization in its redesign of its performance appraisal system. Tool 1–A–3, The Reengineering Times, is an example of a newsletter update format that the organization can utilize in communicating project status reports to its employees. In Tool 1–A–4, Employee Contests, there are examples that can be utilized by the organization seeking to generate enthusiasm and interest in its reengineering project.

NOTES

1. B. Gingerich, Home Health Care Reengineered, *Home Health Care Management and Practice* 8, 2(1996): 1.
2. M. Hammer and J. Champy, *Reengineering the Corporation* (New York, N.Y.: Harper Collins, 1993): 5.
3. R. Allen, Divide and Prosper, *AT&T Shareowners Report* 3rd Quarter. (New York, N.Y.: AT&T, 1995), 3.
4. Allen, Divide and Prosper, 2.
5. Hammer and Champy, *Reengineering the Corporation,* 160.
6. Hammer and Champy, *Reengineering the Corporation,* 161.
7. Hammer and Champy, *Reengineering the Corporation,* 163.
8. Hammer and Champy, *Reengineering the Corporation,* 165.

9. Gingerich, Home Health Care Reengineered, 1.
10. Hammer and Champy, *Reengineering the Corporation,* 165.
11. S. Blancett and D.L. Flarey, *Reengineering Nursing and Health Care* (Gaithersburg, Md.: Aspen Publishers, Inc., 1995): 287.
12. J. Champy, *Reengineering Management* (New York., N.Y.: HarperCollins, 1995): 6.

Appendix 1–A

Tools

Tool 1–A–1 Job Description

Position Title: Quality Coordinator
Program Area: Agency-Wide
Date Approved: ____________________
Review Dates: ________, ________, ________.
Reviewer Initials: ________, ________, ________.

Position Summary:
Responsible for the development, implementation, and revision of organization-wide performance improvement projects and safety monitoring activities. Oversees the infection surveillance and education staff in the areas of infection prevention, safety compliance, and performance improvement.

Reports to: Administrator/Executive Director

Experience and Qualifications
Licensed as a registered professional nurse in the state. Bachelor's degree in nursing, biology, or other health care-related field preferred. Possesses a minimum of three years of clinical experience with one year of experience in quality improvement, safety management, or infection control.

Competency/Skill Requirements
Competency required in the areas of interpersonal communications, excellent verbal and written skills, and knowledgeable of Medicare, regulatory, and credentialing criteria and standards. Able to utilize a telephone for internal and external communications. Knowledgeable of safety standards, spread of organisms, and the adult learning process. CPR certified. IV certified. Phlebotomy trained. Competent in the provision of nursing care.

Key Responsibilities and Duties

1. Develops and implements an organization-wide performance improvement program.
2. Coordinates the organization-wide review process.
3. Facilitates staff education in the areas of safety, infection control, and performance improvements.
4. Identifies quality indicators throughout service delivery areas.

continues

Tool 1-A-1 continued

5. Compiles monthly, quarterly, and annual reports encompassing the areas of infection, safety, and quality.
6. Tracks, analyzes, quantifies, and compares data relative to safety, infection, and quality.
7. Supervises the completion of patient and referral customer satisfaction survey data.
8. Disseminates quarterly reports regarding the customer satisfaction survey data.
9. Oversees the surveillance for infections of staff, patients, and caregivers.
10. Chairs the organization-wide safety and quality improvement project committees.
11. Develops, implements, and revises on an annual basis organization-wide policies relative to safety, infection control, and quality.
12. Maintains policies and procedures in compliance with state, federal, Medicare, and credentialing standards and criteria.
13. Performs other duties as assigned.

Working Environment
Potentially unsafe and unsanitary home environments. Potential travel in times of inclement weather. Office environment.

Position Physical Demands
Driving or riding a motor vehicle, standing, sitting, walking, bending, reaching, and stretching. Lifting up to 50 pounds unassisted and up to 325 pounds utilizing an assistive device in the home. Limited lifting in the office of files not expected to exceed 10 pounds.

Safety Equipment
Flexible goggles with side shields, anti-reflux respirator, protective gowns, aprons, and gloves.

Supervision Responsibilities __X__ No _____ Yes

Nature of Supervision: None

I, ______________________________, acknowledge receipt and understanding of this job description. I realize that this reflects a general list of responsibilities of the position, as well as a general description of the working environment and physical demands.

______________________________ ______________________________
Signature Date

Tool 1–A–2 Performance Appraisal

Employee Name: ______________________________

Date of Hire: ______________________________

Last Evaluation Date: ______________________________

Type of Evaluation:

Annual _____ **Three month** _____

Interim _____

Evaluator: ______________________________

Evaluation Date: ______________________________

Position: Quality Coordinator

Section 1: Key Responsibilities (rate as per organization's scale)

1. Develops and implements an organization-wide performance improvement program. _____
2. Coordinates the organization-wide review process. _____
3. Facilitates staff education in the areas of safety, infection control, and performance improvements. _____
4. Identifies quality indicators throughout service delivery areas. _____
5. Compiles monthly, quarterly, and annual reports encompassing the areas of infection, safety, and quality. _____
6. Tracks, analyzes, quantifies, and compares data relative to safety, infection, and quality. _____
7. Supervises the completion of patient and referral customer satisfaction surveys. _____
8. Disseminates quarterly reports regarding the customer satisfaction survey data. _____
9. Oversees the surveillance for infections of staff, patients, and caregivers. _____
10. Chairs the organization-wide safety and quality improvement project committees. _____
11. Develops, implements, and revises on an annual basis organization-wide policies relative to safety, infection control, and quality. _____
12. Maintains policies and procedures in compliance with state, federal, Medicare, and credentialing standards and criteria. _____
13. Performs other duties as assigned. _____

Section 2: Competency/Skills and Qualification Requirements (rate yes or no)

Licensed as registered professional nurse in the state. Graduate of an accredited school of nursing. Bachelors degree in nursing, biology, or other health care-related field. _____

Possesses a minimum of three years clinical experience with one year in quality improvement, safety management, or infection control. _____

Excellent written and verbal communication and interpersonal relationship skills. Able to utilize a telephone for internal and external communications. _____

Knowledgeable of Medicare, regulatory, and credentialing criteria and standards. _____

continues

Tool 1–A–2 continued

Knowledgeable of safety standards, spread of organisms, and the adult learning process.	____
IV certified.	____
CPR certified.	____
Phlebotomy trained.	____
Competent in the provision of nursing care.	____

Comments, if any:

Section 3: Supervision Responsibilities (if applicable) (rate yes or no)

None

Comments, if any:

Section 4: Employee Development

Section 5: Review of Goals

Status of Current Goals:

New Goals:

Section 6: Employee Review and Comments

Evaluator Comments:

______________________________ ______________________________

Employee Signature **Date**

______________________________ ______________________________

Evaluator Signature **Date**

Source: Courtesy of ADVANTAGE Health Care Management Resources Press.

Tool 1-A-3 Project Update Newsletter

THE REENGINEERING TIMES

VOLUME 1.1

SEPTEMBER 1, 1996

TASK FORCE Members	DEPARTMENT Process	CONTACT PERSON Extension	PERCENTAGE Completed

Complete with the organization's task force members and their telephone extensions, and then distribute. Each edition highlights a reengineering activity.

Tool 1-A-4 Employee Contests

NAME THAT PROCESS—The employee with the most processes/task forces correctly identified and submitted wins.

SHORT 'N SASSY REPORT—A three-part report: PART 1 Job process done; PART 2 Suggestions to improve the process, and PART 3 Name of person who can best accomplish the process change.

WE'RE IN THE VALUES—The employee finds the most day-to-day work examples of people demonstrating the organization value of the week. The most examples found and turned in wins.

NAME THAT PRICE—Selected items are given prices by the employees, the closest price without going over is the winner.

Suggested prizes include gift certificates and/or savings bonds.

Chapter 2

Organization for Integration

Few disagree that along with changing health care reimbursement patterns, there has been an evolution of the organizational structure of home health care. It involves not just talking with our competitors but sharing administrative staff in some cases, and even merging our organizations in other instances. Not more than 10 to 15 years ago, a great majority of home health care organizations were freestanding, independent in their operations, and independent from their referral sources. The pendulum has swung and now institution-based and corporate-based agencies are on the rise. Statistics established by the American Hospital Association show that in 1993, 42.2 percent of hospitals possessed home health care services. In 1983 only 14.8 percent of hospitals provided home health care services. This represents an increase of 27.4 percent.[1] In the dust that settled from this scurry of activity we find program administrators pondering the future of their organizations. Should they consider an alternative structure for their organization? Recognizing the value in vertical integration, many freestanding home health care organizations are faced with a decision. Should they be acquired or remain independent? Likewise should they acquire or be acquired? If the organization chooses to remain independent will it survive the impact when and if its local hospital develops its own home health care services? Is its current referral base, without the hospital, strong enough to support its business? Before we discuss any further the reasons for alternative delivery models, we need to understand the various types of models that prevail in the health care marketplace.

ORGANIZATION TYPES

Figure 2–1 is a linear model that depicts some of the alternative organizational structures found in home health care. It reflects not a stepped progression but rather a continuum of alternative organizational structures requiring progressive amounts of collaboration with other providers.

A freestanding agency is considered to be at the "None" stage, notwithstanding daily situational collaboration efforts. It faces many possibilities including that of becoming a preferred provider for major referral sources or a merging organization, joining forces with other similar or dissimilar, but related, organizations.

Preferred Provider

When an organization recognizes that its customers have needs for services that it does not provide, it may want to develop a special relationship with another organization providing that needed service. Since the federal government's Health Care Financing Administration (HCFA) developed the diagnosis-related group (DRG) reimbursement structure in 1983, the hospital became more responsible for the postdischarge needs of the patient. Previously, when a patient left the hospital with unattended health care needs, there was often resultant rehospitalization, which sometimes cast suspicion on the quality of hospital services. Hospitals therefore began to place increasing emphasis on this area of responsibility. They not only established discharge planning teams and made referrals to home health care organizations, but also began to question the types and quality of the

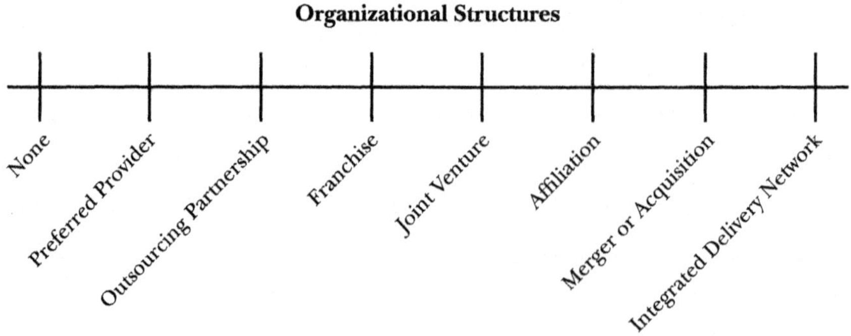

Figure 2–1 Progression of Collaborative Relationships

services they provided. Hospitals collaborated with various providers—commonly home health care and home medical equipment organizations—to ascertain their level of quality. Choosing one organization as the preferred referral source to be used in the event the patient had no preference helped assure the hospital that the patient's needs would be met with an expected level of expertise and quality. The expectation then becomes that the preferred provider works more cohesively with the organization through the development of coordination processes that meet the needs of both organizations and the customer.

Preferred provider relationships have come under public scrutiny for restraint of trade issues. To protect themselves, organizations using preferred providers must assure that the patient's right to choice is respected and that information is documented on the clinical record.

Outsourcing Partnership

At times an organization determines that a vital component of its business can be provided more efficiently by another organization through contracts. These contracts are based upon either a finite service, such as maintenance, or for a portion of the business, such as all therapy services. The contracting organization then delegates all responsibility for that specific area to the outside partner.

Benefits of the outsourcing partnership lie in economies of scale. The outsourced organization may provide an exclusive service—accounting, for example—for which it maintains a staff of 100 traveling accountants. Up to this point, your organization had a part-time accountant on staff, but you suffered from an extremely low retention rate because the accountants resigned as soon as they found full-time jobs. Maintaining a functional part-time position began to cost very large dollars given the high cost of recruiting, interviewing, hiring, and orienting. The organization, however, really does need complete, accurate, and ongoing financial documentation. Through outsourcing with an accounting organization this can be accomplished in a more efficient manner. This differs from contracting services in that the outsourcing agreement provides payment according to the volume, risk assumption, and your organization's profitability. An example includes hospitals that frequently have outsourced management, maintenance, laundry, payroll, and collections.

In developing outsourcing partnerships, the organization should seek the advice of legal counsel since both parties need assurance regarding the fine details relative to risk assumption, quality of services provided, and the maintenance of credentials. This is something worthy of thought and consideration. How will outsourcing affect the quantity of services? The quality of services? Will there be integration problems? Will outsourcing partnerships devalue the service in the minds of other employees? What can the organization do to make certain the outsourcing partner is accepted, respected, and considered an equal in matters of operation? How do we not give away "operational secrets" and thus put ourselves in the position of potential loss of business?

Franchise

Franchising involves one organization contracting with a parent organization for a business opportunity. The parent company has already developed the necessary expertise to operate the business and is available to provide varying degrees of ongoing support as specified in its contract. Franchisers may provide ongoing development, supplies, or services to the franchisee. As a result, the franchiser maintains some of the liability for the outcomes and operations of the business. Franchising requires legal counsel and the completion of well-developed contracts delineating roles and responsibilities of both parties in all aspects of the business operations. Agreements also specify the cost to the franchisee for the opportunity to do business under the franchiser and detail the issues that can result in termination of the franchising relationship. As a franchiser, an organization needs to develop processes to evaluate the quality of services provided by the franchisee, for "one bad apple in the barrel" would be a detriment to the entire organization. As a franchisee, an organization needs to have franchiser support when necessary but likewise the freedom to operate the business independently.

Joint Venture

Joint ventures are the equivalent of partnerships formed for the purpose of conducting one project of common interest. Although it is wise to seek the advice of legal counsel when developing a joint venture it is not required by law. An organization may want to execute a formal agreement to delineate the responsibilities of both parties in decision making, financial matters, and operational issues. If no formal agreement is executed, the court applies the laws of a partnership. Because joint ventures are relative only to one project all parties in a joint venture are ethically and legally responsible only for that one project. All organizations involved in a joint venture are liable for the obligations of the joint business regardless of fault. They must act in the best interest of the joint venture and not necessarily in the best interest of their respective organizations when that action could cause harm to the joint venture. In determining the legality of joint ventures, the court would consider the effects that joint venture may have on competition. The goal is to maintain competition and not restrict consumers' right to choice.

Joint ventures are dissolved when one of the organizations chooses to stop the relationship. Similar to a partnership, this can be done at any time unless it is otherwise stated in a legal agreement. Should one organization desire to dissolve the joint venture, legal counsel is recommended to assist with the liquidation of the assets.

Affiliation

An affiliation indicates some level of collaboration, be it a partnership, association, or preferred provider arrangement. The term *affiliation* simply implies a relationship of some sort among the organizations involved. The specificity of the affiliation is maintained in legal contracts or other documents.

Merger or Acquisition

Mergers or acquisitions occur when two or more organizations unite under one umbrella group and combine their assets and liabilities. (Figure 2–2) The organization being acquired becomes defunct. (For the ease of reading, this text refers to mergers and acquisitions as mergers.) When the organizations are publicly owned, the shareholders of each organization, prior to the merger, become shareholders of the newly formed organization. Mergers require legal consultation and must be approved through the court system for finalization.

Types of Mergers

Figures 2–3 through 2–6 show the three types of organization mergers that can occur: (1) the horizontal merger, (2) the vertical merger, and (3) the conglomerate mergers (for market or product extensions). Horizontal mergers take place when two or more organizations, previously competing to provide the same services, combine.[2] These mergers may sometimes be considered illegal because of the size of the increased market share of the new organization. This occurs especially when the merging organizations

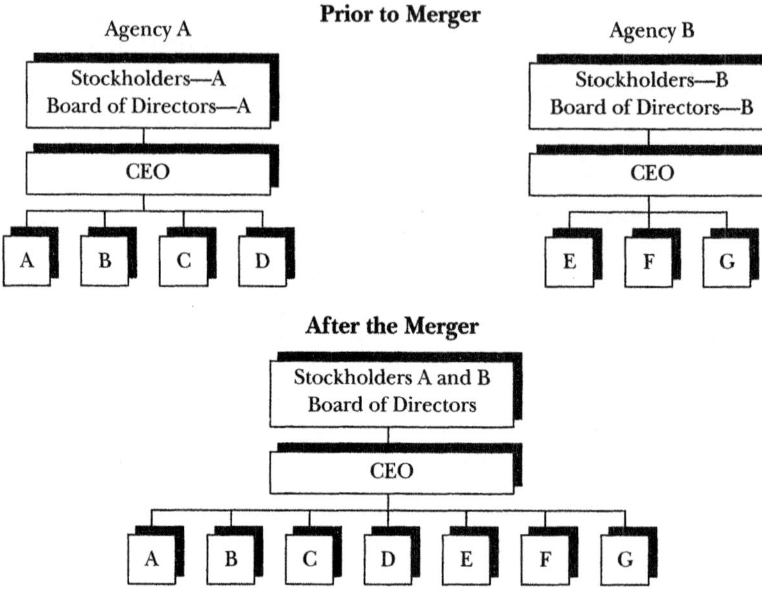

Figure 2–2 Merging Organization

share the same geographic market prior to the merger. The U.S. Justice Department usually considers the following essential factors in its determination of a merger's anticompetitive nature:

1. A trend toward concentration in the relevant market: Has the number of competing firms decreased over time?
2. The competitive position of the merging firms: Are the parties dominant firms despite their relatively small market shares?
3. A past history of acquisitions by the acquiring firm: Are we dealing with a would-be empire builder?
4. The nature of the acquired firm: Is it an aggressive, innovative competitor despite its small market share?[3]

Although the federal government has become less restrictive in its guidelines for merging, it maintains that mergers should not cause probable harm to their competitors. As courts concentrate on the effects of the local market, merger requests are challenged if it appears that the merger might restrain competition. Several exceptions exist, which are seriously considered by the court in the decision process. First, in the absence of this merger will the organization remain viable? If an organization is having financial difficulty or broad-based operational weakness that cannot be

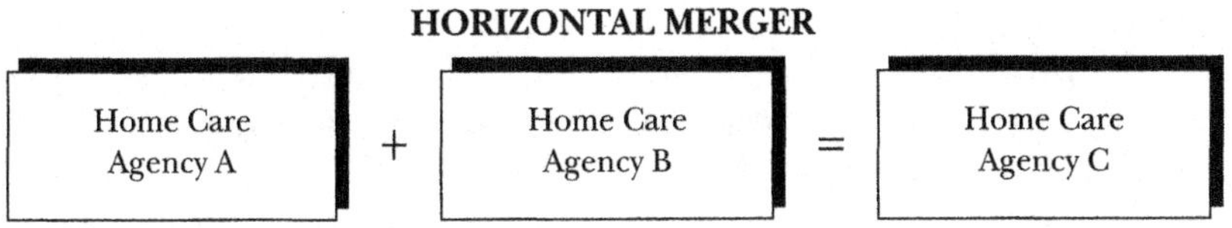

Figure 2–3 Horizontal Merger

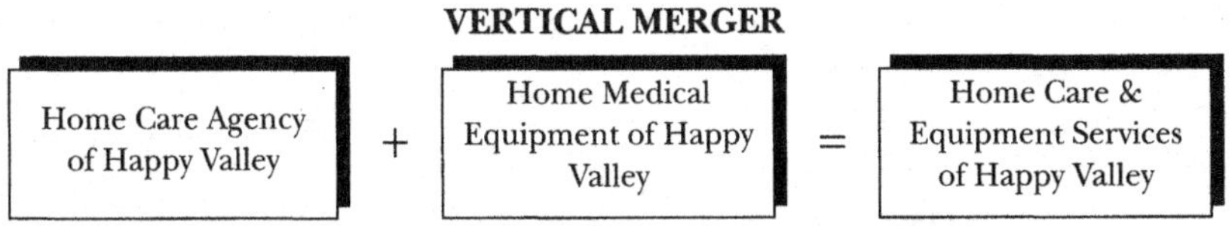

Figure 2–4 Vertical Merger

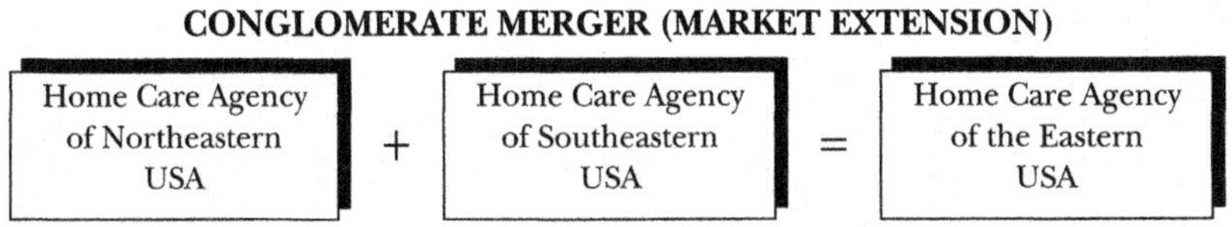

Figure 2–5 Conglomerate Merger—Market Extension

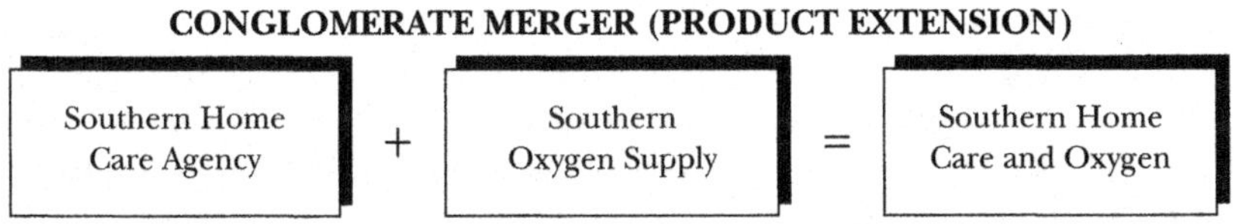

Figure 2–6 Conglomerate Merger—Product Extension

remedied without going out of business or merging, the government will usually permit the merger to go through in order to maintain the business and service for the community at large. Second, if the merger allows a market concentration in a geographic area, as is the case when several small agencies form to create one large organization, will it enable the newly merged organization to compete with larger organizations? Mergers are usually permitted in this scenario because overall restraint of trade may not be a consequence. The court also looks at the past history of the organizations desiring to merge. Have they honored their commitments to the community? Have they partaken in unethical business practices?

Vertical mergers occur when two or more organizations that previously enjoyed a provider-consumer relationship come together, such as a home health care agency and a home medical equipment company. This type of merger provides one-stop shopping and can be a threat to local competition in several ways. Recognizing the inability to compete for any portion of the vertically merged business, other organizations or entrepreneurs may choose not to compete in that particular service. This may create a noncompetitive market and consumers would no longer have the benefit of options. On the other hand, the courts do consider the efficiency of vertically integrated organizations.

Conglomerate mergers occur when two or more organizations that currently do not compete in the same geographic location or that have a supplier-consumer relationship unite under one umbrella. In addition to vertical and horizontal merging, Columbia Health Care has extended its market by merging with other large health care providers throughout the United States. This is called a market extension conglomerate. (See Figure 2–5.) Prior to merging, the individual organizations provided the same product—health care service. When products are added to a business, such as the case of Olsten Kimberly Quality Care, the merger is titled a product extension conglomerate merger. (See Figure 2–6.) Prior to their mergers, Olsten provided staffing services, Kimberly provided medical supplies, and Quality Care provided home health care services. Their merged organization now provides extended services in each of the previous organization's individual markets. When product extension conglomerate mergers are presented to the court, the court considers the customers of the merged organization. If it appears as though the suppliers of the individual organizations will feel coerced into buying more products from the merged organization to maintain their current business relationship, the merger may be denied.

Integrated Care Delivery Network

Currently, many health care organizations are vertically merging with other types of health care organizations along the continuum to develop integrated care delivery networks. Many continue to ask, What is an integrated delivery network (IDN)? Although the definitions may vary somewhat, an acceptable definition for an integrated delivery network is "a network of health care organizations and physicians that provide a coordinated continuum of service to a defined population. It is held clinically and fiscally accountable for the outcomes and health status of the population served."[4] An IDN is the one-stop shop of all one-stop shops. Key to the development of an IDN is the inclusion of the physician, because without the physician as an integral part of the network, the physician portion of the network would be outsourced to someone without the same level of commitment as a network member. Figure 2–7 describes the members of an IDN. The development of IDNs in existence today was driven by a variety of organizational leaders: physicians, hospitals, and payers. In 1994, it was reported that 24 percent of hospitals belonged to an integrated delivery system, with 71 percent in the process of developing such a system and only 5 percent not pursuing IDN involvement.[5] They are doing so to be able to steer their own ship in the future and retain as much of their current market share as possible. Perhaps in the future home health care organizations will generate an IDN!

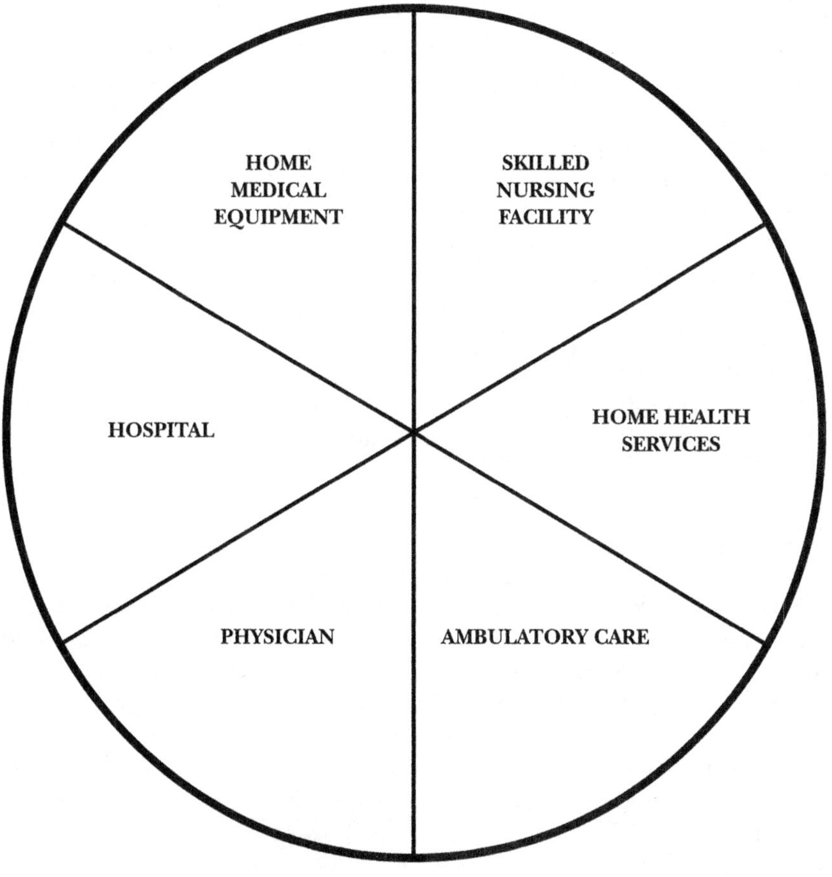

Figure 2–7 Members of an Integrated Delivery Network

Integrated delivery networks do seem to be the preferred health care structure of the future in the minds of managed care organizations that cover a growing percentage of insured lives on a yearly basis. (HMOs alone covered 50.5 million lives in 1994, up from 41.4 million in 1991.)[6] In the fall of 1995, a nationwide research study was conducted by the National Association of Home Care in Washington, D.C., and Fazzi Associates in Northampton, Massachusetts. Fifty managed care companies were asked questions about their current use of home health care. Interestingly, 42 percent of the organizations prefer to contract with vertical networks, if available, assuming they meet their needs. Also, 74 percent of those surveyed believe that they will provide services for Medicare in two years.[7] Given that the respondents included HMOs, point of service organizations (POSs), and preferred provider organizations (PPOs) representing various local, regional, and national markets, one must consider the perspective of the respondents. An independent study of local managed care versus regional managed care versus national managed care may prove to be more accurate in identifying the source of the results. For instance, are the 42 percent of organizations that prefer to contract with vertical networks national companies, or regional or local companies? Overall, the survey comments lead one to believe that vertical integration of quality services will result in more managed care business in the future.

What does all of this mean to the home health care organization of today? It is a loud and clear wake-up call indicating that change is needed to keep pace with the needs and demands of the payers. The need to become as efficient as possible is twofold: (1) either to remain viable as an independent organization, or (2) to become an enticing possibility for a potential acquisition. Acquiring organizations prefer organizations that provide quality services in an efficient manner.

DUE DILIGENCE

Prior to deciding about the level of collaboration or even whether an organization desires to collaborate with another in any form, it is important for the organization under consideration to be evaluated. The process of evaluation involves much investigation into all aspects of the organization to determine its true worth to your organization in dollar terms if a buyout is imminent. This process is known as diligence. The law acknowledges a variety of degrees of diligence, all of which carry different degrees of anxiety and concern. Due diligence is the amount of anxiety that a reasonable person would experience when deciding to merge, acquire, or partner with another organization.[8] The amount of concern and anxiety and the thoroughness of the evaluation conducted is determined by the parties involved, the type of potential collaboration, and the history of both organizations. It is not only acceptable but also expected that organizations preparing to acquire another take a block of time to perform due diligence. The due diligence process incorporates interviews, document review, and direct observation. It is suggested that the due diligence process include an evaluation of the following areas: external environment, internal administrative, human resources, financial, and clinical. Each list below includes specific items that should be evaluated in each of these areas.

External Environment

- Comparison of competitors
- Community needs assessment
- Organization's perceived strengths, weaknesses, opportunities, and threats
- Customer satisfaction levels

Internal Administrative

- Past reports of licensing and accreditation surveys
- Level of expertise and credentials
- Board of directors' level of commitment and expertise
- Structure and style of management
- Ratio of non-revenue producing staff to volume
- Capital
- Information systems
- Process improvement initiatives
- Productivity of staff
- Policies and procedures

Human Resources

- Numbers and types of employees
- Review of all contracts

- Salary and benefit package(s)
- Record maintenance
- Evidence of orientation and ongoing education
- Rate of retention
- Performance correction and review process
- Policies and procedures

Financial

- Assets and liabilities
- Financial ratios
- Condition of receivables and payables
- Policies and procedures

Clinical

- Level of expertise
- Types of programs
- Resources
- Equipment—amount, condition, and maintenance
- Records—presence and content appropriateness
- Utilization review of care to ascertain volume of services delivered versus volume of services needed
- Policies and procedures
- Application of the above to direct patient care

INTEGRATION OF SERVICES

Once the due diligence process is completed, a decision made, and the new structural framework implemented, the real work begins. This important phase involves the integration of processes and care along the continuum of care in a manner that reduces costs and maintains or improves quality. It now becomes clear why efficient and distinguished individual organizations are needed, because only the strong organizations will hit the ground running—prepared, ready, and capable of taking the new integrated organization to higher levels.

Essentially all processes need to be considered in a way that is individualized from the patients' perspective, incorporates the special needs of the level of care being utilized, and is based in integrated thought and process. To explain further, consider an IDN with a hospital, home care agency, skilled nursing facility, outpatient rehabilitation, and physician offices. A method of delivering care to a diabetic patient must ensure that, regardless of where the patient accesses his care, staff of that organization are aware of the IDN's coordinated plan for assessment, patient education, and treatment of the diabetic patient. The patient is diagnosed with diabetes and his primary physician's office staff begins the pathway to health for this patient. The office staff educates the patient about diabetes, specifically the definition and signs/symptoms of hypoglycemia and hyperglycemia. It also educates the patient about insulin administration. Physician offices are responsible to state departments of health for licensing, and as care delivery changes they most likely will become even more regulated. Although the physician office is following the IDN's plan of care for the diabetic patient, it is also attentive to the individual needs of the office to maintain credentials. Several months later that patient develops a subsequent appendicitis and is hospitalized for an emergency appendectomy. The staff in the hospital know the patient's complete history, including what information the patient knows about his diabetes. They do not duplicate the instruction but rather proceed to teach the patient about sick day management and special care needs, such as eye care and foot care. Once again, the hospital is following the IDN's plan of care for the diabetic patient and also other important functions specific to the hospital to maintain state licensure and accreditation status. It sounds simple, but consider all of the processes that need to be integrated: chronic disease care planning or clinical pathways, coordination of services with transfers from one level of care to the next, documentation and information flow, billing, data collection for outcomes measurement, and performance improvement, among others.

Rationale for Integrated Delivery of Care

The stages of changing health care delivery result from the financial influences of managed care. Urban areas with a more concentrated population are faced with higher percentages of managed care forces, forces that present two options: (1) change, or (2) lose the competitive edge and possibly the entire business. Business and industry have made it perfectly clear that they will no longer put up with the high cost of health care. As a result, industry has supported efforts at controlling health care costs and has found that managed care for employees is a bargain. Throughout the United States there are many areas that have been affected by a large volume of managed care and have been forced to change their health care delivery methods. For every area with advanced health care models, there exist other areas delivering care no differently than they did 20 years ago. This creates confusion for health care leaders in all markets. Should they begin to reengineer in anticipation of something that may not come for years, or should they continue to modify their delivery methods, knowing that their highly managed market is going to demand more and more efficiency?

Stages of Managed Care Markets

The managed care market stages have been divided into four categories—Stage 1 through Stage 4. In Stage 1, health care delivery is unstructured, with each level of care provided independent of the others. Perhaps some managed care from PPOs and HMOs exists, but no greater than 10 percent. This market views managed care as "more trouble than it's worth." Organizations do not have processes in place to meet the demands of the managed care companies. Stage 2 markets evolve as the HMOs and PPOs encompass up to 25 percent of the health care delivery. It is at this stage that organizations stop denying managed care's existence and begin to consider some major work to deliver their care more efficiently. Managed care companies are picking up momentum in these areas and soon develop a real foothold in the market. In Stage 3, several very large managed care organizations exist and managed care encompasses up to 65 percent of the market. This stage leads to chaos as organizations recognize an immediacy to their need to reengineer or face the consequences—bankruptcy. This is when the organization recognizes that it has more of the risk than the payer. If it is not efficient, it will suffer costs much higher than reimbursement. This is the stage that weeds out the weak and the ill-prepared.

The first three stages progress to the final stage as we know it today—Stage 4, or managed competition. In this stage, 100 percent of the care is reimbursed by managed care. Industries and other employers unite in their quest for health care coverage and find strength in those numbers. They purchase managed care from the most cost-effective source and contracts for coverage are so large that a loss of a contract may lead to the demise of that particular managed care company. At this stage there is much to be lost for the employers, payer, and the provider. To circumvent their risk, some HMOs are merging with IDNs, something considered absurd in the past. Fortunately for the public, 98 percent of today's managed care companies identify quality as an important factor in contracting with organizations.[9]

CONCLUSION

Although this sounds bleak for home health care providers, there are ways to increase efficiency while maintaining quality and that is what this book is all about. In Chapter 7, we'll look at some of our restraining forces as we perceive them to be. We'll consider the expectations of the HCFA and several of the accreditation bodies. There is hope for a future as a provider and at the end of this journey all consumers of health care will enjoy affordable quality services. Granted, the process may not be pleasant, but it is a process that we must embark upon for survival.

NOTES

1. American Hospital Association, *SACP Trendlines,* October 1995, 2.
2. M.B. Metzger, et al., *Business Law and the Regulatory Environment, Concepts and Cases,* 9th ed. (Homewood, Ill.: Richard D. Irwin, Inc., 1995), 1052.
3. Metzger, et al., *Business Law,* 1053.
4. C. Curran, Developing Integrated Delivery Networks (Presentation at meeting of the American College of Healthcare Executives, Williamsburg, Virginia, August 1995).
5. C. Curran, Developing Integrated Delivery Networks, August 1995.
6. Group Health Association of America, *National Directory of HMOs Database, 1994 HMO Performance Survey,* Washington, D.C.
7. What Managed Care Companies Want and Expect from Home Care (Presentation at annual meeting of National Association for Home Care, October 1995).
8. H.C. Black, *Black's Law Dictionary,* 5th ed. (St. Paul, Minn.: West Publishing Co., 1979), 411.
9. C. Curran, Developing Integrated Delivery Networks, August 1995.

Chapter 3

Meeting Credentialing Expectations in the Restructured Organization

This chapter is one of the most difficult to write in a reengineering book simply because complying with regulations and standards is the foundation of our organizations—it's our bread and butter; our measure of success. People are inherently fearful of change and change that stretches the limits of generally accepted interpretation is beyond comprehension for us where we are most secure... inside our box. Within our organizations we have what we'll term as "sleepers." Sleepers are the employees who come to work on time, do their job, and leave. They never challenge anything or anyone. If the CEO announced that the sky was going to fall at 1300 hours, the sleeper would listen and go back to doing his job as though the announcement was never made. Many consider sleepers to be good employees because they cause no disruptions and pose no challenges. They just do their job. Sleepers feel safe and secure and so they should. Sleepers are rarely the cause of trouble and their personnel files are exemplary. Sometimes sleepers retire and colleagues learn their names for the first time because sleepers always just did what their boss told them to do—they followed all of the accepted rules. But if organizations had only sleepers working for them, our world would soon become stagnant. With only sleepers in our work world there would be no one to stir things up. There would be no challenges to what is known and accepted because everyone would "just be doing their jobs."

Identifying the rules becomes an interesting process. Whose rules are they? Are they rules set out by the accreditation board or by HCFA, or are they the rules as *interpreted* by the state surveyor who visits your region annually? There is a saying, "You are what you were when." This saying is worthy of reflection as we recognize that each of us has a collection of different experiences, experiences that govern how we interpret what we see, read, and hear. These experiences contribute to the fact that only 7 percent of what is communicated is understood. Think about it. You say something to an audience of 100 people and only seven of those people understand the message sent. So we ask, are you interpreting the spoken word of your surveyor as he intended it to be received? Are we interpreting written standards and conditions as regulators intended when they sent their message? Did HCFA interpret the desires of Congress appropriately before it committed them to writing? Consider the legislative changes made in the area of home health aide training. In one state, the Department of Health and the Association for Home Health Agencies conducted regional meetings to explain the newly written regulations. In their explanation they stated that every aide hired after August 14, 1990 was required to meet the personnel qualifications specified in regulation 484.4. This regulation specified the number of hours of formal training an employee needed prior to being certified as a home health aide. One of the authors questioned this interpretation. Her reading and interpretation of the regulation was that the aide needed to complete the structured aide training *or* show evidence of passing a competency test in the outlined areas. A memo was issued within a month indicating that the author's interpretation was correct and that the Department of Health and the state association provided erroneous information at many of the statewide meetings. It was the author's challenge of the message that led to a more relaxed interpretation of this particular standard. In retrospect, we learned that the legislators did not intend to have the certification of home health aides be an either/or scenario. The written standard, however, clearly expressed *either* the training course *or* successful completion of a competency test. This story demonstrates the power of reading the standard, analyzing its content rationally, and then diplomatically challenging the interpretations of others, even our surveyors.

There will be times during the reengineering process that our creativity will take us to a higher ground, a place where the means of delivering care is unfamiliar to us. We need to allow that process to occur and foster the evolution of good ideas that springs us out of the box of past life experiences and out of the box of regulations and standards. (See Figure 3–1.) Creative approaches to the delivery of health care are needed to better face the challenges of managed care with the desire to provide consistency and quality. Sometimes the knowledge of the regulations inhibits the free flow of ideas as doors slam shut in our minds. It is a dichotomy for us as we stretch out of the box that restrains us into a brighter world only to have the barriers still exist when we come back to reality. The challenge is twofold. First, accept the fact that "you are who you were when" and rationally approach the reasons why your thoughts have shut down a good idea. How much of what you think is law and regulation is really your reaction to a

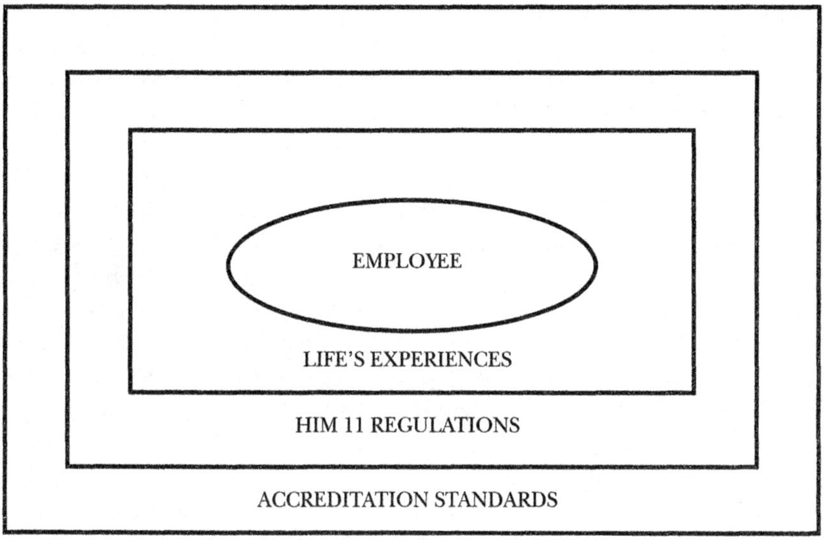

Figure 3–1 Constraints on Free Thinking

surveyor's comment or a presentation you heard years ago that made perfect sense . . . then! The second challenge comes when we recognize that we have a revolutionary idea and the regulations *are* indeed restrictive. This is when we must challenge the regulators to change the binding rules that force us to operate in inefficient ways. Legislative action is surely needed to decrease restrictive regulations and managed care is forcing that issue. It's time for home health care leaders to be proactive in their efforts and influence change. Actual stories of restricted creativity in reducing health care costs and enhancing efficiency because of archaic laws will be embraced by the public. The resulting outcry of the public and industries undoubtedly will speed the revision process. But, to avoid confusion, do not expect that all of your reengineering ideas will hit a brick wall due to law and regulations, because in reality the biggest brick wall is none other than ourselves.

HISTORICAL PERSPECTIVE OF THE HEALTH INSURANCE MANUAL 11

Home health care has as its roots the beginning of society. Traditionally, ill patients were treated by a visiting physician and the patient's family until health care workers started visiting patients' homes to provide assistance. At the start of the twentieth century, the first hospitals were founded as charitable organizations largely for the care and treatment of communicable diseases. Patients only entered hospitals when family members could not provide their care or if they were indigent. Community health departments were established in response to the patient needs within the community. Some of the agencies provided home health care as we now know home health nursing, but most community health services were geared toward the care, treatment, and prevention of communicable diseases. Visiting Nurse Associations (VNAs) were established in communities to provide preventive care and well-child immunizations as well as health care for patients with all types of illness. Up to this point payment for health care services was provided from patient donations and the benevolence of others.

As a result of the Great Depression (1929) many people found themselves in poverty despite having worked long and hard. Savings were either lost or depleted and people were destitute. To circumvent the financially devastating effects of the depression, President Franklin D. Roosevelt declared that the U.S. government would help the poor and indigent with their health care needs in the form of social welfare. Shortly thereafter, in the 1940s, a great majority of the male work force entered military service to fight for the country in World War II, leaving industry in a state of chaos. With the male work force called to active duty, this country experienced a shortage of workers available to maintain factory operations. To entice women to work, factory leaders began to offer health care benefits in addition to salaries. This was a turning point in health care's history in the United States. It was at this juncture when the population at large began to expect that the employer or the government was responsible to provide for people's health care needs.

In 1966, Medicare was established to provide for the health care needs of the elderly. The federal government adopted parameters specifying which services would be reimbursable for various levels of care. The HCFA, which is the federal agency that administers the Medicare program, developed the Health Insurance Manual—Section 11 (HIM 11) to address the qualifying criteria for receiving and providing home health care. Despite drastic changes in the delivery of health care over the past several decades, most of the HIM 11 regulations have remained unchanged since their inception in 1966. For example, regulations still require the beneficiary to be "essentially homebound" to qualify for Medicare-reimbursed home health care services. These regulations were developed at a time when the average length of hospitalization was close to three weeks as opposed to today's rate, which is fast approaching three days. Hospital admission criteria have also become more restrictive, creating a crack in the service continuum. Many people in need of health care services find themselves without health care coverage.

HIM 11 Synopsis

The HIM 11 is divided into sections that include conditions, standards and billing information. Beginning at 2180, the HIM 11 describes the types of home health agencies, which include public, nonprofit, and proprietary. General requirements then specify the regulation for an agency to consider itself a home health agency (HHA). These requirements must be considered as background knowledge when reengineering home health care organizations because they mandate what organizations need to do to operate as HHAs. For example, an HHA must:

1. Primarily provide skilled nursing services and other therapeutic services.
2. Have policies established by professional personnel to govern the services that it provides. The group of professional personnel needs to include one or more physicians and one or more registered professional nurses.
3. Have a physician or registered professional nurse who supervises the skilled nursing and other therapeutic services.
4. Document and maintain clinical records on ALL patients.
5. Be licensed and maintain licensure requirements in the state in which it operates.
6. Compile and utilize an overall plan and budget.
7. Meet the conditions of participation to provide for the safety and well-being of all patients.
8. Meet additional requirements as determined by the regulator.
9. Protect and promote the rights of each patient receiving services.
10. Disclose ownership and management information as required under law.
11. Only use appropriately certified home health aides. Certification requirements are also defined in the HIM 11 in Section 1861.
12. Provide services in compliance with all applicable local, state, and federal laws.
13. Provide services in compliance with accepted professional standards.
14. Include the patient's plan for care as part of the clinical record.
15. Maintain written policies and procedures respecting advance directives in compliance with law and regulation.

16. Accept patients for care only by the primary HHA.
17. Obtain an appropriately written contract for services provided for agency patients by an individual who is not an employee.

Excluded from the definition of HHA is an organization that primarily provides mental health services.[1]

In general, all home health agencies certified by Medicare need to provide skilled nursing and at least one other service from the following list: physical therapy, occupational therapy, speech-language-pathology, medical social services, and home health aide services. The HIM 11 then provides definitions and characteristics of organizations, such as parent agencies, subunits, and branches and also specific information about policy needs, annual review needs, and clinical record retention in branch and subunit offices.

The HIM 11 details the types of surveys conducted by individual state departments of health or designee on behalf of the Medicare program. It explains various components of the survey process including the manner for selecting patient visits and clinical records for review. It includes definitions of personnel, which will be discussed in more detail in Chapter 5.

The crux of the HIM 11 is contained in the Conditions of Participation and Standards, the regulations with which certified home health agencies must comply. Although the conditions and standards are both important, condition level deficiencies can lead to punitive results, such as loss of approval for training potential aides for the organization. A threat of financial sanctions is periodically considered but none have materialized as of this writing.

Exhibit 3–1 lists the Medicare Conditions of Participation, which must be familiar to those responsible for the reengineering process. Standards are subdivisions of the conditions and some of the standards are detailed in sample applications of the reengineering process throughout the ensuing chapters.

HISTORIC PERSPECTIVE OF THE JOINT COMMISSION ON ACCREDITATION OF HEALTHCARE ORGANIZATIONS

Accreditation is a voluntary credential that provides more validity to the services offered by the organization and is becoming an organizational requirement for many third-party payers. The genesis of accreditation lies with the Joint Commission on Accreditation of Hospitals (JCAH). As a response to fears related to poor surgical techniques leading to unneces-

Exhibit 3–1 Medicare Conditions of Participation

Medicare Conditions of Participation for Home Health Care Agencies

1. The patient has the right to be informed of his or her rights. The Home Health Agency (HHA) must protect and promote the exercise of these rights.
2. The organization complies with federal, state, and local laws regarding disclosure and ownership information, and accepted professional standards and principles.
3. Organization furnishes services. Administrative control and lines of authority for the delegation of responsibility down to the patient care level are clearly set forth in writing and are readily identifiable. Administrative and supervisory functions are not delegated to another agency or organization, and all services not furnished directly, including services provided through subunits, are monitored and controlled by the parent agency. If an agency has subunits, appropriate administrative records are maintained for each subunit.
4. A group of professional personnel, which includes at least one physician and one registered nurse (preferably a public health nurse), with appropriate representation from other professional disciplines, establishes and annually reviews the agency's policies governing scope of services offered, admission and discharge policies, medical supervision and plans of care, emergency care, clinical records, personnel qualifications, and program evaluation. At least one member of the group is neither an owner nor an employee of the agency.
5. Patients are accepted for treatment on the basis of a reasonable expectation that the patient's medical, nursing, and social needs can be met adequately by the agency in the patient's place of residence. Care follows a written plan of care established and periodically reviewed by a doctor of medicine, osteopathy, or podiatric medicine.
6. If the agency furnishes medical social services, those services are given by a qualified social worker or by a qualified social work assistant under the supervision of a qualified social worker. In accordance with the plan of care, the social worker assists the physician and other team members in understanding the significant social and emotional factors related to the patient's health problems, participates in the development of the plan of care, prepares clinical and progress notes, works with the family, uses appropriate community resources, participates in discharge planning and in-service programs, and acts as a consultant to other agency personnel.
7. Home health aides are selected on the basis of factors such as a sympathetic attitude toward the care of the sick, ability to read, write, and carry out directions, and maturity and ability to deal effectively with the demands of the job. They are closely supervised to ensure their competence in providing care. For home health services furnished (either directly or through arrangements with other organizations) after August 14, 1990, the HHA must use individuals who meet the personnel qualifications specified in 484.4 for "home health aide."
8. An HHA that wishes to furnish outpatient physical therapy or speech pathology services must meet all the pertinent conditions of this part and also meet the additional health and safety requirements set forth in 405.1717 through 405.1721, 405.1723, and 405.1725 of this chapter to implement section 1861 (p) of the Act.

continues

Exhibit 3-1 continued

9. A clinical record containing pertinent past and current findings in accordance with accepted professional standards is maintained for every patient receiving home health services. In addition to the plan of care, the record contains appropriate identifying information: name of physician; drug, dietary, treatment, and activity orders; signed and dated clinical and progress notes; copies of summary reports sent to the attending physician and a discharge summary.
10. Clinical record information is safeguarded against loss or unauthorized use. Written procedures govern use and removal of records and conditions for release of information. Patient's written consent is required for release of information not authorized by law.
11. The HHA has written policies requiring an overall evaluation of the agency's total program at least once a year by the group of professional personnel (or a committee of this group), HHA staff, and consumers, or by professional people outside the agency working in conjunction with consumers.

sary patient complications, the JCAH began to accredit surgeon performance in the 1950s by evaluating it against established standards. Soon the surgeons complained that, regardless of their individual or collective quality of services, patients still suffered complications. They suggested that the JCAH broaden its scope to include hospital personnel, which the JCAH responded to by establishing hospital personnel criteria. This expanded focus was a natural blend for JCAH's mission with improving the quality of health care delivery to the public. As health care evolved, the JCAH once again responded by developing program area standards for other settings, such as ambulatory care, mental health, long-term care, and home health care. Home health care accreditation began in June 1988 after the development of standards specific to this field. The JCAH changed its name to the Joint Commission on Accreditation of Healthcare Organizations (JCAHO, otherwise known as the Joint Commission) in recognition of its awareness of the changing health care environment.

The Joint Commission's standards are developed through a national consensus of the home care field that includes agency representatives, surveyors, and other knowledgeable professionals. Standards are continually evaluated and revised when necessary. Standards are initially developed over a two-year process and undergo field reviews, advisory committee suggestions, pilot studies, and final approval prior to implementation. A home care organization is then evaluated against their application of these high standards. This evaluation consists of documentation review; home visit observation; and staff, patient, and caregiver interviews. When an organization does not fully meet the intent of a standard a recommendation is made by the Joint Commission. Accreditation decisions are based upon the number and weight of the recommendations. Organizations receiving accreditation are respected for having voluntarily achieved such high standards of excellence.

Joint Commission Manual Overview

The Joint Commission provides two manuals for use by home health care agencies. Volume I contains base-line information about the survey process. It describes the types of organizations that are eligible for survey under the standards, the application process, types of surveys, and scheduling parameters, and specifies a variety of polices pertaining to the accreditation process. In the event that a requirement is rewritten, moved in its entirety, or placed within a different standard, Volume I also lists the standards and provides a cross reference from the previously published standards to the current published standards. Knowledge of the information in this volume is vital to the organization seeking accreditation.

Volume II provides an in-depth review of the standards and expectations of the Joint Commission. It is organized into functional chapters, which are not based on services but on functions, such as assessment, which crosses multiple service lines. Section one consists of five patient-focused functions:

1. rights, responsibilities, and ethics
2. assessment
3. care, treatment, and service
4. education
5. continuum of care

It also includes six organization-focused functions:

1. improving organizational performance
2. leadership
3. management of the environment of care
4. management of human resources
5. management of information
6. surveillance, prevention, and control of infection

Volume II also lists key Joint Commission staff phone numbers, publications, and video information to assist organizations in their pursuit of accreditation.

Specific standards are listed within each functional chapter to take the mystery out of the survey process. To assist the organization further with understanding the standard, the Joint Commission provides an intent statement and specifies the guidelines used by the surveyor for scoring. Some examples are offered for the various types of home care organizations (home health, pharmacy, support services, personal care, respiratory, hospice, and home medical equipment). Organizations can then read the actions they need to take to implement each individual standard.

Joint Commission Decision Outcomes[2]

Recommendations made by the Joint Commission surveyor include one of the following:

Supplemental recommendation. This indicates that the organization has met most of the intents of the standard in appropriate numbers. This recommendation indicates that only "rare instances" of noncompliance exist and that the Joint Commission need not take any official follow-up action.

Type I recommendation. This indicates that the organization either has not addressed the standard or meets only minimal compliance of the standard through their established mechanism. This recommendation requires follow-up activity in the form of written reports or additional on-site surveys. Outcomes of the follow-up action do affect the final accreditation decision.

Outcomes of the survey process lead to the following types of decisions:

- Accreditation with commendation is awarded to agencies that comply significantly with all standards. Agencies in this category may have supplemental recommendations but no Type I recommendations and their overall score is 90 or above.
- Accreditation with or without Type I recommendations is awarded to organizations with an overall compliance with the standards. This outcome is the most common outcome of the survey process.
- Conditional accreditation is awarded to organizations with multiple Type I and supplemental recommendations. It requires a follow-up survey to focus on the most significant areas of noncompliance.
- Provisional accreditation is awarded to those organizations selecting the Early Survey Process upon successful completion of the first survey in this two-survey process.
- Not-accredited status is granted to organizations that choose to withdraw from the Joint Commission accreditation process or those organizations with minimal compliance with all standards.

HISTORICAL PERSPECTIVE OF THE COMMUNITY HEALTH ACCREDITATION PROGRAM

Like the Joint Commission on Accreditation of Healthcare Organizations, the Community Health Accreditation Program (CHAP) is driven by a similar mission—to improve the quality of health care. Born out of a desire "to counter public fears about a quality crisis in this increasingly crucial health care arena,"[3] its scope is narrower in focus and solely encompasses home health care. CHAP is a subsidiary of the National League for Nursing and surveys a variety of community health care organizations. Its standards are written with a customer focus in mind while emphasizing the management of the organization and the patient's outcomes of care.

CHAP Manual Overview

The CHAP Manual is titled *Standards of Excellence for Home Care Organizations.* The foreword provides its philosophy, purpose, and objectives as well as information about administration. Accreditation policies and procedures address eligibility criteria, information about payment schedules, deemed status, survey process, and definitions. For ease of application by the organization and the surveyors, the CHAP manual is subdivided into essential core standards required of all home health care organizations and then standards specific to the type of services offered by the agency, such as professional services, paraprofessional services, hospice services, infusion therapy, home medical equipment, and pharmacy services. Information provided with each standard includes:

1. the standard's purpose
2. justification for the purpose of the standard
3. expectation for evidence to show implementation of the standard

For example, if the surveyor interviews staff to assess compliance with a standard an "I" will appear to indicate that interviewing is used by the surveyor. Other methods include documentation, observation, or survey by phone or mail. To assist the organization in understanding the intent of the standards, CHAP lists specifically *what* documentation, *what* observation, *what* survey, and *what* interview topic will be covered.

CHAP Decision Outcomes[4]

Full accreditation is granted to those organizations significantly complying with the standards. These organizations may have to provide follow-up actions to the recommendations. Deferred accreditation is awarded to those organizations that must provide additional information or undergo an additional survey to focus on areas of deficiency. Denial of accreditation occurs when the organization does not comply with a majority of the standards set forth in the CHAP manual.[5]

NATIONAL COMMITTEE FOR QUALITY ASSURANCE OVERVIEW[6]

Given changing health care configurations, a discussion of the National Committee for Quality Assurance (NCQA) may be worthwhile. NCQA, established in 1990, is a private, nonprofit organization that evaluates and provides information about the quality of managed health care. Its purpose is twofold: (1) accreditation of managed care companies and (2) measurements of patient care outcomes.

To be accredited by NCQA, the managed care company must meet the intent of standards in a variety of divisions. Information about these areas comes about from the Health Plan Employer Data and Information Set (HEDIS), which was initially developed by a coalition of HMOs and turned over to NCQA. The HEDIS information pertains to the following areas:

1. Quality of care: Review includes preventive medicine, prenatal care, acute and chronic disease, and mental health.
2. Member access and satisfaction: Includes statistics regarding access and usage of services by members, availability of enrollment, and the results of patient satisfaction surveys.
3. Membership and utilization: Includes membership data; high occurrence procedures; high-cost procedures; and utilization statistics for acute inpatient care, ambulatory care, nonacute inpatient, mental health, chemical dependency, outpatient prescriptions, maternity, and newborns.
4. Finance: Surveys the overall financial performance including generally accepted financial ratios.
5. Descriptive information on health plan management and activities: Surveys other processes that measure the value and accountability of the managed care company.

NCQA Decision Outcomes

Decision outcomes of the NCQA survey may be full accreditation, one-year accreditation, provisional accreditation, denial for accreditation, or the organization may be placed under review. More than half of all HMOs in the United States have been reviewed by the NCQA.

There are several reasons why home health care organizations need to be cognizant of the NCQA. First, home care organizations may be merged with or developed by managed care companies. Second, an understanding of other accreditation programs helps related organizations recognize what may be important to their consumers and accreditors within the near future. Third, an understanding of the standards that must be met by the contracted managed care organization we contract with allows us, as home care providers, to understand the needs of the managed care company and to develop and market services that meet their needs. Finally, HEDIS requires specific outcome and utilization data collecting and reporting from the managed care company, some of which is requested from the home health care organization.

HEDIS is the basis of all available comparisons of HMOs today. In fact, the framework for HEDIS has been mimicked and used by state health departments to compare hospitals on a regional level, a future possibility for home health care in the future.

APPLICATION OF CREDENTIALING REGULATIONS AND STANDARDS TO THE REENGINEERING PROCESS

As an organization proceeds with reengineering, it needs to consider the consumers of the care and the payer mix involved, not just currently but in the future. Medicare is the major source of health care payment for the over-65 age group. Traditionally, services were provided under a cost-based reimbursement structure, however, nontraditional reimbursement rates such as managed care and capitation are on the rise.

The HCFA is in the process of evaluating some options for prospective payment for 100 percent of Medicare recipients. Although this has been under discussion for more than a decade, it appears to be imminent based upon the longevity and thoroughness of the planning. It is hoped that the final product will include necessary revisions in eligibility criteria and standards conducive to alternative home health care delivery processes.

Managed care in some form is rapidly replacing traditional indemnity insurance and per-visit reimbursement for state Medicaid programs. This covers a majority of this population group. As discussed above, more than 50 percent of these health care organizations are somewhere in the process with complying with the NCQA standards for accreditation purposes and must report HEDIS-related information.

The reengineering organization must also consider the services it plans to provide in the future. The needs and expectations may not be the same for the personal care organization and for the nursing organization. Agencies that are not Medicare-certified may want to establish a goal for accreditation. If this is the case, it would behoove such organizations to consider the standards of the accreditation body of their choice during the reengineering process. While recreating the organization that is right for you, you need to lay all of the cards on the table to make well-informed decisions. The operational elements discussed below compare the major credentialing organizations' criteria. This information is not all-inclusive, but it is intended to be thought provoking. It does not replace the value or need for the official publications, which can be purchased through the following locations:

HIM 11
Superintendent of Documents
Government Printing Office
Washington, DC 20402-9371

Joint Commission Manual for Home Care Accreditation
Joint Commission on Accreditation of Healthcare Organizations
One Renaissance Boulevard
Oakbrook Terrace, IL 60181

CHAP Manual
National League for Health Care, Inc.
350 Hudson Street
New York, NY 10014

OPERATIONAL ELEMENTS

Although the HIM 11 specifies *criteria for payment* of home health care services and the Joint CHAP specifies *standards for the provision of quality services,* we often consider them to be of equal weight in our decision making. It is imperative for the reengineering team to consider its customers—both present and future. Knowing the direction in which the organization is moving allows the organization to choose which regulators and/or accreditors it needs to consider in its reengineering process. During reengineering efforts it is sometimes frightening to go outside the norm or outside the traditional paradigms.

The intent of this section is not to provide the solutions or the direction your organization *needs* to take to reengineer. This book is not a paved road but rather provides the machinery and mechanical principles the organization could use in its quest for a more efficiently run operation. This section compares some common operational elements from each of the selected regulatory and accreditation bodies. Comments are provided to help the reader interpret the meaning of these standards and regulations, moving outside of the grooves to which we have become accustomed and to decide how best to meet their requirements.

Admission Process

HIM 11 Regulations. Care must be provided to the Medicare recipient in the same manner as any other patient. The organization is permitted to establish policy and procedure, however, the policy and procedure must be consistent regardless of the payment source.

Joint Commission Standards. The organization is permitted to admit patients within the parameters of its admission policies. The organization needs to establish its admission process that must address the patient's needs relative to the organization's services. The organization needs to establish a process that includes the appropriateness of a referred patient to obtain services, the minimum amount of information obtained at the time of the referral, and finally, the qualifications of the evaluator and time frame for completion of the initial patient assessment. Some of this information is to be committed to policy.

CHAP Standards. Clients are admitted for services only when a reasonable expectation exists for the organization to meet their needs. The organization must develop policies governing the admission process. Physicians must provide proof of terminal illness for all hospice patients.

Comments. These regulations and standards do not restrict the organization to any specific admission process; rather they require the organization to consider the essential process of entry into care. Note that none require a nurse to admit the patient and none require an intake coordinator to coordinate the admission process. Although these vehicles may be the most efficient method of processing referrals, they are neither dictated nor required.

Annual Evaluation

HIM 11 Regulations. An annual review of the operating budget and capital plan must take place and be coordinated by a group of professional personnel, usually referred to as the professional advisory committee (PAC) or professional advisory board (PAB). The annual total program evaluation needs to include all services furnished to the patients, the administration, and the management of the organization. This includes policies and procedures, contract management, personnel management, clinical record review, patient care, and assessment of the home care organization relative to its established goals.

Joint Commission Standards. In addition to complying with state and federal regulations, if appropriate, for annual evaluations the Joint Commission expects organizations to evaluate its performance in relation to its established goals, missions, and values. Goals need to encompass all of the functional chapters of the manual. Thus an annual evaluation will include the assessment of aggregated data from areas such as patient satisfaction, complaints and grievances, incidents, infection surveillance, environmental safety, utilization review, and quality improvement. This evaluation is then used for the planning process.

CHAP Standards. The organization must conduct periodic internal and external SWOT (strength, weakness, opportunities, and threats) evaluations. An annual organization evaluation needs to be conducted and reviewed by the governing board. The organization's policies and procedures, organizational structure, goal accomplishment, patient census evaluation, human resources, financial resources, and all programs must be included in the scope of this evaluation.

Comments. Of importance in this operational element is the need to incorporate data collection activities into the routine of the organization. Some administrators believe they need to hire additional staff just to collect, trend, and aggregate data needed for an agency evaluation. How can comprehensive data be collected in the least troublesome and most efficient manner? Can the reengineering principle of technology be used for this? Perhaps it would be more beneficial for the organization to hire an information system specialist rather than another person solely to track information manually.

Application Process

HIM 11 Regulations. The agency must develop the policies, procedures, and processes required and provide services to a Medicare beneficiary for a period of two weeks prior to the survey. Staff for all services must be available either directly or through contract. The state department of health must be notified of the agency's intent for certification to assist it with its schedule planning. The agency has no guarantees about when the state department of health will arrive for the survey. To assist with the initial survey process, organizations have the option of paying either CHAP or the Joint Commission to conduct the survey in states where they are approved for deemed status. Subsequent surveys are conducted on an unannounced basis. The survey frequency is based on the organization's past survey outcomes and varies from every 9 months to every 36 months.

Joint Commission Process. The organization must prepare for the Joint Commission survey by developing policies, procedures, and processes. An application form needs to be submitted at least six months in advance of the desired survey date. The organization is permitted to request specific dates for its survey. There is no guarantee that the request will be honored by the Joint Commission, although an attempt is made to meet customer expectations. Subsequent visits occur, with notice, on a triennial basis. (Those organizations in the deemed status program receive annual unannounced surveys.)

CHAP Process. Organizations must request an application and submit their completed application to the CHAP. CHAP provides the organization with a contract and a self-study for completion to ensure it is prepared for its initial survey. Organizations then prepare for the CHAP survey by developing policies, procedures, and processes. The self-study is to be returned to CHAP within six months of the initial contract signing. A site visit is then conducted. Subsequent surveys are unannounced and occur annually.

Comments. Preparing for a survey requires time and commitment regardless of the regulator or accreditation body. The organization's staff needs to understand the regulations and standards to justify why its creative processes or services or methods meet the intent of the standards. Remember that surveyors are human and may themselves have trouble thinking "out of that box."

Care Planning

HIM 11 Regulations. The plan of care is considered to be the HCFAs 485 form and must be completed, reviewed, and signed by a physician at least once every 62 days. Every locator must be completed in the 485. It is expected that the various disciplines caring for the patient will establish discipline-specific care plans relative to the care needed by the patient. The organization may choose to include this information in the 485 or use a separate form. Verbal orders are considered to be included in the plan of care. Coordination among caregivers must occur to ensure that the plan of care is appropriate and complete. Prior to providing care, the organization must advise the patient of the plan for care, the disciplines involved, frequency of visits, and changes in the plan.

Joint Commission Standards. An entire chapter is devoted to the care planning process in the Joint Commission manual. The organization must define its care planning document, which may be the 485 supplemented by verbal orders, one page of multidisciplinary care planning, or one page per discipline for discipline-specific patient care planning. Care planning must include the evaluation of any assessments as appropriate. Care plans need to identify the patient problems, list the actions, and specify the goals for care. The care plan must reflect all changes in the patient's condition.

CHAP Standards. There must be a policy statement regarding the plan of care. CHAP standards mirror the HIM 11 regulations in that they require information from all locators of the 485 to be included. Each patient must be informed of the plan of care and the care needs to be coordinated by all members of the patient's care team.

Comments. The HIM 11 can be confusing as it interchanges the plan of care with the care planning process. Department of health surveyors expect the organization to do care planning and the organization is wise to identify exactly what it considers to be its care planning document. As you reengineer your organization, consider the pros and cons of care planning. Do you really need to have a nonfunctional piece of paper for the staff to complete and update or can you make it a useful tool and part of the documentation system? Remember, the care plan includes the patient's problems, agency interventions, and goals for care. None of the credentialing bodies requires it to be any one specific piece of paper.

Consent for Surveyor Home Visit

HIM 11. State department of health (DOH) surveyors obtain written consent from all patients on forms provided by their department. Consent forms are maintained by the health department.

Joint Commission Standards. Organizations are required to obtain verbal and written consent forms from the patient. Signed consents are placed within the organization's patient record.

CHAP Standards. Organizations are required to obtain written consent forms from patients. A sample consent form is included in the appendix of the CHAP manual.

Comments. Although each credentialing body has its own take on the consent form issue, the organization is at liberty to determine its own process. The organization is not prohibited from making copies of the consent form from the department of health for the organization's patient record, nor is it prohibited from asking the patient to sign a different consent form in addition to the CHAP required form. In keeping with the reengineering principles, the organization needs to question the process and validity of its self-directed processes.

Contract Services

HIM 11 Regulations. All contracts must be written and contain the following:

- description of the services being contracted
- frequency of the review of the contract
- termination date of the contract
- information about the need to provide care in accordance with the plan of treatment established by the physician and agency staff
- description of the contractor's standards for personnel, which includes qualifications, functions, supervision, and in-service training
- description of the agency's method for determining reasonable costs and reimbursement for the specific services to be provided by the contractor
- assurance that the contracting organization will comply with the Federal Civil Rights Act

Joint Commission Standards. Written contracts/agreements are required for services provided to the patients on behalf of the organization. The contract must include:[7]

- name of the contractor
- services provided
- rights and responsibilities of each party in the coordination, supervision, and evaluation of the patient's care
- roles of each, if any, in the admission process, initial assessment, reassessment, development, review and revision of the care plan, scheduling of patient visits, discharge planning process
- process and responsibility for submission of documentation

- responsibility of the contractor to adhere to policies and procedures
- charges for services
- terms of agreement
- conditions for renewal

In addition, hospice contracts need to specify the roles of each in the interdisciplinary team conferences and provision of nursing care 24 hours per day.

CHAP Standards. Contracts must be reviewed annually and include:[8]

- orientation to the applicable program
- maintenance of current licensure and certification, if appropriate
- need to document the day of service and submit documentation within seven days (72 hours for infusion nurses)
- malpractice insurance coverage
- mechanism to evaluate contract services
- placement of paraprofessionals within 24 to 48 hours
- process for backup paraprofessional staff
- assurance that personnel are educated about the hospice services, if appropriate
- mechanism for communicating with the rest of the hospice team
- competency credentials for infusion nurses
- patient education responsibilities for home medical equipment (HME) companies
- referral response time for HME requests
- delegation of responsibility for assessment, contracting, delivery, cleaning of equipment, and payer verification
- delegation of responsibilities regarding assessment of the needs for pharmaceuticals, pharmacy contact, drug profiles, and maintenance of a medication profile
- process for obtaining pharmaceuticals including after-hour procurement and time frames for filling prescriptions

Comments. The intent behind these regulations is to help ensure that the quality of care provided to the organization's patients is the same whether provided by a direct employee or by a contractor. Note that contracts are not required for direct employees. Some organizations spend many hours in contract management activities for all employees. Do the benefits of contracts with current employees outweigh the expense of contract management? Is this an efficient use of time? These are questions to be addressed when reengineering this process.

Discharge Process

HIM 11 Regulations. Patients must be notified of the plan to discharge prior to actual discharge. A summary of the care provided needs to be forwarded to the attending physician.

Joint Commission Standards. The patient must receive discharge planning. At the time of discharge, the patient is to be provided with discharge instructions, if applicable. A discharge summary needs to be completed within the organization's established time frame and include a written summary of the status of the patient throughout the course of care, current patient status, and the date and reason for discharge.

CHAP Standards. CHAP requires that a plan be developed by the patient, family, organizational care team, and outside agencies to meet ongoing needs after discontinuation of services. Discharge planning process must be outlined in organizational policy.

Comments. To make the discharge planning process more efficient and to provide for continuity of patient care, the reengineering team may want to conduct a survey of community resources to establish protocols for referrals. The team also should address the question: How can the discharge planning process be coordinated and include the entire care team?

Documentation of Wound Care

HIM 11 Regulations. For reimbursement purposes, the size, depth, nature of drainage (color, odor, consistency, and quality), condition, and appearance of skin surrounding the wound needs to be documented to allow the fiscal intermediary to evaluate the ongoing need for skilled nursing intervention.[9]

Joint Commission Standards. These standards require documentation of an assessment of the patient's condition. The organization is responsible for establishing the assessment content and reassessment frequency.

CHAP Standards. No specific requirements exist in the CHAP standards.

Comments. Although the organizations providing Medicare and Medicaid services need to comply with documentation requirements from the HIM 11, they are not required to comply with these specificities for all patients. What **is** in the best interest of the organization? Consider all perspectives: regulatory, financial, legal, and standards of care. The reengineering team needs to consider the HIM 11 requirements when evaluating the documentation process. A computerized program prompting responses or choices to the specific HIM 11 requirements may be the most efficient way of assuring that this regulation is met. Or is it? What does **your** team think?

Documentation Process

HIM 11 Regulations. Each patient assessment needs to include the patient's condition and functional status. Much of the demographic and assessment information is incorporated into the HCFA form 485, such as name, age, birth date, sex, referral date, hospital discharge date, start of care date, all current diagnoses, functional impairments, medications, prognosis, service type, and frequency required and goals. Other required information includes: patient risk factors, family situation, living arrangements, primary informal caregivers (presence and ability to understand instructions), living environment, advance directive information, aide assignment sheet and supervisory visit notes, discharge planning activities, outcomes for services, and progress notes. There is no specified frequency for progress notes in the HIM 11, however, it is expected that the organization has established a policy for progress note frequency.

Joint Commission Standards. For all care provided, the following items need to be documented: disciplines involved, diagnosis, name, sex, address, phone number, date of birth, legal guardian, height and weight as appropriate, emergency contact, safety measures, suitability/adaptability of home, visit notes for each visit, identity of others involved in the care, discharge instructions, transfer forms/copies, consent forms, terminal illness consent for hospice care, functional limitations, activity restrictions, and ongoing changes in condition. For home health and hospice patients the following must be documented: physician name, medical-surgical history, allergies, food-drug interactions, diet restrictions, initial assessment (which includes nutritional risk and functional assessment), learning needs, reassessments, medication profile, plan for care, aide instructions and supervisory visits, ongoing education, impressions and conclusions from assessments, communications, actions, and interventions about patient's status, signed and dated progress notes, treatments and procedures, relevant test results, patient response to treatment and care, signed physician orders, advance directive discussion and copy (if appropriate), experimental treatment information, copies of physician reports, referrals, and discharge summaries. The reassessment frequency and content need to be defined by the organization in policy and a note must exist for every visit.

CHAP Standards. Documentation must be made regarding the referral source; reason for service; diagnosis; prognosis; family database; physical, psychosocial, and environmental data; emergency contact; patient problems; plan for treatment; short- and long-term goals; safety measures; functional limitations; physician's name; dietary, treatment, and activity orders; medication profile including adverse reactions, side effects, drug allergies, and contraindications; medical orders; consent forms; evidence of advance directives; copies of summary reports sent to the physician; progress notes including the attitudes and responsiveness of client and family to care and the availability and adequacy of care; coordination of care; and discharge summaries.

Comments. The organization has latitude with the format of documentation, frequency of documentation, and process for documentation. For example, none of the regulators or accreditors dictate a reassessment with every visit. The reengineering team may want to ask what documentation its organization wants to require for every visit. Does the organization need to document a note with every visit? Why or why not?

Fiscal Planning

HIM 11 Regulations. The organization must have an annual operating budget and a three-year capital expenditures plan that includes the year of the annual operating budget. The annual operating budget includes all expected income and expenses based on generally acceptable accounting practices. The capital expenditure plan includes projected sources of revenue and all expenses in excess of $100,000.

Joint Commission Standards. The budget and capital expenditure planning process must consider input from all levels of the organization including management, staff, contractors, and volunteers. The planning process must be based on sound judgment, including, for example, a review of the prior year's budget and a projected statistical analysis of the upcoming year's patient population.

CHAP Standards. Many standards deal with the financial planning and evaluation of the organization's financial status. Ratios must be analyzed. Budgeting includes the board and management staff and includes input from the strategic planning, various programs, functions, products, and services. The capital plan must identify expenditures of $600,000 or greater. Accrual-based accounting is used for financial reporting.

Comments. The regulatory and credentialing bodies' intent with these regulations is to ensure the agency's financial viability and thus its ability to continue providing needed services to the community at large. In reengineering, the organization may want to consider creative ways to ensure that input is gathered from all sources and based in reality. Perhaps this input can be gathered via a touch-tone phone survey of all employees. Perhaps the information system specialist can create a program that prompts answers to financial questions to create a projected capital and budget plan.

Mental Health Services

HIM 11 Regulations. Psychiatric evaluation and therapy may be provided to patients with psychiatric disorders that necessitated active treatment in an institution by qualified registered nurses. Nurses must be trained or possess experience in addition to standard nursing curriculum and their resumes must be sent to the Medicare fiscal intermediary for approval prior to submitting bills for psychiatric care.

Joint Commission Standards. The Joint Commission requires additional assessment criteria for this patient population. Assessment of the patient's emotional and behavioral status and specific parameters of the patient's psychosocial status must be documented in the patient's clinical record.

CHAP Standards. No specific standards related to this patient population are included in the CHAP standards.

Comments. Again, the regulations and standards provide the organization with some requirements but do not restrict the expansion into other markets. Perhaps a needs assessment of the organization's external environment shows that an increase in chemical dependency exists in the adolescent population. The reengineering team may choose to develop an outreach program or organize group therapy sessions for this population. Some other regulations may apply with this program expansion, but there are no boundaries as to what can and can't be done. Reengineering possibilities are limitless.

Orientation Content

HIM 11 Regulations. The HIM 11 does not specify parameters for orientation. In the interpretive guidelines, a probe questions the organization's process for orienting the contracted staff about the organization's goals, policies, and procedures.

Joint Commission Standards. The organization must have documentation showing that all supervisory personnel were oriented to the care they are supervising, otherwise there need only be evidence of orientation. Orientation evidence needs to be present for the types of care provided; home and community safety; confidentiality; infection control; equipment management; the storage, handling, and access to supplies, gases, and drugs; hazardous waste disposal; patient abuse and neglect; community resources; the referral process; advance directives; the dying process; care of the dying; specific tests administered by that discipline; the emergency preparedness plan; and any other patient care related responsibilities. It must also be evident that employees were oriented to policies and procedures affecting themselves and their positions. Hospice employees must show evidence of orientation to psychosocial and spiritual issues, grief and bereavement, pain and symptom management, stress management, handling death in the home, and communication skills.[10]

CHAP Standards. All contract staff must be oriented to the program. Orientation evidence must be incorporated into all personnel records, however the content of the orientation is not specified.

Comments. Note that the Joint Commission does not require written documentation of the orientation. Is there any efficiency gained in not documenting the orientation needs? Consider all perspectives. From a credentialing perspective, perhaps not. From a legal and personnel management perspective, perhaps yes. These are all decisions for your reengineering team to consider. Based solely on credentialing bodies' demands, the personnel record for a Joint Commission organization would look different than the personnel records of a CHAP organization.

Paraprofessional Services

HIM 11 Regulations. Aide services are reimbursable by Medicare provided that the aide meets the qualifications and the patient is in need of personal care services. Patients meeting home health care criteria, receiving skilled services, and unable to care for themselves with no available, able, capable, or willing caregiver to provide personal care services for them qualifies the individual for Medicare-reimbursed aide services. The organization must have proof of the aide's level of competency via successful completion of a home health aide training course or competency evaluation and ongoing continuing education as defined in regulation.

Joint Commission Standards. Surveyable Joint Commission services include nonprofessionals providing direct or indirect patient care, such as home health aides, nurses aides, homemakers, personal care aides, companions, and live-in companions. The Joint Commission requires compliance with state and federal requirements, where applicable.

CHAP Standards. An entire section of the CHAP manual addresses the services provided by paraprofessionals. The professional administering the paraprofessional program must have a bachelor of science degree, although a masters of science degree is preferred, plus a minimum of two years of home care or community care experience. Paraprofessionals may be:

- Level I home health aides, responsible for personal care, ambulation assistance, medication assistance
- Level II home health aides, responsible for support to patients receiving high-technology services
- homemakers
- chore service staff
- other titles of staff providing environmental support[11]

Comments. As our population ages, paraprofessional services will become more important for chronic disease management. Potential paraprofessional services should receive concentrated time and respect from the reengineering team. There are a variety of areas the team may want to consider, not just for the traditional homebound elderly but for the partially dependent elderly. Consider expansion of services performed by other providers, not just home health care. Services such as transportation, grocery shopping, medical bill processing, and adult day care activities are only a few of the nontraditional services that paraprofessionals can provide. For the fiscal managers reading this, consider that most of the wealth in the United States lies with our elderly population—ergo the elderly often desire to purchase such services. Health care of the future may pay for chronic disease management services, such as those listed above, in lieu of alternative services.

Performance Appraisal

HIM 11. The organization needs to complete a performance review of home health aides at least once every 12 months. Other reviews are based upon the organization's logical and reasonable personnel policies.

Joint Commission Standards. Annual performance evaluations based on the specific job description are required.

CHAP Standards. Performance appraisal must be completed annually and include:

- employee self-evaluation
- supervisor's assessment of employee
- employee development planning
- employee goals
- quality achievement review
- on-site employee evaluation reports for direct care providers
- employee response to evaluation[12]

Comments. This is yet another area for the reengineering team to consider. Is the performance appraisal process effective? Is it conducted in an efficient manner? Does the performance appraisal provide a complete picture of the employee's performance or is it done just to meet the regulation? Is there value to the current method of performance appraisal? Do the appraisals contain all of the information required by the accreditor or the organizational policy?

Personnel Records

HIM 11. Personnel records must contain current license and certification, where appropriate.

Joint Commission Standards. In addition to the HIM 11 requirements, the organization must show that employees who meet the requirements of the job description are hired. Employees are aware of the content of their job descriptions and were hired as a result of an organized hiring process. The employee's file must show that the employee was interviewed after completing an application and that the organization has obtained at least two references. Evidence of competence needs to exist for all direct care providers. Personal care staff files must demonstrate a level of expertise and understanding of the elements of body function, techniques for bathing, taking vital signs, oral hygiene, shaving, feeding, dressing, transfer, assisting with specific exercises, treatments, and ambulation. Health status must also be documented as required by law. The organization also needs to show evidence of continuing education and any other organizational requirements. Annual performance appraisals based upon the employee's job description need to be contained within the personnel record. Personnel records must be collated in a consistent manner for ease of locating information.

CHAP Standards. Records must include

- individual qualifications
- reference checks (more than one)
- police record search, if required by state law
- current licensure
- health records, if required by organizational policy
- performance appraisals
- competency evaluations, if applicable
- malpractice insurance for all staff
- orientation documentation
- continuing education documentation
- other information as required by state and federal requirements[13]

Comments. To assist the organization in personnel file management, the reengineering team may want to consider using a computer system to track information.

Physician Certification Process

HIM 11 Regulations. Physicians must certify at least once every 62 days that the patient meets homebound criteria and has an acute illness necessitating home skilled services. The HCFA 485 form must be used to complete this process.

Joint Commission Standards. The physician must sign orders certifying the patient's diagnosis, need for services, and goals for treatment in compliance with state and federal regulations. Physician orders are required for all direct patient care only. The content of the physician certification mimics the HIM 11 and must be signed within the parameters of organizational policy but no greater than every 30 days.

CHAP Standards. Physicians are responsible for developing a plan of treatment and necessary revisions. The plan of care must be reviewed by the physician at least once every 62 days and when necessitated by a change in the patient's condition. The plan of treatment requirement mimics the HIM 11 HCFA 485 form locators.

Comments. The reengineering team needs to consider the requirements of the appropriate credentialing bodies as it plans for the physician certification process. Problems commonly occur with the retrieval of physician orders. Electronic signatures are accepted at this time, however the paper with an original signature needs to be retrievable by the organization. The reengineering team may want to ask several physicians to assist them with creative processes to obtain the signed certifications.

Policy Requirements

HIM 11 Regulations. Although it is inferred that the agency has other policies, the following list constitutes the specific policies required by HIM 11 regulation:

- admission
- advance directive
- annual agency evaluation
- clinical records including retention of same in the event that the agency discontinues operations
- discharge
- disclosure of clinical records
- emergency care
- medical supervision
- personnel policies, including qualifications
- plans of care
- program evaluation
- scope of services offered

Joint Commission Standards. Policies are required that address the following areas:

- accountability for controlled substances
- administrative policies and procedures
- advance directives
- adverse drug reactions
- appropriate staff response in the event of cardiopulmonary arrest
- care planning process

- clinical medication monitoring
- clinical policies and procedures
- clinical records
- confidentiality
- conflict of interest
- continuity of care
- discontinuation and discarding of medications and products
- documentation in the clinical record
- initial assessment and reassessments
- lab-related
- management of hazardous medications, materials, and wastes
- medication and blood product administration
- medication and product selection, procurement, storage, preparation, and dispensing
- patient rights and responsibilities
- performance evaluation
- physician responsibilities
- provision of care
- record retention
- referral process
- release of information
- resuscitation of patients
- roles of the patient/representative and home care agency/personnel in decisions
- routine and emergency response procedures
- selection, procurement, distribution, and administration of medications
- staff assignment
- staff rights
- withdrawal of life sustaining care or service

CHAP Standards. Organizational policies must include the following:

- all programs
- admission
- care coordination
- clinical records

- continuation of service
- discharge
- financial
- infection control
- notification of referral sources if the patient does not meet eligibility criteria
- patient education
- patient rights and responsibilities
- personnel policies including conditions of employment, employee/employer obligations, grievance process, and nondiscrimination stipulations
- physician orders
- public disclosure statement
- quality improvement
- reporting of unusual occurrences
- safety
- service delivery and products, including medical direction, emergency care, and practice standards for each discipline
- timely assignment of staff
- timely patient assessment for eligibility

Comments. The reengineering team may want to find a comfortable middle position between the massive policies the organization is accustomed to and the few that are actually required. Policies and procedures are developed to direct organizational activity in a consistent manner. Although policies may provide a comfort to organizational staff, too many policies unnecessarily restrict the creative nature and flexibility needed in a changing industry environment.

Public Disclosure

HIM 11 Regulations. The Public Information Act authorizes HCFA to release the official Medicare report, statements of deficiencies (after January 31, 1973), plans of correction, and comments submitted by the provider relative to deficiencies. Prior to the release of any information, the agency has up to 30 days to review the requested information and submit written comments as to the accuracy of the information. If pertinent, the comments are included with the written report sent to the requester.

Joint Commission Policies. For surveys conducted on or after July 1, 1995, the Joint Commission releases copies of the final and most recent accreditation report for a fee when requested in writing. The organization is provided with the name of the requesting party and an opportunity to review the information to be sent to the requester. The surveyed organization has 30 days to submit written comments to accompany the accreditation report sent to the requester.

CHAP Policies. CHAP requires the organization to release information about its philosophy and purpose, licensing, credentialing, and accreditation reports upon request.

Comments. The organization needs to be aware of the credentialing body's policies about public disclosure.

Qualifying Services

HIM 11 Regulations. Nursing services and at least one of the following are required:

- physical therapy
- occupational therapy
- speech therapy (speech/language pathology)
- medical social services
- home health aide

Joint Commission Standards. Home health or personal care services that include any of the following can qualify:

- nursing
- physical therapy
- occupational therapy
- speech therapy (speech/language pathology)
- medical social services
- home health aide
- support services
- equipment management
- pharmaceutical services
- hospice services
- respiratory therapy services

CHAP Standards. Community health services that include any of the following:

- professional services
- hospice care
- home infusion therapy
- home dialysis services
- home medical equipment
- pharmacy services
- private duty nursing
- supplemental staffing
- pediatric home care
- public health programs
- community nursing centers

Comments. Due to incongruent terminology, the organization needs to look at its services from a multidimensional perspective. For example, pediatric home care, although only listed under CHAP, is a covered service under the HIM 11 and Joint Commission with some qualifiers. The Joint Commission covers the professional and paraprofessional services of the pediatric patient and the HIM 11 covers nursing, physical therapy, occupational therapy, speech pathology, medical social services, and aide services as long as the child meets eligibility requirements. Also, although we know what is covered by these credentialing bodies, this does not restrict the programs we can offer.

Quality/Performance Improvement

HIM 11 Regulations. No requirements.

Joint Commission Standards. The organization is required to improve performance and is offered great flexibility in the process. A written plan is required outlining the process the organization chooses to utilize. The organizational improvement process needs to encompass 10 of the functional areas (or more easily understood, chapters) outlined in the manual: rights, responsibilities, and ethics; assessment; education; care, treatment, and service; continuum of care; leadership; management of the environment of care; management of human resources; management of information and surveillance; and prevention and control of infection. The process must also consider the dimensions of performance, for example the effects of the action, the appropriateness of the process, the timeliness of the study, the effectiveness of the change, the continuity of the care, the safety of the patient, the efficiency of the staff, and the respect and caring provided to the patient.[14]

CHAP Standards. A written quality improvement plan must exist, which is understood by all organizational management and staff. The plan contains goals, standards, time frames, responsibilities, and follow-up actions. The results of activities are used to improve processes, products, and services. Service quality is determined by patient outcomes to care.

Comments. There is much flexibility provided to the organization. This is an area that will be further discussed in Chapter 8. The challenge for the reengineering team is how to comply with the regulations while making the process effective and meaningful rather than just another job to be done.

CONCLUSION

We hope this section nudged some thoughts from the recesses of your mind. Although regulations are black and white, do-or-die requirements, organizations need to make certain they aren't reading more into the regulation than what is there. Have you ever proofread and signed off on a memo because it read as you intended, only to discover later that a vital word was missed or the contraction was used rather than the affirmative word? This example of looking at the black and white of the HIM 11 or other accreditation manuals is a vital part of the reengineering process. Does that regulation really say what we always thought it said or have we applied a commonly held interpretation, restricting ourselves unnecessarily?

No, we can't bill Medicare for nonqualifying services but that doesn't mean that those nonqualifying services would not meet a need or be a viable market. It simply means that Medicare is not a potential reimbursement source. So often we refuse to budge from what is comfortable because we want to wait for the next external force. Clinical pathways, in their true sense, limit the number of visits provided to the patient. Few home care organizations in a nonmanaged care market have chosen to limit the number of visits and work with the content of the visits to become efficient. The reason is quite simple—until the need exists for managed care why shoot ourselves in the foot and reduce our visit numbers and revenue? Attitudes such as this will allow us to survive for a little while but some day we will wake up and find ourselves in cultural shock. Evolutionary time spans from a Stage I market to a Stage III market took up to three years in the early 1990s but now it happens in half of that time. Eighteen months is enough time for some organizations to begin to realize that they are in serious trouble with higher costs than payers are willing to reimburse. Once this realization hits, organizations have an average of one year to reengineer themselves into more efficient operations. If this sounds like it could be your organization, do you have a large enough endowment to support this last-minute effort and defensive positioning?

NOTES

1. U.S. Department of Health and Human Services, *A Provider's Guide to the Home Health Certification Process,* Sect. 2180 (Washington, D.C.: 1993).
2. Joint Commission on Accreditation of Healthcare Organizations, *1995 Accreditation Manual for Home Care,* Vol. 1 (Oakbrook Terrace, Ill.: 1994), iii.
3. National League for Health Care, Inc., and Community Health Accreditation Program, Inc., *Standards of Excellence for Home Care Organizations* (New York, N.Y.: 1993), Foreword 1.
4. National League, Policies and Procedures, in *Standards of Excellence,* 8.
5. National League for Health Care, Inc., and Community Health Accreditation Program, Policy and Procedures, 9.
6. National Committee for Quality Assurance, *HEDIS, Executive Summary* (Washington, D.C.: February 1995).
7. Joint Commission, *1995 Accreditation Manual,* 204–205.
8. National League, Core 34–37, in *Standards for Excellence.*
9. U.S. Department of Health and Human Services, *A Provider's Guide,* Section 205.1.
10. Joint Commission on Accreditation of Healthcare Organizations, *1995 Accreditation Manual for Home Care,* Vol. II (Oakbrook Terrace, Ill.: 1994), 290–291.
11. National League, Para Professional 5, in *Standards of Excellence.*
12. National League, Core 33, in *Standards of Excellence.*
13. National League, Core 32, in *Standards of Excellence.*
14. Joint Commission, *1995 Accreditation Manual,* Vol. II, 162.

Chapter 4

Gaining Control of Costs

When we hear that we need to gain control of our costs, our initial response is, "Of course I know what my organization's costs are." But do we really know the true costs of providing each service offered by our organizations? Many in the home health industry believe that as long as we are making a profit we have no need to know the exact cost for each service. With the reimbursement purse strings tightening in the health care marketplace, gaining control of costs is a critical aspect of doing business.

While there is no single proven method to determine the validity of the financial analysis reports being generated, no matter what the system, the output is only as good as the input. If the organization desires valid financial information then time and resources must be dedicated to its pursuit.

Why do we seek to gain control of costs when the future of home care reimbursement is up in the air? At this writing, our federal legislators and elected executives have not agreed upon any health care reform measures, nor on the federal health care budget. There are days when they are unable to agree who should be present at the discussions. We are certain, however, that by the time you read this book, they will have agreed on some changes and we will be in the midst of new topics of debate. They do agree on the need to cut health care costs and on the need to make changes in the Medicare covered services and total Medicare program expenditures. As health care providers, our concern must be to preserve home care for the residents of our communities and to ensure a reasonable rate of reimbursement for home care services.

REIMBURSEMENT TRENDS

Insured coverage programs that provide home care today form a kaleidoscope of alternatives and methodologies. The American Managed Care and Review Association (AMCRA) of Washington, D.C., recognizes three primary types of managed care organizations: (1) health maintenance organizations (HMOs), (2) preferred provider organizations (PPOs), and (3) point-of-service (POS) plans. HMOs consist of physician and hospital services that are paid a fixed fee for these services. The HMO providers normally must provide these services to the HMO's insured population groups. Access to services is via the primary care physician selected by the insured individual from the HMO's approved list of participating physicians.

The PPO also has a fixed fee established for services provided by its network of providers. This fee is a percentage discount off the usual and customary fees for services. To receive services outside the provider network means that the insured individual becomes responsible for paying the charges beyond the usual fees established (fixed) by the network of preferred providers.

The POS plan has a fixed fee for services, as well as a primary care physician who serves as the gatekeeper to services by specialists, inpatient hospitals, emergency rooms, and an entire cadre of health care related services. Significant increases in cost are incurred by the insured individual if he or she chooses to receive services outside the network of providers.

Another managed care organization that has surfaced recently is the physician-hospital organization (PHO), a network developed to provide services at a discount to the insured population. This organization is made up of hospitals and physicians with a shared interest in maintaining and enlarging the enrollment area in which they practice.

Primary modes of Medicare reimbursement currently being proposed by the U.S. Congress and executive branch (which will affect home health care payment) include the following:

1. *Fee-per-Visit Methodology.* This preestablishes a cost cap limit per discipline based upon 1995 figures. This is aimed at maintaining a budget-neutral position for the home care Medicare benefit services.
2. *Rate-per-Episode Methodology.* This proposes to establish a flat rate for all covered services delivered in any 120-day period relative to the initial admission date for services. There is also a proposed 45-day period for a break in services in order to qualify the Medicare recipient for a new episode of care. This in essence puts the agency at financial risk for the provision of services for these additional 45 days. Planned case mix adjustment outlines 18 case categories. The episodic rate is designed to be set low enough to limit growth and is based upon mean cost consistent with the 1995 prospective payment system (PPS) demonstration project.[1]
3. *Bundling.* Although this concept appears to be growing out of favor at the moment, it seems appropriate to include this concept of reim-

> bursement for future reference. This proposal provides for a 20 percent add-on to the current DRG rate paid to acute care providers (hospitals) in order that they assume the responsibility for the provision of post-acute care services such as home care, durable medical equipment, hospice care, skilled nursing facility care, and prescriptions. Analysis of this proposal by the Hospital Home Care Association of America (HHCAA) demonstrated a significant fiscal deficit to the home care provider by this reimbursement methodology as it had been proposed in 1995.[2]

In the PPS's per-visit episode model of reimbursement, 50 percent of the home health organization's savings (i.e., payments that are below an anticipated annual aggregate per episode) are returned to the home care organization at the end of the fiscal year. Exceptions can be sought for extended care cases but those outliers that exceed the 120-day limit count against the annual aggregate caps established and the amount of the above 50 percent returned dollars.

Other less popular reimbursement models proposed in 1995 included a proposal for co-payments to be made by patients after a certain number of visits were provided in each calendar year. Also proposed was a change in Medicare home care reimbursement, to a Part B 80/20 reimbursement model with an annual deductible.

Prospective payment in the acute care setting (DRGs) and in the ambulatory setting (APGs) is reality. The far-reaching effects of the APG system have yet to be realized fully.

The trend in care delivery is toward health care providers becoming part of provider networks and establishing integrated care delivery models. This networking and integration of care is focused on quality, nonduplicative, cost-efficient services. This focus correlates closely with the goal of organizational reengineering and supports the position that reengineering and restructuring for the present and future is vital and relevant to home care providers. How else can we assure ourselves a vital role in integrated care delivery?

One major reimbursement trend yet to be discussed—but one causing the most internal unrest for home health care administrators—is capitation. Managed care organizations predict that by the year 1998 greater than 50 percent of their reimbursement will be via the capitation model.[3] What does capitation mean to home health care providers? In basic terms it is a dollar amount paid per insured life for the total number of insured lives—for example, $5.00 per month per enrollee, multiplied by 2,000 enrollees equals $10,000.00 per month, or $120,000.00 per year. What will $120,000.00 per year provide in terms of services? This question is one of the most important aspects of negotiating a capitation agreement. What are the specific services that are included in the capitation rate? Let's take just home nursing care as an example and consider various ways in which home nursing care is provided. It could include not only intermittent nursing but private duty. Is the included intermittent nursing a one-hour per day visit, or is it any amount of time up to 23 hours per day? Is this intermittent nursing provided by a registered professional or a licensed practical nurse? Does it include high-tech assisted home nursing or only chronic long-term supportive nursing care? Does it include home nursing specialist care such as psychiatric or maternal-child nursing? Is personal care included in the managed care organization's definition of nursing care? Does the capitation agreement include the provision of supplies for the nurses to provide wound dressing changes? Does it include the cost of the medications the nurse administers? Does it include the provision of the intravenous fluids, medications, and supplies she administers? Does it include family counseling, dietary instruction, and community agency referrals for services? Does the nurse need to provide the walker the patient needs? The catheters, the drainage bags, the ketodiastix, the glucometers? All of these questions arise merely about the service provision of nursing. Without complete clarification of included services, it is impossible to know what that $120,000.00 per year equates to in services and expenses. In order to develop and project agency cost data effectively and project expenses, much more needs to be known about the capitation process.

A variation of capitation—global capitation—takes the capitation for a single service even further, and in fact is the terminology used to describe an all-inclusive capitation rate. This rate will be negotiated with the hospital or health care system and includes hospitalization, physician fees, and other related health care expenses.[4] It is important to establish risk corridors with the global capitation contract, so that the boundaries of risk are established prior to finalization of the contract. This risk corridor provides reimbursement to the payer if the volumes are below preestablished levels and vice versa, should the service volumes exceed the preestablished payment levels.[5]

CONTRACT PREPARATION

How can we begin to gather the data regarding our costs in preparation for reengineering? And for the future anticipated reimbursement model of capitation?

Examining the organization's current utilization and costs as they relate to the managed care arena is only one small segment of the organization's future volumes. The successful negotiation of a contract requires much more. For example, when we look at our current volumes for managed care organization XYZ, we are looking at only one piece of the pie. The total home care service provision includes all of our competitors' volumes and alternative care delivery modalities that will revert to home care. In other words, if your home health care organization is seeing 10 congestive heart failure(CHF) admissions per 1,000 enrollees of managed care organization XYZ, and home care agency A is seeing 5, home care agency B is seeing 4, and home care agency C is seeing 2, the total home care volume per 1,000 enrollees is really 21 admissions to home care for the diagnosis of CHF per 1,000 enrollees. The figures available to us within our own organization are not sufficient for projections of this nature.

How can we determine more realistic utilization volumes in order to increase the accuracy of these projections and our capitation rates for these proposals? Gathering referral data for all acute care, primary care, and community referral sources to the home care arena is one step in the process. Seeking these data from the managed care organization is another, as is collaborating with other home health organizations to gather data and working with the state's home health care association. Comparison of these numbers against national standards is another important aspect of verification and collection of utilization data.

It is important to realize that the volumes anticipated will exceed current utilization volumes, and in a capitation agreement *you* become the gatekeeper to visits, meaning that you determine the total number of visits provided per admission to your home care organization. Increases in visits do not increase the monthly and annual reimbursement.

Further safeguards in the capitation agreement or integrated care delivery negotiations that the organization should include are measures that limit or reduce the organization's risk. Future rate adjustments based on the Consumer Price Index (CPI) is but one method of risk management of care delivery contracts. Whether the CPI index rises or not, you will want to secure a risk limit per case clause for a maximum number of cases on an annual basis within the signed agreement. The level of limits in this clause can vary significantly and be as low as 1,000 cases per year or $1,000 per year. They can also vary significantly from agreement to agreement according to individual negotiations. Additional safeguards can be put into place relative to changing demographics within the insured population groups, increased incidences of epidemics, natural disasters, and advancements in technology and practice. In an organization's eagerness to obtain the contract or to be included in the provider network, it's important not to "give away the farm."

How do we take a calculated risk as opposed to being a gambler throwing the dice and hoping for a winner? Through the reengineering/restructuring process, the analysis of our business processes and the identification of our costs are key to future win-win negotiations. Once costs are clearly identified and quantified, we can earmark changes appropriate to today's Medicare reimbursement model and proactively plan for future changes based on proposed prospective payment methodologies and the percentage of managed care's anticipated impact within our region.

MANAGED CARE'S IMPACT

The term *managed care* had its inception in the early 1980s. The spread of managed care throughout the United States, while slow at first, now has gained momentum. The highest managed care market penetration is present in the West and Northwest regions of the United States with Minneapolis recording a high managed care market penetration.[6] Since the early 1990s we have provided audiences with a definition of managed care. By defining the two words *care* and *managed,* we have developed a definition of managed care. To us, *care* means "watchful attention and responsibility" and *managed* means "to direct or control." In the area of health care, we interpret the combination of these two words as directing with watchful or careful attention the health care of those enrolled. The stages of managed care penetration in the health care market ranges from the unstructured Stage 1, when penetration hovers around 10 percent, to Stage 4, where integrated delivery networks (IDNs) form and managed care is estimated to be greater than 80 percent.

Stage 2, where loose care delivery networks and HMOs increase in terms of numbers of enrolled lives, to Stage 3, where the consolidation of the health care networks begins, vary in estimated market penetrations from 15 to 60 percent. This progression is well diagramed by McKeon in *Home Health and Fiscal Management.*[7]

How long it takes to get from Stage 1 to Stage 4 is anyone's guess, but the initial progression is always the longest with future progressions occurring much faster. Currently, the northwestern regions of the United States have an estimated 88 percent managed care market penetration rate. How can other parts of the country benefit from this knowledge?

The East, Midwest, and southern regions of the country have the distinct advantage of looking to and gaining knowledge from our counterparts in the Northwest. Utilizing their experiences to plan proactively for our future is what a learning organization is all about.

As a learning organization in the throes of a reengineering project, we need to identify our value-added work, our true costs, and find creative ways to continue providing quality services within the resources and future reimbursement available to us.

COST IDENTIFICATION

There exist two primary categories of costs: direct and indirect. The direct costing of expenses is usually the easiest and most objective to visualize, assign, and track, since these costs include salaries and supplies. The indirect costs are less clear and often more subjective in their distribution, allocation, and application and include facility costs, utilities, marketing, and administrative expenses.

Often ideas and opinions about allocation of costs are as numerous as your employees. How can costs be appropriately pro-rated into the reimbursable service and program centers? How can the costs that originate in an external parent corporation or principal office be realistically evaluated as part of the member or subsidiary organization's financial picture? How valid are the figures assigned from the external sources?

Living in the retrospective charge, cap, and cost era of home care as we have done in the past and continue to do in the present, we often found it advantageous to add costs to the direct service centers, cost allocate from the parent organization's administrative and general accounts, and cost shift whenever possible. In today's world of managed care and integrated delivery systems, we need to reanalyze the figures in light of the new reimbursement and health care delivery systems. It is becoming imperative that the true costs of doing business be determined as they relate to the individual services being provided.

Traditional Medicare Cost Reporting

Previously the cost reporting method acceptable to Medicare allowed for all charges to be assigned to one discipline—i.e., one service would be combined on one line of the cost report, with this combined sum being further combined with a total of the administrative and general cost of the organization. This total administrative and general cost often included the filtered down or step-down costs from the parent organization, as well as the administrative and general costs of the organization itself. These allowable administrative and general costs were spread across the various disciplines (i.e., services according to the volume percentages of each discipline relative to the total reimbursable volume of the organization). This reimbursable unit of measure in this traditional Medicare reimbursement arena is the home or site visit. For an example of this step-down cost allocation see Table 4–1.

Using these figurative examples, the total administrative and general costs are added to each of the reimbursable services according to the percentage of the total volume. For example, in the area of nursing visit volume, this percentage is obtained when the number of nursing visits is divided by the total number of visits. It is important that the combined direct care costs and administrative and general allocated costs do not exceed the Medicare allowable caps for the discipline. (See Table 4–2.)

Standardized Methodology for Cost Accounting

There are other, more traditional methodologies of costing and some organizations, such as St. Paul Fire and Marine Insurance Company (a

Table 4–1 Cost Allocation Example

Total administrative costs	$100,000.00
Total general costs	$ 50,000.00
TOTAL	$150,000.00

Discipline	*Visit Numbers*	*Percent*
Nursing	25,452	72.5
Physical therapy	824	2.4
Speech therapy	212	.6
Occupational therapy	489	1.4
Medical social work	120	.3
Home health aide	8,003	22.8
TOTAL	35,100	100.0

Table 4–2 Medicare Caps versus Charges versus Costs

Discipline	*Visit Cap (in $)*	*Cost (in $)*	*Charge (in $)*	*Medicare Reimbursement (in $)*
Nursing	91.56	69.91	95.00	69.91
Physical therapy	93.72	78.23	95.00	78.23
Speech therapy	93.72	66.28	95.00	66.28
Occupational therapy	93.72	67.89	95.00	67.89
Medical social work	112.88	128.23	125.00	112.88
Home health aide	54.13	27.30	55.00	27.30

middle-market commercial insurance organization), in its reengineering project, developed and used its own standardized methodology for costing of expenses relating to reimbursable services. St. Paul Fire chose to gather and spread these data into identified categories. Staffing costs were the first costs identified by determining and analyzing all the staff time of the individuals who contributed to the process.[8]

An example of this application could be found by analyzing the process for admission to home care. The percentage of time that each contributing member of the home care team spends in order to complete the admission process is calculated. For an admission to be complete, each contributing staff member must determine the amount of time spent in the process. (See Table 4–3.)

This table identifies the direct salary costs of both the direct caregiver and the office support staff needed for the admission of one patient. Added to the direct salary costs are other direct costs of the visit, such as the supplies needed to complete the visit (i.e., chart paper, medical supplies, teaching materials, tools and equipment), travel, and proportionate employee benefits.

As the additional resources needed to complete the admission visit are identified and quantified, the actual direct cost of each admission visit can be calculated. This, added to the percentage of the collective indirect costs appropriate to utilization volumes, becomes the total cost of the admission visit. Nondirect costs include items such as facility expense (i.e., rent, utilities, mortgage, and maintenance), marketing, public relations, telephone, postage, depreciation, and other expenses of doing business. This method of step-down costing can provide the home health executive much needed cost/expense versus service reimbursement information, but it also poses additional questions. Questions relative to how the organization's marketing dollars are being spent, how much rework of billing is occurring, or

Table 4–3 Admission Process Time Analysis

Staff Member	*Travel**	*Visit**	*Office**	*Hourly Rate (in $)*	*Cost (in $)*
Admitting nurse	20	60	20	19.36	32.35
Intake office			30	18.48	9.24
Medical records			10	7.97	1.35
Data entry clerk			20	8.28	2.76
Billing/registration clerk			15	8.14	2.04
TOTAL					47.74

*Time is expressed in minutes.

whether the facility's expense is justified in light of the organization's current reimbursement picture are a few examples of such questions.

There are various cost accounting methodologies that can be implemented within a home health care organization. What is best at any one time depends on the organization's specific needs and the reimbursement arena in which it operates.

Activity-Based Costing (ABC)

Activity-based costing (ABC) costing is the current costing model being applied to the home health care setting. This system of accounting identifies the resources needed to provide each activity (i.e., service). The cost of operations of the home health care organization identified by the ABC accounting method are resources that appear as activities within the general ledger of the organization. These are identified as they are used in the provision of reimbursable services. (For an example of this concept application, please see Table 4–4.)

Expenses in the ABC method of costing are combined according to unit, batch, business, and enterprise. The following are brief explanations of each of these expense groups.

Unit

Expense examples include direct care, workers' salaries, benefit expenses, insurance, workers' compensation, taxes, equipment, and supplies. These expenses fluctuate with volumes.

Table 4–4 Resource Activity Allocation

	Resource/Staff Salaries
Activity Categories	*Average Salary Cost per Discipline per Hour*
Nursing	$19.36
Physical therapy	$21.42
Speech therapy	$17.36
Occupational therapy	$18.54
Medical social services	$16.42
Home health aide	$8.14
Homemaker	$7.10
Management	$22.95
Clerical support	$11.42
Community liaison	$21.15

Batch

This includes activity costs such as billing process, scheduling, medical records, infection control, safety, quality assurance functions, and supervision of staff.

The following expenses are semifixed in nature.

Business

This level assigns the expenses of the management staff to the service lines they manage (i.e., therapy coordinator to physical, speech, and occupational therapy based on time percentages). Billing expenses are assigned based on total claims submitted and collection and receivable activities.

Enterprise

This level's expenses include administrative expenses and senior management expenses that cross over programs, branch offices, multiple product lines, and more than one company or corporation. These are fixed, nonfluctuating expenses.[9]

In today's health care organization, the program manager wants to know the total costs for each service unit provided. For that reason it becomes increasingly important to quantify the number of visits, the level of the care provided (i.e., RN versus LPN), the travel expenses related to distance from the organization, and supply usage to the minutest detail (i.e., one 4 × 4 gauze or one dozen 4 × 4 gauzes for each dressing change). Once figures are assimilated and totaled and costs per service decided upon, informed decisions regarding resource allocations can be made.

REENGINEERING COST REDUCTION EXAMPLES

In order to provide examples of savings achieved through the reengineering process within the organization, we will make some outcome assumptions for the purposes of this book. In doing so, we are able to compare costs before the reengineering project and with costs after changes were implemented as a result of the reengineering.

Example 1: Direct Care Costs

For the purpose of illustration, it will be assumed that XYZ Home Health Care has been well into the throes of reengineering and has decided to streamline its documentation process. Instead of the current narrative nurse's progress note, they have agreed to develop a checklist and to circle relevant data on a formatted nurse's progress note.

The average nurse's salary was computed to be $19.36 per hour and the average amount of time currently spent in documenting a regular nursing care visit was found to be 35 minutes. These are the base line figures to be utilized in establishing the amount of cost savings. The documentation task force projected the savings gleaned as a result of this task revision. (See Table 4–5.)

It is important to note at this point in the discussion that this is only a true savings if the registered nurse spends this available time is providing additional reimbursable services. The time saved in the documentation of care can be accumulated at the rate of seven minutes per visit, totaling 42 minutes each day. With this additional time, one additional daily visit could be provided. Table 4–6 illustrates the potential additional visit volume generated by each registered nurse in a year when this number is annualized. Table 4–7 in turn equates the increased number of visits to the additional revenues utilizing the revenue figure of $80.00 per skilled registered nurse visit.

These figures assume that all visits made are reimbursable visits. As one can see, in terms of direct cost savings as well as revenue generation, this simple reengineering project of redesigning the documentation forms of the organization can make a significant positive impact on the organiza-

Table 4–5 Documentation Process Revision Savings

Registered Nurse Documentation Time				
RN Hourly Rate $19.36			*RN Minute Rate $.32*	
Documentation time before reengineering		17 minutes	Cost/Visit	$5.44
Documentation time after reengineering		10 minutes	Cost/Visit	$3.20
Savings	Time/Visit	7 minutes	Cost/Visit	$2.24
COST SAVINGS:				
Per Visit		$2.24	Per Day	$13.44
Per Week		$73.20	Per Year	$3,806.44

Table 4–6 Nursing Visit Volume Comparison

Pre- and Postdocumentation Redesign		
RN Visits per Day	*Per Week*	*Per Annum*
6	30	1,560
7	35	1,820

Table 4–7 Nursing Revenue Comparison

Pre- and Postdocumentation Redesign		
Daily	*Visits*	*Revenue*
	6	$480.00
	7	$560.00
Weekly	*Visits*	*Revenue*
	30	$2,400.00
	35	$2,800.00
Annual	*Visits*	*Revenue*
	1,560	$124,800.00
	1,820	$145,600.00

tion's bottom line. In addition to the direct salary cost savings, there are related savings in benefits, training, and orientation.

Example 2: Skill Mix

Another potential outcome of a reengineering project might be the decision to increase the utilization of licensed practical nurses (LPNs) for the provision of skilled nursing visits. This is a revision in the skill mix of employees. If we assume that the average salary of the LPN is $12.48 per hour, we can visualize the direct salary cost saving of this reengineering redesign by using the same visit number presented above in Tables 4–6 and 4–7. Since the difference between the hourly rate of the registered professional nurse and the LPN is $7.88, this is the dollar amount used to project and calculate this cost savings. (See Table 4–8.)

These two tables (Tables 4–7 and 4–8) correlate a direct salary expense as a result of a reengineered documentation process first to a potential increase in annual revenues and second, to an increase in visits made by

Table 4–8 Skill Mix Cost Savings

Licensed Practical Nurse		
8-Hour Day	*40-Hour Week*	*2,080-Hour Year*
$63.04	$315.20	$16,390.40

Note: This figure calculates only the direct salary costs and does not include the percentage benefits savings.
Savings per Hour = $7.88

each field nurse. In the second example, a change in the skill mix, in conjunction with the redesigned documentation process, again demonstrates the effects of this reengineering strategy.

Table 4–9 compares the direct field staff salary cost per reimbursable visit of care provided by a registered professional nurse to the direct field staff salary cost per reimbursable visit of care provided by the LPN before and after the redesign of the documentation system.

The spread of direct salaried costs per visit range from a low of $22.13 after documentation redesign to a high of $25.81 before documentation redesign for the registered nurse visit. The spread of the LPN visit cost ranges from the low of $14.26 after documentation redesign to a high of $16.64 before documentation redesign. The spread from the high to the low with the utilization of a different skill level for the provision of nursing visits is $11.55. This is a significant amount when projected against the annual nursing visit volume of any organization. (We do not mean to imply by this example that all skilled nursing visits can be provided by a licensed practical nurse.)

Example 3: Clinical Pathway Practice Model

Another viable health care expense reduction can be seen as a result of the implementation of clinical pathways. With the use of clinical pathways the number of visits can be decreased, while consistency and quality of services can be retained and enhanced.[10]

There will also be a related decrease in the organization's direct salary costs and utilization of temporary per diem and per visit staff for each course of patient care—from admission to discharge from home care. Gingerich and Ondeck have discussed this principle of cost savings in their publication, *Clinical Pathways for the Multidisciplinary Home Care Team.*[11] In that work, the costs per discipline per visit are multiplied by the total num-

Table 4–9 RN versus LPN Cost per Visit Comparison

	Before Documentation Redesign		
Staff	*Visits/Year*	*Salary*	*Direct Salary Costs/Visit*
Registered nurse	1,560	$40,268.80	$25.81
Licensed practical nurse	1,560	$25,958.40	$16.64
	After Documentation Redesign		
Registered nurse	1,820	$40,268.80	$22.13
Licensed practical nurse	1,820	$25,958.40	$14.26

ber of visits provided to determine the episodic costs for each admission. The primary diagnosis or clinical pathway was used to make these projections. Outcomes and variances are addressed by the total clinical pathway system. Variances are tracked, trended, and analyzed for care and outcome, and fiscal implications are also included as they relate to patient care and costs. In Table 4–10, the preclinical pathway visit numbers and correlated costs are projected and compared to the postclinical pathway visit numbers. The clinical pathway used in this table is for the diagnosis of cerebral vascular accident (CVA). Gingerich and Ondeck believe that the number of clinical pathway visits presented in this comparison will continue to be compressed as a result of changing health care reimbursement and patient care needs. The projections presented in Table 4–11 are these initial savings projections. With the anticipated decrease in the number of visits per admission to home care, these savings will continue to grow.

In addition to the cost savings per episode of care, there are other benefits to the agency from the implementation of the clinical pathway practice model. These benefits include decreased staff orientation and

Table 4–10 Home Care Cost: Diagnosis of Cerebral Vascular Accident (CVA)

	Preclinical Pathways				
Discipline	*Visits*	×	*Cost/Visit*	=	*Total Cost*
Nursing	11		$73.40		$804.40
Physical therapy	18		$77.69		$1,398.42
Occupational therapy	21		$70.25		$1,475.25
Speech therapy	22		$70.20		$1,544.40
Medical social work	3		$80.49		$241.47
Home health aide	53		$24.63		$1,305.39
TOTAL					$6,769.33

Table 4–11 Home Care Cost: Diagnosis of CVA

	Postclinical Pathways				
Discipline	*Visits*	×	*Cost/Visit*	=	*Total Cost*
Nursing	9		$73.40		$660.60
Physical therapy	15		$77.69		$1,165.35
Occupational therapy	19		$70.25		$1,334.75
Speech therapy	22		$70.20		$1,544.40
Medical social work	4		$80.49		$321.96
Home health aide	49		$24.63		$1,206.87
TOTAL					$6,233.93

documentation time, enhanced customer satisfaction, and marketing and public relations benefits. These aspects are discussed in more detail in Chapter 6.

Example 4: Restructuring the Hierarchy

A final example of cost savings that can be gleaned as a result of reengineering is presented in this case study about the redesign of XYZ Home Health Care Corporation and the redesign of its management structure. This is a fictitious example presented for discussion purposes only, but the concerns presented can be found within home care organizations nationwide. The background of this corporation is included in the case study discussed in the following pages. Tool 4–A, Organizational Self Study, provides the format of this case study to be used within the reader's organization. After reading the case study provided, the organization's information can be inserted into Tool 4–A and evaluated as part of its reengineering project.

Case Study: XYZ Home Health Care Corporation

Background. This agency was developed in 1985 in rural upstate New York. The community's managed care penetration is at Stage 2. There is strong competition in the community in terms of numbers of home care organizations, several of which are hospital based.

Certification Status. This is a Medicare-certified home care agency that is preparing for a Joint Commission certification survey.

Volume. This agency is strictly a provider of traditional intermittent services and conducts approximately 35,000 visits per year. (See Table 4–12 for a breakdown of costs per visit by disciplines.)

Organizational Structure. This traditional home care agency has an organizational hierarchy structure with many middle management positions added

Table 4–12 Case Study: Cost per Visit by Discipline

	Cap	*Cost*	*Charges*	*Reimbursement*
Nursing	$91.56	$69.91	$95.00	$69.91
Physical therapy	$93.72	$78.23	$95.00	$78.23
Speech therapy	$93.72	$66.28	$95.00	$66.28
Occupational therapy	$93.72	$67.89	$95.00	$67.89
Medical social work	$112.88	$128.23	$125.00	$112.88
Home health aide	$54.13	$27.30	$55.00	$27.30

as the agency's operating environment changed, or as staff gained seniority and no longer wanted to work in the field. (See Figure 4–1.)

As a result of the reengineering project, which took a close look at the referral/admission process within the organization, a decision was made to flatten and condense the organizational chart. In the existing admission/referral process, the administrator served as the hospital liaison, providing discharge planning for two hospitals that referred to the home care agency. The intake coordinator coordinated the start of therapy services and provided the coordination of ongoing team and progress report updates. The nursing coordinator was responsible for coordinating the start of nursing services and the ongoing team and progress reports. The community coordinator (the master's prepared social worker [MSW]), coordinated the start of personal care and homemaker services and provided team and ongoing report updates. The MSW also provided approximately half of the social work visits for the organization. The total number of social work visits per year is 256. It is clear that the admission/referral process can be streamlined, and as a result of this streamlining, several other positions were closely evaluated. The new organizational structure for the management level of the organization now consists of the positions listed in Figure 4–2. This restructured organizational chart eliminates two full-time positions: the community services coordinator and the assistant administrator. It also realigns responsibilities of the remaining positions and elevates an existing business office position into the organizational management structure.

The restructured/reengineered admission/referral process results not only in more coordinated referral intake and admission of patients, but also in enhanced scheduling of services and communication of the patient's status and changing needs. It also frees the administrator from the hospital and community liaison work, allowing her to remain in the office more consistently. The newly designed community liaison coordinator is available in the hospitals and visits physician offices and other refer-

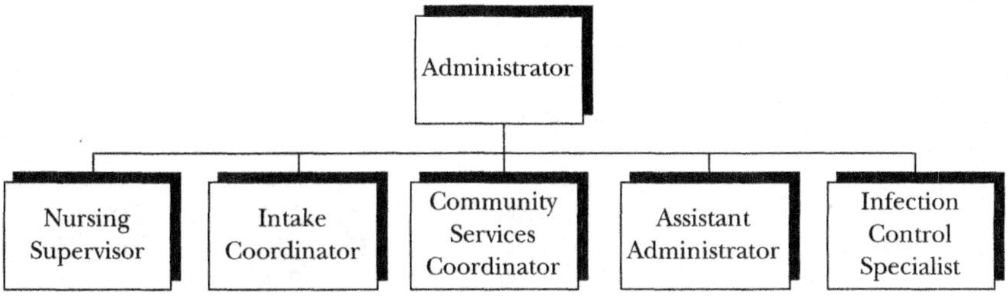

Figure 4–1 Case Study: Original Organizational Chart

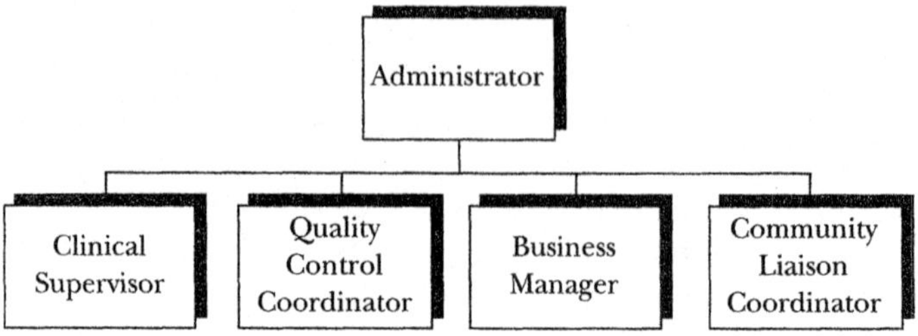

Figure 4–2 Case Study: Restructured Organizational Chart

ral sources on a regular basis. This enhanced quality and consistency of care is an important effect of the reengineering process. The expansion of the infection control specialist's role to quality control coordinator provides a further dimension to the organization. All of the social work visits are provided by contract professionals. Tables 4–13 and 4–14 demonstrate the effects of the restructured organizational chart on administrative salaries and benefits, pre- and postredesign. The decreased effects of the reduced administrative overhead, which is a part of the administrative and general cost shifting of cost allocation in the cost report are readily seen. The cost per visit allocation after redesign is seen in Table 4–15.

The preceding examples of fiscal expense reduction are made possible via the successful application of reengineering of a variety of processes within the organization. Several of these examples will be discussed in Chapter 6, which will also examine the impact of these reengineered processes on operational efficiency and customer expectations. Although additional examples could be used to demonstrate cost savings and efficiencies, these were selected because of their agency-wide implications and diversification of reengineering strategies.

Table 4–13 Administrative Salaries and Benefits

	Preredesign		
Position	*Salary*	*Benefits (27%)*	*Total*
Administrator	$60,000.00	$16,200.00	$76,200.00
Assistant administrator	$52,000.00	$14,040.00	$66,040.00
Nursing supervisor	$45,000.00	$12,150.00	$57,150.00
Infection control	$42,000.00	$11,340.00	$53,340.00
Intake coordinator	$40,000.00	$10,800.00	$50,800.00
Community services	$35,000.00	$9,450.00	$44,450.00
TOTAL	$274,000.00	$73,980.00	$347,980.00

Table 4–14 Administrative Salaries and Benefits

	Postredesign		
Position	*Salary*	*Benefits (27%)*	*Total*
Administrator	$60,000.00	$16,200.00	$76,200.00
Clinical supervisor	$45,000.00	$12,150.00	$57,150.00
Quality control coordinator	$42,000.00	$11,340.00	$53,340.00
Community liaison coordinator	$44,000.00	$11,880.00	$55,880.00
Business manager	$28,000.00	$7,560.00	$35,560.00
TOTAL	$219,000.00	$59,130.00	$278,130.00

Table 4–15 Administrative per Visit Cost Allocation

Discipline	*Visit (%)*	*Add On Before/After*	*Total Variance*
Nursing	72.5	$9.91/$7.93	$50,394.96
Physical therapy	2.4	$9.91/$7.93	$1,631.52
Speech therapy	.6	$9.91/$7.93	$419.76
Occupational therapy	1.4	$9.91/$7.93	$968.22
Medical social service work	.3	$9.91/$7.93	$237.60
Home health aide	22.8	$9.91/$7.93	$15,845.40
TOTAL	100%		$69,497.46

INVENTORY COSTS

Many of the previous examples have presented reductions in the area of direct costs, administrative salaries, and benefits related to salary costs. Another fiscally significant aspect of the reengineering project is the analysis of the organization's processes for maintaining materials and supplies and inventory levels. When analyzing these processes, the organization often learns that utilization levels of supplies greatly exceeds reasonable expected levels of utilization based on patient visit volumes. Length of time "on the shelf" or in the office equates to length of time the money spent to obtain those shelf items was not available to be put to work for the organization.

Selection of inventory often is found to be a reflection of individual staff preferences, which, in many cases, no longer correlates to individuals currently on staff. The expense of purchasing a multitude of brands of any one item is significant in the area of loss of volume purchasing, storage space usage, and caregiver decision time selecting which product to use. The obsolescence and outdating of supplies contribute to fiscal deficit in inventory control practices of organization. A secondary loss related to inventory is providing excessive quantities in homes, which can result in overutilization by the agency caregiver.

Both in the managed care arena and when using ABC methodology, the actual supply cost per patient visit type has been carried out to the actual numbers of 4×4 dressing pads utilized per patient relative to the wound stage.

BILLING PROCESS

In the area of business administration, the billing process is key to the health of any organization. The number of days in receivable, turnaround time from billing to actual receipt of payment, time dedicated to collections, claim volumes, billing errors, receivable levels, and billing delays all enter into this equation.

Accounts payable also can pinpoint process improvement areas such as length of time in payables, expectations of suppliers, and early payment options. The provision of customer discounts in return for prompt payment is one incentive being utilized by organizations seeking to enhance cash flow.

In this area, with reengineering efforts the organization is often able to gain better control of the receivables/payables process. This, in turn, enhances the overall fiscal viability of the organization. The study of the process from service delivery to billing is vital to the success of the reengineering project.

VALUE-ADDED WORK

As the reengineering project team reviews and analyzes tasks and processes, the newly reengineered processes must retain the components of the work that is value-added.

In the process of task breakdown and review of the steps in a work process, the project team will identify work or tasks that do not add value to the finished product/service. These are the steps to be targeted for redesign or elimination. With the "leaning" of the organization's workforce, all work being performed must add value to the product or service.

Examples of value-added work can be work needed to meet funders and third-party payers' expectations. A prime example of this type of work is the ongoing communication with the managed care insurer to report the patient's progress toward meeting goals established and progress in physical/medical status. Expectations of third-party payers vary, but in order to maintain your organization's viability as a provider of home care services to these populations, the individual managed care/insurer organization's expectations must be met.

A similar example is the liaison work with physician offices performed by the organization's staff. If the referring physician expects the nurse to deliver his orders for signature on a specific day, at a specific time, this task could be considered value-added work. Work and tasks essential to the viability of the organization are value-added work. A further refinement of this definition would be that value-added work includes those elements of tasks or processes that, if eliminated, would negatively affect the outcomes. Rework and duplication of efforts and tasks is *not* considered value-added work and in fact is considered by many quality initiatives to be detrimental to the process outcome and to the viability of the organization.

CAPITAL EQUIPMENT, FACILITY, AND SPACE

In a reengineering project's attempt to evaluate and gain control of costs, it is essential to include task forces assigned to the following three major areas of expense and strategic planning of the organization: capital equipment, facility, and space.

The capital equipment task force team reviews the capital request and acquisition process to determine the steps and tasks needed for this vital organizational process. Cycle time, cost comparison, request for proposal process, and distribution and allocation of available financial resources for capital are considered by this task force. The ratio of expense to revenue generation and the depreciation schedule for newly purchased capital is also reviewed. An important aspect of the depreciation schedule is the consideration given to the life cycle of equipment acquired in relationship to its anticipated obsolescence. (Tool 4–A5, included in Appendix 4–A can be used to adapt and evaluate computer systems.)

Facility and physical space assignment necessary for the uninterrupted flow of work among the services and the proximity to departments that have frequent interaction is part of the overall design and process analyzed by this task force. Maximum utilization of space for the maximum reimbursement through the step-down costing methodology is the current focus of facility/space assignment. Besides analyzing the current facility, this task force must be visionary and consider the future program and geographic expansions of facility and space needed to support it.

These issues involved in reengineering and redesign will be discussed in greater detail in Chapter 6.

CONCLUSION

The fiscal analysis that is a primary component of organizational reengineering is essential to the long-term success of the project. To be counted among the 30 percent of organizations that succeed in their reengineering efforts, the fiscal organization's analysis must be conducted with the organization's mission and values serving as the backdrop to decision making.

Cost expense reduction, allocation of resources, and facility planning is essential to the long-term health of the home care organization. The efficient organizational operations that result from the reengineering project enhance the organization's competitiveness in its quest to be ready for prospective payment. The streamlined organization will find itself among those chosen to negotiate for managed care contracts. Quality, efficiency, and customer satisfaction are the keys to success within the managed care arena. These are the desired outcomes for the reengineering project of the home care organization.

The following tools are intended as a guide for the measurement of anticipated cost savings to aid the organization as it works through the reengineering process. Tool 4–A–1 should be completed with organization specific data and costs. Within the organizational structure boxes, insert the titles of your organization's positions and in Tool 4–A–2 insert the corresponding salary and benefits in dollars for each position. The next step is the completion of this same process for the post-reengineering management positions (Tool 4–A–3). Now calculate the administrative add-on savings as a result of these exercises and place these into Tool 4–A–4 according to the visit percentage spread of the organization. This exercise provides the organization with the exact dollar savings to be achieved as a result of redesigning the organization's management structure.

Tool 4–A–5, a computer analysis form, is intended for use in comparing home care computer companies and programs. The boxes are checked to indicate the computer and program capability of the company listed at the top of each column. This tool places essential information on one sheet of paper and quickly provides a comparison of computer companies. Since there are more than five computer companies, it might be necessary to utilize more than one of these forms.

NOTES

1. National Association of Home Care, *Prospective Payment,* Report 625b, II (Washington, D.C.: August 18, 1995), 5.
2. Hospital Home Care Association of America, *Efforts to Block Bundling in the House Meet with Success,* Special Bulletin no. 2. (July 3, 1995), 7.

3. *What Managed Care Companies Want and Expect from Home Care* (Northampton, Mass.: Fazzi Associates, 1995), 1.
4. W. Simione, Capitation, *Caring Magazine* 14, no. 6 (1995): 25.
5. Simione, Capitation, 25.
6. *Developing Integrated Delivery Networks.* Paper presented at the College of Health Care Executives. (Williamsburg, Va., August 1995).
7. T. McKeon, *Home Health Fiscal Management* (Gaithersburg, Md.: Aspen Publishers, Inc., 1995), 469.
8. K. Swendsen and A. Barnett, Light at the End of the Tunnel, in *Corporate Reengineering: Strategies for Growth* (New York, N.Y.: The Conference Board, 1994), 18.
9. T. McKeon, Activity Based Cost Management, *Journal of Home Health Care Practice* 7, no. 4 (1995): 73.
10. W. Maturen and K. Van Dyck, Using Outcome-Based Critical Pathways To Improve Documentation, *Home Health Care Management and Practice* 8, no. 2 (1996): 53.
11. B. Gingerich and D. Ondeck. *Clinical Pathways for the Multidisciplinary Home Care Team* (Gaithersburg, Md.: Aspen Publishers, Inc., 1995), 7.11.

Appendix 4–A

Tools

Tool 4–A–1 Organizational Self Study Case Study

Background:

Certification Status:

Volume:

	Cost per visit by discipline			
	Cap	**Cost**	**Charges**	**Reimbursement**
Nursing				
Physical therapy				
Speech therapy				
Occupational therapy				
Medical social work				
Home health aide				

Example of Organizational Structure*
(Preredesign)

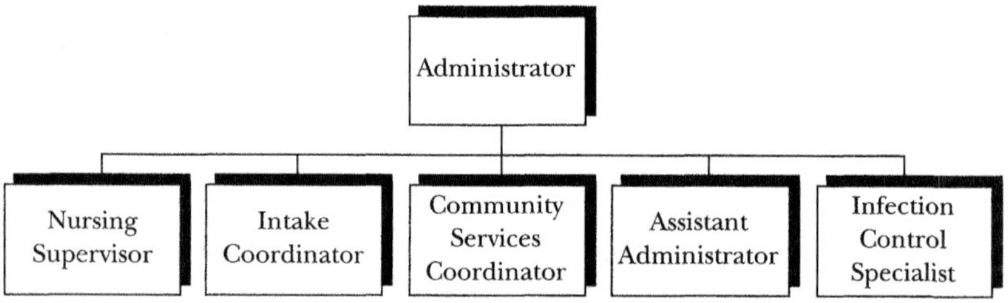

**Insert your organization's titles and positions in the chart above.*

Restructured Organizational Chart*
(Postredesign)

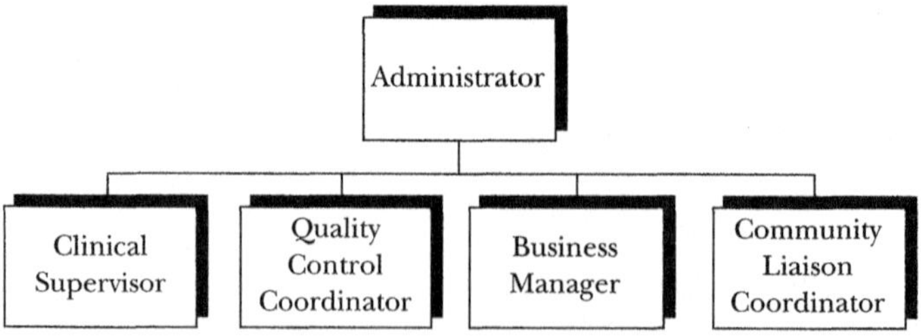

**Insert reengineered organization's titles and positions in the chart above.*

Tool 4–A–2 Administrative Salaries and Benefits

Preredesign

(Replace these titles and costs listed below with your preredesign organization chart in Tool 4–A–1.)

Position	*Salary*	*Benefits (27%)*	*Total*
Administrator	$60,000.00	$16,200.00	$76,200.00
Assistant administrator	$52,000.00	$14,040.00	$66,040.00
Nursing supervisor	$45,000.00	$12,150.00	$57,150.00
Infection control specialist	$42,000.00	$11,340.00	$53,340.00
Intake coordinator	$40,000.00	$10,800.00	$50,800.00
Community services coordinator	$35,000.00	$9,450.00	$44,450.00
TOTAL	$274,000.00	$73,980.00	$347,980.00

Tool 4–A–3 Administrative Salaries and Benefits

Postredesign

(Replace these examples with your titles listed in the restructured organization chart in Tool 4–A–1.)

Position	*Salary*	*Benefits (27%)*	*Total*
Administrator	$60,000.00	$16,200.00	$76,200.00
Clinical supervisor	$45,000.00	$12,150.00	$57,150.00
Quality control coordinator	$42,000.00	$11,340.00	$53,340.00
Community liaison coordinator	$44,000.00	$11,880.00	$55,880.00
Business manager	$28,000.00	$7,560.00	$35,560.00
TOTAL	$219,000.00	$59,130.00	$278,130.00

Tool 4–A–4 Administrative per Visit Cost Allocation

(Use the numbers for the organization administrative costs divided by the total visit volume to determine the add-on before and after reengineering. Then calculate the variance.)

Discipline	*Visit (%)*	*Add-On Before/ After*	*Total Variance*
Nursing	72.5%	$9.91/$7.93	$50,394.96
Physical therapy	2.4%	$9.91/$7.93	$1,631.52
Speech therapy	.6%	$9.91/$7.93	$419.76
Occupational therapy	1.4%	$9.91/$7.93	$968.22
Medical social service work	.3%	$9.91/$7.93	$237.60
Home health aide	22.8%	$9.91/$7.93	$15,845.40
TOTAL	100%		$69,497.46

Tool 4-A–5 Computer Analysis Form

Computer Company ⟶ Components					
One-Time Entry					
485 series					
Coding					
Verbal orders					
Billing UB92					
Edit Screen					
Electronic Capabilities					
Payroll Contractor					
Employee					
Accounting Ledger					
Accounts Payable					
Accounts Receivable					
Budget					
Documentation One-Time Entry					
Care Plans					
Clinical Pathways					
Forced Entry					
Summaries					
Medication Profile					
User Friendly					
Electronic Mail					
Word Processing					
Report Writing					
Scheduling					
Personnel Credential Tracking					

Chapter 5

Identifying Staffing Needs

Staffing is one of the most critical factors leading to the success or failure of an organization's reengineering process. We must continue to ask an extremely important question: Why? Why do we need *X* number of office support staff? Why do we need an MSN for this position or an MBA for that position? Why do our therapists report to a rehab supervisor? Why do we maintain the current organizational structure? Why do we say that we are the leading providers of quality health care in our community? Why do we consider our employees to be competent? How do we assess that competency? Answering these questions allows us to evaluate the way our organization operates and also provides the project team with an opportunity to stretch its brain, jump out of the box, and develop a staffing structure that enhances operational efficiency.

DEFINING OUR SERVICES

Perhaps the first step in staffing an organization lies with defining its services. Home health care agencies typically list their services as nursing, therapy, social work, and aide care. In challenging this response, let's consider the perspective of our customers, an important consideration for maintaining a customer-focused service!

In Exhibit 5–1 we see that patients want to feel like they matter—that they are people, not just numbers. These customers want someone to show them how to care for themselves, support them through the acute phase of illness, and teach them what they need know for long-term health. They want to be pain free and know that someone is available to meet their needs whenever they arise. Patients don't have a preference for an aide, a registered nurse, a physical therapist, or a physical therapy assistant as long

Exhibit 5–1 Customer Perspectives of Home Health Care Services

Customer	*Product/Service*
Patient	Direct care Education: how to get well and stay well Support through illness A "hometown" feeling about the provider
Payer	Patient satisfaction Healthy client base Cost-efficient, quality health care for clients in ill health Timely and complete information
Physician	Patient care: assessment education direct care Timely information Patient satisfaction Cost-efficient care (influenced by managed care)
Staff	Job satisfaction Autonomy within individual positions Support from leadership, when necessary Resources to do the job well
Referral sources	Timely responses to requests Continuity of patient care Patient satisfaction
Industry	Cost-efficient quality health care services A health care cost freeze without a loss of services

as the caregiver is considerate and respectful of them as individuals and meet their needs in a competent manner.

The payer is another consumer of our care. As our customer, the payer is looking for an overall healthy client base to reduce its expenditures. Its business is contingent upon "happy clients," therefore it wants the home care organization to be customer-friendly. The payer wants us to consider the most cost-effective way to provide competent and caring staff for its client base. It wants to receive timely communication and work closely as part of the team. In breaking out of that box, we must realize that the payer has no preferences as to the number or frequency of visits—but simply a preference for the cost of the care needed by the patient. Low-cost providers allow the payer the capacity to spend limited dollars on a greater amount of health care for increasing numbers of clients.

The physician desires credible and competent staff to assess the patient and report necessary and accurate information in a timely manner. Ease in their working relationship with the home care organization is appreciated by the physician's office staff as they coordinate care between multiple providers and patients. Committed to the patient's care and expecting to be included in care planning, the busy physician wants to be able to call the right person when there is a free moment and discuss a patient's case.

Home health care employees are also customers. They want not only to provide services but the opportunity to make a difference in the lives of their patients. This opportunity, from a direct caregiver perspective, requires time with the patient. While interviewing home health staff across the United States, the leading factors promoting job satisfaction and staff retention were stated as autonomy and the availability of leadership support, when needed. Good leaders are able to balance this dichotomy and find that their employees are content and satisfied as they continue to develop in their positions.

Individuals and organizations referring patients to home health care seek timely assistance for those referred. Often referral sources are reluctant to relinquish their feelings of responsibility until services are initiated and the patient's needs are satisfactorily met.

The home care industry seeks to provide quality health care services in a cost-efficient manner. Maintaining current services that meet the needs of all customer groups without straining the health care budget is one goal of the industry. Another goal is to increase the amount and types of services provided within the home care setting in lieu of the more costly service arenas, such as the hospital setting.

Now let's go back and consider what services home health care agencies provide. This time let's use "full brain thinking." Home health care organizations provide:

1. symptom intervention
2. patient and caregiver education and support
3. patient assessment
4. direct patient care
5. communication and coordination of care among patients, caregivers, referral sources, physicians, organization personnel, and in a larger sense, the entire community
6. human resource recruitment, development, and retention to meet the needs of other customers

The staff we select for our reengineered home health care agency need to be the vehicles for the provision of our newly stated services. They may have position titles that are foreign to our traditional way of thinking but they will provide the core services perceived as our role by our customers.

STAFFING REQUIREMENTS OF CREDENTIALING BODIES

Certainly, the organization does not want to restructure itself out of compliance with HCFA or lose its accreditation with the Joint Commission or CHAP. Therefore, it needs to thoroughly investigate the regulations and standards set by these credentialing bodies to use as support beams in renovating its staffing structure.

A review of the Medicare Conditions of Participation for Home Health Agencies uncovers little. According to Medicare rules, the home care agency must provide skilled nursing *services* and at least one of the following: physical therapy, occupational therapy, speech therapy, medical social service, or home health aide. Only one of those services must be provided by employees of the agency and all others may be contracted. In building an organizational structure, the Conditions of Participation provide few support beams for our redesign process allowing us much more flexibility in our creative approaches.

As a CHAP-accredited organization, the home care agency must have a governing body or governing individual, administrative and management positions, and a CEO. Note that CHAP does not dictate the numbers of positions, only the presence of staff filling these roles and responsibilities. These requirements do not restrict organizations in the area of reengineering. In fact, CHAP's core standard number 57 specifies at CIV.7a. that "As a leader in the industry, the CEO is a role model fostering innovation within the organization."[1] The intent of this standard is for CEOs to be creative and drive legislative change to meet the ongoing and changing needs of customers. For those of us still wanting to kick and argue that we must do it the way it has always been done, let's look a little further.

The Joint Commission offers no requirements regarding the organizational structure. A review of its standards shows that the organization must have leadership and direct care staff. In standard HR 2.1, the Joint Commission requires that the organization have staff of sufficient numbers, types, and qualifications to meet the needs of patients relative to the scope of services advertised as provided by the organization.[2] Although some would argue that this standard dictates a comfortable level of staffing to meet any contingency, the intent of this standard is for the organization to provide qualified physical therapists for services that can only be provided by licensed physical therapists, for example, and to provide adequate numbers of staff to meet the needs of their current patients. The organization must be in compliance with the Medicare Conditions of Participation requirements *if* it is a Medicare-certified agency.

It is clear that credentialing bodies provide us with few barriers to looking at our organization's structure and challenging the way we operate.

Perhaps we can provide the services we advertise, meeting the needs of our patients with only 75 percent of our current staffing by changing the way we operate. Perhaps we can change the staff mix and still provide quality services or better yet, *improved* services to all of our customers. Perhaps we can look beyond what we have today and spread our focus far and wide. What new technology is available that will help us to restructure our organization for cost efficient care?

Mandated Personnel Qualifications

The Medicare Conditions of Participation dictate personnel qualifications for only direct care staff and the agency administrator. Medicare regulation 484.4 spells out the specific qualifications for various positions, which are described below.

- The agency "administrator" is a person who
  1. Is a licensed physician, or
  2. Is a registered nurse, or
  3. Has training and experience in health service administration and at least one year of supervisory or administrative experience in home health care or related health programs.
- The "audiologist" is a person who
  1. Meets the education and experience requirements for a certificate of clinical competence in audiology granted by the American Speech-Language-Hearing Association, or
  2. Meets the educational requirements for certification and is in the process of accumulating the supervised experience required for certification.
- A "home health aide" is a person who
  1. Successfully completes a state-established or other training program that meets the requirement of regulation 484.36(a), and
  2. Completes a competency evaluation program or state licensure program that meets the requirements of regulation 484.36(b), or
  3. Completes a competency evaluation program or state licensure program that meets the requirements of regulation 484.36(b), and
  4. Has furnished home health services, in accordance with regulation, for compensation within the past 24 consecutive months.
- An "occupational therapist" is a person who
  1. Is a graduate of an occupational therapy curriculum accredited by the Committee on Allied Health Education and Accreditation of

the American Medical Association and the American Occupational Therapy Association; or

2. Is eligible for the national registration examination of the American Occupational Therapy Association, or
3. Has two years of appropriate experience as an occupational therapist and has achieved a satisfactory grade on a proficiency examination conducted, approved, or sponsored by the U.S. Public Health Service, except that such determinations of proficiency do not apply with respect to persons initially licensed by a state or seeking initial qualification as an occupational therapist after December 31, 1977.

- An "occupational therapy assistant" is a person who
  1. Meets the requirements for certification as an occupational therapy assistant established by the American Occupational Therapy Association, or
  2. Has two years of appropriate experience as an occupational therapy assistant, and has achieved a satisfactory grade on a proficiency examination conducted, approved, or sponsored by the U.S. Public Health Service, except that such determinations of proficiency do not apply with respect to persons initially licensed by a state or seeking initial qualification as an occupational therapy assistant after December 31, 1977.
- A "physical therapist" is a person who
  1. Is licensed as a physical therapist by the state in which the therapist is practicing, and
  2. Has graduated from a physical therapy curriculum approved by
     (a) The American Physical Therapy Association (APTA), or
     (b) The Committee on Allied Health Education and Accreditation of the American Medical Association, or
     (c) The Council on Medical Education of the American Medical Association and the APTA, or
  3. Prior to January 1, 1966,
     (a) Was admitted to membership by the APTA, or
     (b) Was admitted to registration by the American Registry of Physical Therapy, or
     (c) Has graduated from a physical therapy curriculum in a four-year college or university approved by a state department of education, or
  4. Has two years of appropriate experience as a physical therapist, and has achieved a satisfactory grade on a proficiency examination conducted, approved, or sponsored by the U.S. Public Health Service,

except that such determinations of proficiency do not apply with respect to persons initially licensed by a state or seeking qualification as a physical therapist after December 31, 1977, or

5. Was licensed or registered prior to January 1, 1966 and prior to January 1, 1970 had 15 years of full-time experience in the treatment of illness or injury through the practice of physical therapy in which services were rendered under the order and direction of attending and referring doctors of medicine or osteopathy; or
6. If trained outside the United States,
   (a) Was graduated since 1928 from a physical therapy curriculum approved in the country in which the curriculum was located and in which there is a membership organization of the World Conference of Physical Therapy, and
   (b) Meets the requirements for membership in a member organization of the World Conference of Physical Therapy.

- A "physical therapy assistant" is a person who
  1. Is licensed as a physical therapy assistant, if applicable, in the state where practicing, and
  2. Was graduated from a two-year college program, approved by the APTA, and
  3. Has at least two years of appropriate experience as a physical therapy assistant, and has achieved a satisfactory grade on a proficiency examination conducted, approved, or sponsored by the U.S. Public Health Service, except that these determinations of proficiency do not apply with respect to persons initially licensed by a state or seeking initial qualification as a physical therapist assistant after December 31, 1977.

- A "physician" is a doctor of medicine, osteopathy, or podiatry legally authorized to practice medicine and surgery by the state in which such function or action is performed.

- A "practical (vocational) nurse" is a person who is licensed as a practical (vocational) nurse by the state where practicing.

- A "public health nurse" is a registered nurse who has completed a baccalaureate degree program approved by the National League for Nursing for public health nursing preparation or registered nurse study that includes content approved by the National League for Nursing public health nursing preparation.

- A "registered nurse (RN)" is a graduate of an approved school of professional nursing, who is licensed as a registered nurse by the state where practicing.

- A "social work assistant" is a person who
  1. Has a baccalaureate degree in social work, psychology, sociology, or other field related to social work, and has had at least one year of social work experience in a health care setting, or
  2. Has two years of appropriate experience as a social work assistant, and has achieved a satisfactory grade on a proficiency examination conducted, approved, or sponsored by the U.S. Public Health Service, except that these determinations of proficiency do not apply with respect to persons initially licensed by a state or seeking initial qualification as a social work assistant after December 31, 1977.
- A "social worker" is a person who has a master's degree from a school of social work accredited by the Council on Social Work Education and has one year of social work experience in a health care setting.
- A "speech pathologist" is a person who
  1. Meets the education and experience requirements for a certificate of clinical competence in speech pathology or audiology granted by the American Speech-Language-Hearing Association, or
  2. Meets the educational requirements for certification and is in the process of accumulating the supervised experience required for certification.[3]

Similar to the Conditions of Participation, CHAP defines the qualifications of direct care staff. CHAP has an additional aide classification for the home health aide. This expanded role, home health aide II, is available to aides with at least one year of home care experience and an additional 40-hour training period related to high-tech patient services.[4] In the home infusion arena, CHAP specifies the educational qualifications and prior work experience prerequisite for pharmacists and also defines parameters for the qualifications of the infusion nurse supervisor.

CHAP has no requirements regarding the types of services provided and the employment/contractor status of those providing the services other than for Medicare-certified agencies that must meet the Conditions of Participation. Supervisory parameters are specified. For instance, the organization must have a registered nurse visit the patient at least once every two weeks when care is being provided by a licensed practical/vocational nurse. The organization's reengineering team should thoroughly analyze the accreditation standards that apply *after* brainstorming activities. This sequence prevents barriers from interfering with the free flow of thoughts.

The Joint Commission allows more flexibility in personnel qualifications. Naturally, the Medicare-certified organization must meet the prerequisites defined in the Conditions of Participation as previously outlined.

The non-Medicare-certified home health agency must ensure that its staff has current licensure, where appropriate, and that verification of education and training is completed, if required by law or organizational policy.[5] The Joint Commission also has supervisory requirements, such as its requirement that paraprofessionals be supervised in the home at least once every six months.

The Joint Commission requires ongoing competency testing of all direct care practitioners to assure a competent staff. This testing requires direct skills observation by a like discipline, with the exception of paraprofessionals who are tested by a registered nurse.[6] The core competencies for each position are defined by the organization. In reengineering, the organization has much flexibility in establishing the manner in which competency is evaluated.

Assuring Staff Competency

Organizations have always considered the competence of their staff in one way or another. Most organizations, either by regulation, surveyor interpretation, or desire, have gathered written documents or observed skills in the field as proof of competency. Although the HIM 11 and CHAP standards require the organization to hire competent staff, the guiding light for home care's need for a planned and systematic approach to staff competency is found in the Joint Commission's 1995 revisions to its human resource standards. Again, these standards offer wide latitude to the organization as they develop their competency program. They do require periodic (as defined by the home care organization) skills observation of all direct care staff.

In planning for an overall competency program, the organization may want to consider three important aspects:

1. printed information
   a. copies of licenses, certifications, and educational degrees
   b. orientation checklists
   c. ongoing individual and organizationally mandated inservice education records
2. orientation
   a. must take place prior to direct patient care
   b. must take into account all regulatory and accrediting requirements
   c. must include an orientation to services provided, the organization, regulatory requirements (i.e., advance directive legislation), all new equipment, and skill requirements

3. skills observation of direct care staff
   a. direct observation of skills by a qualified person by or on behalf of the organization
   b. the organization defines the core skill competencies required for all direct care positions.

The organization needs to utilize a consistent process to ensure that all services are provided with accuracy and skill. Developing and implementing a competency program for each staff position assists the organization in its attainment of this goal and also assists in the professional development of the individual staff members. As the organization defines the roles and responsibilities within each job description, the organizational structure will become easier to define.

ORGANIZATIONAL STRUCTURE

The organization must decide how many layers of hierarchy it wants. Unlike a seven-course dinner, already reengineered organizations find that the recipe for success requires fewer layers within the organization. In fact, three or four layers are perfectly sufficient. Consider your current structure. Figure 5–1 represents a partial organizational structure that is quite typical of home health care organizations today. As you review this structure, consider the layers of staff—there are seven layers between the licensed practical nurse (LPN) and the CEO. As children, most of us learned how communications can be misconstrued as a message is whispered down the line from one person to another. This is part of the problem with a multilayered organizational structure. Most obvious to external customers (and to some of our staff) is the slow reaction time of the multilayered organization to changing market needs. This slowed reaction time can even affect the more successful organization in that the delay in response places it in a vulnerable position given market competition.

Another factor to consider is the long-term application of today's decision making. An organizational structure deemed perfect for today may be totally wrong for tomorrow. In many hospitals, for example, during the mid- to late 1980s, LPNs were replaced with RNs. This was an appropriate reaction to the changing acuity level of the acute care patients as a result of Medicare's changed reimbursement methods. Most recently, however, those same hospitals have reevaluated their practitioner mix again and are replacing their RNs with LPNs or multiskilled workers (cross-functional positions).

Organizations must constantly reevaluate their staff positions and the best time to do that is with each vacancy. Does this vacant position need to be replaced with a staff member who has the *same* or *different* qualifica-

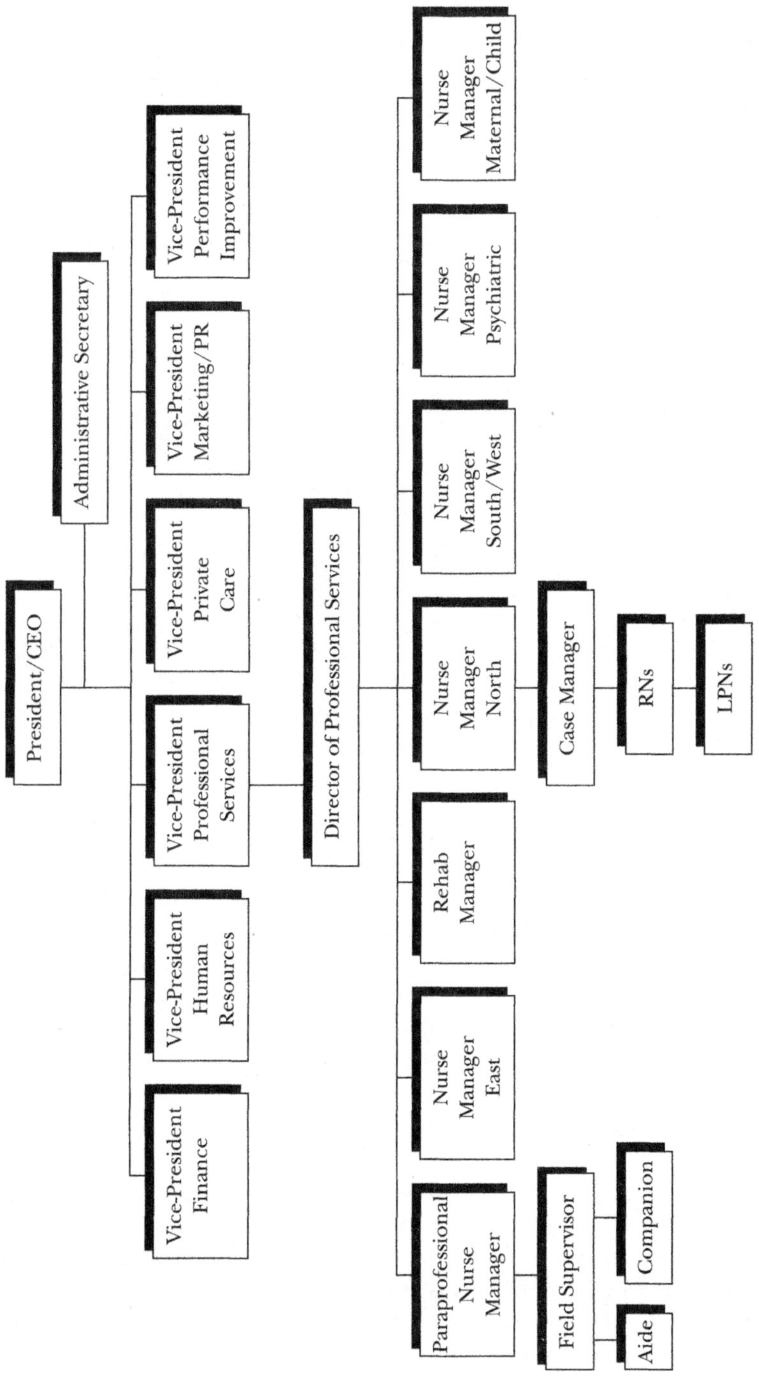

Figure 5–1 Organizational Structure (Partial)

tions? Do we even need to fill this vacant position? Are our customers' needs the same? What do they perceive our role to be? As we answer these and other questions, we need to keep in mind that proactive—rather than reactive—thinking will keep our organizations on the cutting edge.

Today's home care organizations share common ground in their organizational structure with many agencies having similar staff positions. Although a national database is not available to define their roles, the following positions are often identified by home care organizations:

accounts manager
administrative director
administrative secretary
administrator
billing clerk
chief executive officer
data entry secretary
director of clinical operations
director of professional services
financial officer
human resource director
human resource manager
information systems director
manager of clinical services
medical records manager
medical records secretary
MIS technologist
payroll supervisor
personnel director
quality assurance director
quality control specialist
quality improvement coordinator
receptionist
reimbursement coordinator
telephone operator
vice-president of finance
vice-president of human resources
vice-president of professional services
vice-president of quality

A well-known acronym comes to mind here. In reengineering we need to use the KISS method—Keep It Simple, Silly! In other industries in the business world, it is common to maintain only half as many position titles as employees. Think about the amount of energy and time expended maintaining such a volume of job descriptions and performance appraisals. Consider the complicated chain of communication among all of those positions. Worse yet, consider the bureaucratic process required to get a simple answer back to a valuable customer. In an attempt to be customer-oriented and responsive to the marketplace, Toyota compressed all of its positions into only seven position titles. Columbia/HCA is reengineering and plans to operate all of its facility types with only 40 position titles, including the CEO.

Understanding the qualifications and prerequisites that credentialing bodies require of home care organizations allows us next to consider the home care organization's structure using some of the reengineering strategies discussed in Chapter 1. It is at this point that brainstorming becomes essential as we examine and rethink the skill levels that currently exist. In retrospect, we can see that home care agencies have utilized the cross-training strategy at the practitioner level with nurses providing phlebotomy, electrocardiograms, and usually the admitting/discharge process; whereas the aides provide for the housecleaning, laundry, and meal preparation needs. Application of this strategy at the office support staff and management levels is a viable alternative for most agencies.

Cross training provides many staff with more broad-based knowledge and it is that broad understanding of the organization that allows staff to assist organizational customers better. Decisions about how various staff positions dovetail with each other must consider the customers of each position. For example, the physician "customer" works closely with the clinical staff and clinical managers. The patient works with the clinical staff and also the receptionist and billing office. The insurance company works with the billing and accounts receivable departments. Recognize that the decisions you make in your organization may not be the decisions I make in mine. What may be logical and appropriate in your agency is not necessarily logical and appropriate in another. Given this discussion, are there any positions within the organization that logically can be combined?

At the practitioner level of the organization, consideration must be given to the use of clinical specialists versus nurse generalists versus LPNs. What is the current and projected patient diagnosis mix? Do the clinical specialists possess a knowledge and desire to provide care external to their area of expertise? Can efficient care be provided by specialists? On the other hand, do generalists possess the in-depth acute care knowledge needed for today's home health care patient? For tomorrow's home health care patient? What care can safely be delegated to the LPN? Is there a difference in the quality of care provided by specialists, generalists, or LPNs? Is there value added if the organization decides to hire only clinical specialists at a higher cost? Is that value measurable? Is there value added by replacing current clinical specialists with generalists? Is that value measurable? Is there value added by replacing all RNs with LPNs? Is that even a possibility? What state regulations exist that dictate the skills that *must* be performed by a registered nurse? By an LPN? Can we use volunteer professional staff? In Chapter 4, in the skill mix example of cost reductions, the reader can see the fiscal savings that result from using this strategy. At this point the reader is thinking "...but...but...but." There is no need to have a coronary. The authors are simply asking some of the questions that may surface in a thorough brainstorming session.

Reengineering the Organization Staff

In order to apply the reengineering principles (as discussed in Chapter 1) to the staffing component, an abbreviated discussion is provided here of one of the central aspects of reengineering: brainstorming. Participants in the reengineering process need to make use of brainstorming. Some ideas may not be well thought out but every idea is documented by a group secretary. The only rule states, "No idea is a bad idea." In fact, all ideas are quickly documented, allowing maximum time for more ideas. If a negative thought is verbalized (such as "That won't work. Remember the time we tried that?"), the facilitator needs to document the negative thought for future discussion, thus allowing the brainstorming to continue. Participants can improve upon others' ideas. The beauty of brainstorming is the variety of ideas and perspectives shared by the participants, and their willingness to avoid holding back. One person generates a thought that sparks another idea, that creates a totally new and radical change for the reengineering organization.

Another strategy that comes to mind here is to promote efficiency at all staff levels. At this point, many participants become offended, citing their track record of working long, hard hours. The problem is that we equate efficiency with labor intensity. Efficiency means an organization works smarter, not harder, and attains both quality of services and planned, measurable outcomes with the least amount of resources. This can be realized through technical support, such as computerization and through expanded technical-based services, such as in-home cardiac monitoring. On a more basic level, however, this can be achieved by streamlining processes, evaluating job positions, and cross training employees.

A byproduct of decentralization may actually be enhanced flexibility and autonomy in service delivery. Consider the governments of countries without states or provinces. Everything must go back to the central government, which can only operate efficiently with one structure and set of rules that apply to all. The central government must maintain a unified approach to its operations regardless of the situation and the desire of the citizens. School systems in the United States operate similarly. The level of intelligence, speed of the learner, or interest in the subject often has little bearing on the curriculum, a curriculum set in stone. With such an approach, quick learners become bored, slow learners become frustrated, and all learners develop dislikes for subjects that were forced upon them. Transferring this same principle to home health care, can we not develop self-managed teams? Do we really need a scheduler in the main office or can we empower our employees to communicate directly with their patients to set a mutually convenient visit schedule? Do the patients really need to be seen during the hours that the office is open? Would the pool of available staff be larger in a controlling rather than controlled environment? Could there be a benefit to replacing several middle managers with a liaison nurse in the office? Certainly all of these questions lead to "but what about's . . . ". As the project team approaches its decision point, it needs to think seriously about all of the pros and cons.

In reengineering the staffing of the organization, the project team is encouraged to evaluate the market's technological advances aimed at promoting efficiency. An organization doesn't need millions of dollars to computerize. Personal computers are relatively inexpensive and can provide the smaller organization with ease in information management. Many companies have developed software packages specifically for the home care organization. Linking is available to allow one computer to talk with another. Consider the impact when the direct care staff member enters patient data, which can then be accessed immediately by office staff. Linkage with physician office staff is yet another possibility of computer networks. Aside from information management, consider the advances in technology that provide assessment information at the push of a button. Some examples include protime and glucose monitors, and cardiac monitors. We are on the verge of reaping the real value of telecommunications. Technology to evaluate the functional status of pacemakers and fax machines that relay important information from one office to the next are only two examples of telecommunication technology in existence. Communications with field staff is effortless through the use of cellular phones. The possibilities of telecommunications are explored further in Chapter 10.

Establishing the Hierarchical Structure

Although we've looked at the qualifications and prerequisites that the HIM 11 identifies for several of the positions, it is the organization that ultimately identifies each position's qualifications and prerequisites. Prior to setting those qualifications and prerequisites, however, the organization needs to establish the hierarchical structure under which it plans to operate and the position responsibilities. Application of the reengineering strategies may result in an organizational structure similar to that in Figure 5–2. This reengineered organization has a three-layered hierarchical structure that ensures ease of communication, minimizes steps in the decision-making process, and helps to streamline workflow involving human resource intervention. At first glance, one may lament the compression of the middle management staff. Let's look a little closer. Exhibit 5–2 shows some of the management positions within the organization prior to reengineering. A list of responsibilities, although incomplete, includes the major tasks for each position. Again, it is imperative for the organization

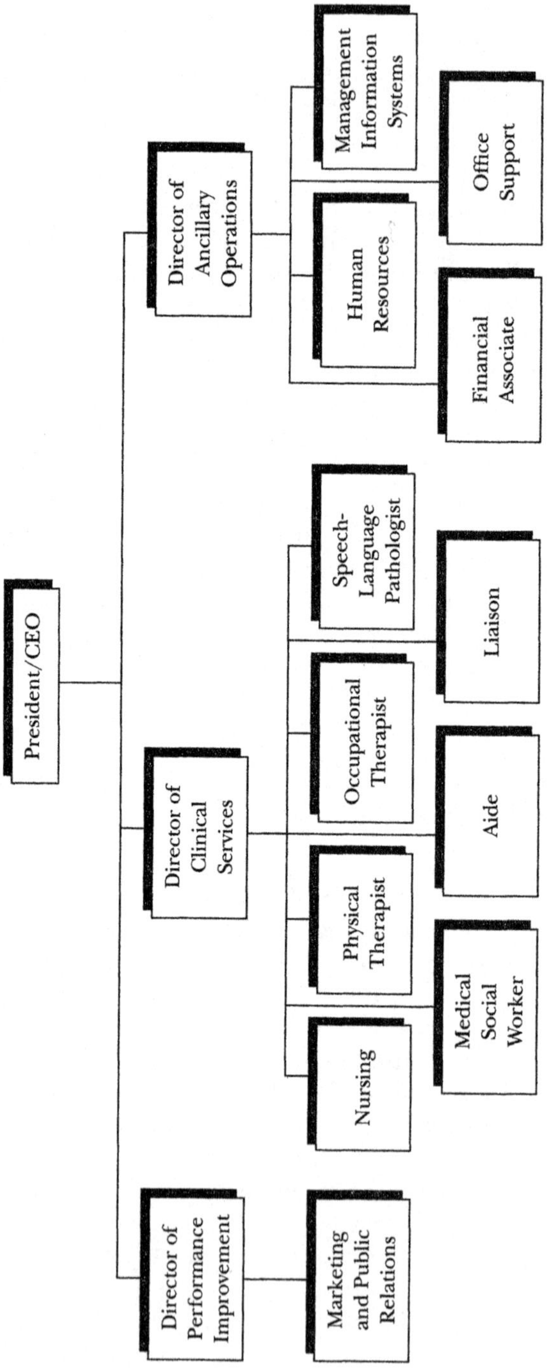

Figure 5–2 Organizational Structure (Reengineered Organization)

Exhibit 5–2 Prereengineering Management Position Responsibilities

Position	*Responsibilities*
President/CEO	• Oversees operational and fiscal management. • Liaison between the organization, board of directors, and community at large. • Coordinates the formation of an agency-wide strategic plan. • Establishes and models the organization's culture. • Periodically evaluates the agency in relation to its mission, values, and strategic goals.
Vice-President of Professional Services	• Researches and develops new programs. • Internal resource for professional staff. • Oversees the management of daily operations. • Establishes policy and procedures. • Liaison between the organization and professional associations.
Director of Professional Services	• Oversees daily operations. • Develops and implements work processes. • Implements quality initiatives, accreditation standards, and policy/procedures. • Liaison between the organization and third-party payers. • Hires professional and paraprofessional staff.
Nurse Manager	• Manages the day-to-day operations. • Assigns patients to individual case managers. • Collects performance improvement data. • Conducts utilization review and chart audits. • Liaison between organization management and staff. • Participates on committees and task forces as needed
Case Manager	• Assigns and schedules patient visits. • Admits patients for service. • Liaison between agency staff, patient, and physician. • Promotes continuity of patient care. • Assigns patients to direct field staff for care. • Coordinates all patient care. • Assists with the evaluation of the direct field staff. • Resource for agency staff, physicians, patient, and caregiver.
RNs/LPNs	• Provide nursing care to patients, as directed. • Admit patients for service, if needed (RNs only). • Liaison between the patient and agency.

to question all of these. What value is there for the agency to have six layers of customer liaisons? Why does it require two positions to assign and schedule patient visits? Is there a reason for having so many management staff positions? If so, what is the value of such restricted responsibilities? Can any of these positions be consolidated? Finally, if we consolidate positions, how many full-time equivalents (FTEs) do we need to hire for each newly structured position?

In Exhibit 5–3 the results of the reengineering process are manifested in two streamlined and condensed management positions with a reshuffling of responsibilities both upward and downward. The CEO takes on more operational activities by establishing policy and procedure and overseeing the management of daily operations. The director of clinical services assists in the development and implementation of new programs and processes, while the RNs and LPNs achieve more autonomy through self-scheduling. Essentially, all staff within the organization become a part of the changing organizational structure and gain new opportunities to develop skills in otherwise restricted areas.

Exhibit 5–3 Varied Competencies Within the Professional Nurse Position Description

Position Title: Professional Nurse

Position Summary: Performs nursing admission and follow-up visits. Responsible for the observation, education, and continuity of patient care. Collaborates with the patient's care team in the coordination of home health care.

Reports to: Director of Clinical Services

Qualifications and Prerequisites: Licensed as a registered professional nurse in the state of employment. Graduate of a National League for Nursing accredited school of nursing. BSN preferred. Minimum of two years of institutional nursing experience required.

Competency: Knowledgeable of nursing assessment and evaluation skills appropriate to the patient population served. CPR certified. Competent with phlebotomy and venous access. Able to read and write in English. Articulate in written documentation. Able to use a telephone and computer keyboard. Utilizes positive customer service skills. Population-specific competencies are as follows:

- Rehabilitation Nurse: knowledge of the principles and practice of rehabilitation nursing in all age groups.
- Psychiatric Nurse: knowledge of the psychosocial assessment for mental health disease in the preteen through adolescent age group.
- Maternal-Child: knowledge of the prenatal, antepartum, and newborn phases of growth, development, and care.
- Pediatric: knowledge of growth and development, disease processes, and psychosocial assessment for the age group from birth to 18 years of age.

While brainstorming and considering alternative position responsibilities and titles, the organization needs to find the common threads among current positions in order to define new positions. This process is especially effective in restructuring the office support staff. For example, Figure 5–3 depicts an organization with the following positions: accounting, billing, computer analyst, data entry, medical records, payroll, receptionist, scheduler, and secretary. This organization currently has at least one FTE in each position. Rather than considering them separate positions, the reengineering organization viewed them as *functions.* In this light, it became easier to find the common threads existing among them. This organization chose to consolidate the billing, accounting, and payroll functions under one position, which was retitled "Financial Associate." It cross trained the medical records secretary, data entry secretary, and computer analyst in each of these functions and retitled the position "Information Technologist." The newly created position of "Customer Service Representative" had qualified personnel able to function as schedulers, receptionists, and secretaries. Keep in mind that every organization is different. There exists no universal pattern, only principles to guide the reengineering process.

Tools 5–A–1 and 5–A–2 are included in the Appendix for the organization to conduct time studies for current staff positions. Tool 5–A–1 can be provided to all employees for their subjective completion. For example, a

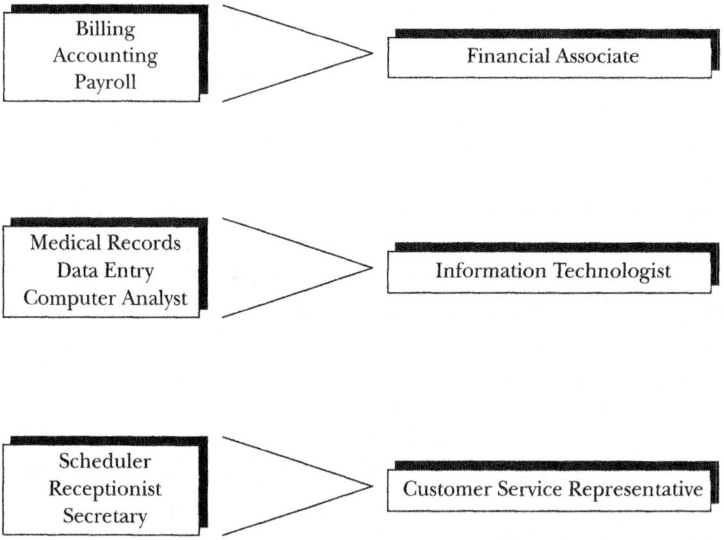

Figure 5–3 Position Consolidation

physical therapist may indicate the following activities and proportion the following percentages to each activity:

Referral communication	5 percent
Travel	15 percent
Direct patient care	45 percent
Answering pages	7 percent
Coordination of care activities	5 percent
Restocking care supplies	5 percent
Documentation	18 percent
Total	100 percent

Note that the percentages must add up to 100 percent. Completion of these forms by every physical therapist allows the agency to identify the activities currently performed by each position that can be delegated to another position. This type of streamlining then utilizes staff time in the best possible way promoting more efficiency of time usage.

Tool 5–A–2 is a more refined time analysis tool. Staff members are asked to note their activities at five-minute intervals. This is especially helpful for positions entailing coordination of activities as staff are often pulled away from one activity to intervene in another area. In other applications, this tool identifies opportunities for improvement of individual time management. Due to the time intensity of such a study, application of this tool is usually limited to a one- to two-week period.

Similarly, organizations can examine their current practice of multiple position descriptions within the same personnel level. It is not at all uncommon for today's home health care organization to have separate job descriptions for the rehabilitation nurse, maternal-child nurse, psychiatric nurse, registered nurse, on-call nurse, public health nurse I, and public health nurse II. Why can't this position be titled Professional Nurse? The responsibilities essentially encompass the functions of assessment, observation, evaluation, patient education, coordination, and documentation. Some readers may question the appropriateness of condensing these varied positions into one—after all, shouldn't the descriptions distinguish among varied competencies? Exhibit 5–3 is one solution to this problem. It shows a portion of the position description for professional nurse that accommodates the varying degrees of required nursing competencies. Note that the psychiatric nurse is competent only in the preteen and adolescent age group, as compared to the rehabilitation nurse, who is competent in all age groups. This organization set specific standards of competency levels to correlate with its rehabilitation and adolescent psychiatric programs.

As new positions are created, the organization needs to commit time, energy, and resources to cross train current staff into new roles. Following through with the example of the financial associate outlined above, each employee hired for that position must obtain training and be deemed competent in the billing, accounting, and payroll functions. By no means does this consolidation indicate that one FTE is replacing three FTEs. It simply means that each FTE in the financial associate position is capable of handling the payroll process, completing the financial ledgers while making payments, and accepting remittances and processing patient bills to a variety of payers. Staffing numbers need to be determined through a specific individualized analysis.

Determining Organization-Specific Qualifications, Prerequisites, and Job Responsibilities

It is at this point that the qualifications, prerequisites, and job responsibilities for each position can be identified. Recalling the position qualifications and prerequisites mandated by the HIM 11, it is evident that HCFA mandates no specific requirements for most management staff and office support staff. There needs to be, therefore, an organization-specific qualification, prerequisite, and competency established relative to the types of care provided. It is essential for the organization to ask why a specific prerequisite or qualification is required, because establishing parameters that prevent potentially excellent employees from joining your organization would be a disservice to the organization.

What qualifications are required for the financial associate? After contemplation, this organization decided that a high school diploma or equivalent is the only qualification required, although a certificate or degree in business is preferred. Some argued that the minimum entry should include a business degree, thus bringing a certain knowledge base to the organization and reducing the expense of training and orientation. Others argued that they had friends, who despite not completing high school, were very capable of performing the functions of billing, accounting, and payroll. The group discussed the pros and cons and set the qualifications based upon consensus.

In a similar manner, the prerequisites were evaluated. To establish the prerequisites for the financial associate, the group considered the maturity of its organization, seniority of its employees, market demands, and the current level of expertise versus the desired level of expertise. A newly formed organization in a rapidly growing environment may choose to require a minimum of five years of work experience, while a more mature organization with a known and stable in-house financial expert may require no previous work history. In this scenario, the organization decided a minimum of two years work history in a related position was essential.

Exhibit 5–4 depicts a position description for the newly created financial associate position. The position description specifies the required knowledge base to meet informational and regulatory needs. Position descriptions assist job applicants in understanding the core role of the position, reporting mechanisms, and requirements. The Federal Ameri-

Exhibit 5–4 Position Description: Financial Associate

Position Title: Financial Associate

Position Summary: Responsible for the entry of charges, payables, and receivables that result from daily operations. Generates patient bills and coordinates the collection process. Produces periodic reports utilizing generally acceptable accounting principles showing agency activity. Prepares payroll ledger and issues payment for all agency accounts payable.

Reports to: Director of Ancillary Operations

Qualifications and Prerequisites: High school diploma or equivalency required. Certificate or diploma in a business-related field preferred. Minimum of two years experience in an accounting, billing, or payroll position required.

Competency: Competency in billing, payroll, and accounting practices. Able to read and write in English. Able to use a telephone. Computer literate. Utilizes positive customer service skills.

Working Environment: Office setting

Position's Physical Demands: Sitting with occasional mobilization. Limited lifting of files not exceeding 10 pounds. Moderate stretching, bending, and reaching for filing of records. Extended time at computer.

Responsibilities and Duties:

1. Enters daily service-related and business-related charges and costs into the computer.
2. Posts receivables and payables.
3. Verifies account balances for patient charges and organization accounts.
4. Compiles management reports at least monthly and as requested.
5. Coordinates reimbursement activity for all outstanding accounts.
6. Verifies and prepares payroll ledger.
7. Enters and generates accounts payable checks.
8. Performs other duties as requested.

cans with Disabilities Act (ADA) mandates that reasonable accommodations be made for employees with disabilities. Listing the work environment and the position's physical demands not only educates the applicant about the position but also sets a foundation for the organization to ascertain the applicant's ability to perform the job's essential functions. Should the applicant not be able to meet one or more of the demands, the organization must make reasonable accommodation or justify an exemption based on undue financial hardship in making such an accommodation. The responsibilities and duties for this position are a combination of responsibilities from the previous billing, accounting, and payroll positions specific to this organization.

ACUITY LEVEL OF PATIENTS AND SCHEDULING

Now that the organization has streamlined its processes and determined a hierarchical structure and position responsibilities, it needs to consider the amount of output that can reasonably be expected per FTE. We must keep in mind that we are not working with widgets on a conveyer belt but instead, with people who have varying needs and expectations, and with a work environment laden with unknowns, such as traffic and extreme weather conditions. Some organizations have developed patient acuity levels to assist with scheduling field staff visits. This involves (1) determining the critical factors that must be considered in caring for the patient, (2) conducting a time study to determine the amount of time required for each patient encounter, and (3) categorizing the types of visits.

Critical factors to consider are elements such as travel time, patient care time, preparation time, and documentation time. Every agency must determine its own travel times relative to the speed limits, amounts of traffic, and parking conditions. In a small urban area in Pennsylvania a home care organization found that the city nurses required 15 minutes to travel one mile, whereas the country nurses traveled eight miles in that same 15 minutes. The number of miles, therefore, is not necessarily the deciding factor. In large urban areas the probability of traffic jams can be determined by evaluating time studies. Patient care times can be categorized into various levels. For example, a patient requiring assessments of physical conditions may require 10 minutes of the field staff's time, whereas a patient requiring an intravenous antibiotic administration may require 60 minutes of the field staff's time. Preparation time will vary depending on the roles and responsibilities of the field staff. Nurses who must physically access the computer for lab results, go to the files for patient education material, and restock their own nursing bags will require more preparation time than nurses working in agencies with an office support clerk who completes these functions for the field staff. Again, documentation time will vary from agency to agency depending on the level of computerization and simplicity of the documentation process. Although no acuity system is foolproof, an agency can target a productivity expectation of 90 to 95 percent. Once the organization has obtained time study data, they need to categorize the individual patients based on an aggregate time projection. The following categories provide an example of an acuity system:

Category 1: total time expenditure of up to 19 minutes

Category 2: total time expenditure of 20–30 minutes

Category 3: total time expenditure of 31–45 minutes

Category 4: total time expenditure of 46–60 minutes

Special: total time expenditure for a period greater than 60 minutes. This category requires close monitoring and payment arrangements based on special costing factors

These times and categories will vary by agency, depending on operational processes, technological support, and environmental factors. A time study format is included in Appendix 5–A for use by the organization.

ESTABLISHING AND MAINTAINING COMPETENCY

Competency must exist at all levels of the organization: the board of directors, management, staff, and volunteers. Although this seems like a logical statement, organizations sometimes find themselves suffering from poor leadership or organizational dysfunction as a result of poor hiring decisions. This can occur as a result of dire need when there is limited availability of applicants. Organizations must carefully establish position competencies, commit them to writing, seek qualified individuals to fill the positions, and evaluate those competencies on an ongoing basis. Interventions may be needed to ensure that all levels of the organization remain competent.

The basic question to ask when developing a competency tool is, What are the skills and areas for which this position is responsible and must maintain a thorough knowledge base? The best place to start is with the employees in the current positions. Ask each employee to list the skills he or she has and knowledge needed to perform the job. Exhibit 5–5 shows two completed forms, one for the information technologist and one for the physical therapist. Note that the credentialing requirements from the HIM 11 and organizational requirements were included on the list. The

Exhibit 5–5 Sample Staff Position Competency Lists

Position: Information Technologist	**Position:** Physical Therapist
Competencies/Skills Required:	**Competencies/Skills Required:**
1. Knowledge of ICD9 coding	1. Graduate of an approved physical therapy school
2. Principles of filing	2. Minimum of two years of experience
3. Computer literacy	3. Licensed to practice in this state
4. Knowledge of computer programming	4. CPR certification
5. Use of copier, including adding toner	5. Assessment skills
6. Customer service skills	6. Development of exercise program specific to patient condition
7. Use of multiline phone	7. Application of adult learning principles
8.	8. Electromuscular stimulation
9.	9. Setup of continuous passive range of motion machine
10.	10. Joint immobilization
11.	11. Use of goniometer
12.	12. Setup of TENS machine
13.	13. Use of ultrasound machine
14.	14. Use of laptop computer
15.	15.

employee then added essential skills and competencies from his or her individual perspective. Such a list can be used for every position within the organization. The Joint Commission requires direct observation of skill competencies at periodic levels for all direct care staff. This includes nurses, therapists, social workers, delivery persons, aides, homemakers, companions, and any other position providing hands-on care, education, or direct service. Competency observation is not required for the office support staff and the management staff, however, the organization may choose to assess the competency of all positions on an ongoing basis. At minimum, the staff's input regarding necessary skills and competencies can be sought during interviews to help establish prehiring capabilities and render the best hiring decision possible among the applicants.

A competent board of directors assists the successful organization in its pursuit of quality services in many ways. Often, the board's expertise brings new information and innovative ideas to the organization. Individual competencies for board membership may include an understanding of the history of the organization, its mission, values, and objectives and also the needs of the community at large as well as an understanding of public relation principles. Aggregate board competencies can include knowledge of business, health care law, human resource management, marketing, public relation strategies, medical science, finances, and consumer use of home care.

Traditionally, volunteers have been used in office support or fund raising roles. The upsurge of hospice organizations has led to expanded roles for volunteers in direct patient care related activities, such as simple home maintenance and ambulation assistance. While reengineering, the organization should consider other uses for volunteer workers. Who is available in the community? Perhaps there are retired nursing instructors willing to make postdischarge phone contacts with patients or periodic phone contacts with current long-term patients who receive less frequent visits. Possibly the organization can tap into community resources, such as the Senior Council of Retired Executives (SCORE), for task force coordination of a special project. Maybe former caregivers want to volunteer their time in the capacity of a home health aide or can help your organization expand into nontraditional services, such as grocery delivery or transportation. Once the functions are defined, the volunteer's list of competencies can be developed and utilized to elevate the organization's level of service.

Generally, staff in all levels of the organization want to do a good job. Conflict may arise at times related to the performance of an individual and it behooves the organization to have a basic list of needed skills outlined for each position. The organization may also need to offer orientation, inservice education, or long-term training about some of the basic competencies. It is only through identifying the skills and assessing employees' capabilities that management can determine the need for intervention.

DESIGNING ORIENTATION AND ONGOING EDUCATIONAL PROGRAMS

Developing a list of skills and competencies required for all staff is the first step in preparing a position-specific orientation and inservice education program. In order to assure a competent staff, the organization needs to provide both general and specific information to the newly hired employee. But first, let's expand on the requirements for employee orientation as discussed in Chapter 3. The HCFA specifies no orientation requirements in the HIM 11 but does require that the organization show evidence of licensure and certification of direct care givers, when appropriate. The CHAP standards specify the following requirements for orientation:

- Personnel records must show evidence of an orientation.
- A formal orientation program outlining important aspects of the organization must exist for newly hired employees.
- Contracted personnel must be oriented to the organization in addition to employees.[8]

The Joint Commission presents very detailed elements for inclusion in the orientation of the staff and contractors of the home health care organization. These elements are found throughout the Joint Commission manual and include:

- waste disposal of hazardous and infective material
- infection control practices
- confidentiality of patient information
- essential policies and procedures
- community resource availability for the organization's area
- referral process
- staff safety concerns and practices in the home and community
- home safety assessment
- actions to take in the event of a natural or man-made disaster
- advance directive practices
- care of the terminal patient
- information data collection
- use of equipment
- services provided by the agency
- patient care responsibilities[9]

The previously established list of skills and competencies can be used for a position-specific orientation to the employee's patient care responsibilities. Exhibits 5–6 and 5–7 are sample orientation checklists developed by the authors. Each new employee is provided the general orientation and the applicable position-specific orientation.

Exhibit 5–6 General Home Health Agency Orientation

General Home Health Agency Orientation Checklist

Employee Name ______________________________

Hire Date ______________________________

General Orientation Item	Oriented by:	Date Oriented:
Mission		
Values		
Goals		
Services		
Strategic Plan		
Organizational Structure		
Confidentiality		
Community Resources		
Referral Process		
Disaster Plan (natural or man-made)		
Policies and Procedures Administrative Human Resource Infection Control Clinical		
Communication Process		
Payroll Process		
Staff Meetings		
In Service Education		

My signature indicates that I have participated in the above orientation.

______________________________ ______________________________

Employee Oriented by

The reengineering organization also needs to consider its current processes. How cumbersome are they? A flowchart is an excellent tool for mapping out the steps in a process. Be careful to list each and every step to allow for a critical analysis of how processes within the organization unfold. The shapes in a flowchart indicate specific points in the process, as follows:

Exhibit 5–7 Position-Specific Orientation

Physical Therapist Position Orientation Checklist

Employee Name ______________________________

Hire Date ______________________________

Position-Specific Orientation Item	**Oriented by:**	**Date Oriented:**
Reporting Structure		
Documentation Requirements		
Assessment		
Development of Exercise Program		
Adult Learning Principles		
Electro-Muscular Stimulation		
CPM Machine		
Joint Immobilization		
Goniometer Use		
TENS		
Ultrasound Machine		
Laptop Computer		

My signature indicates that I have participated in the above orientation.

______________________ ______________________

Employee Oriented by

- oval: demonstrates information
- rectangle: demonstrates a task or activity
- diamond: demonstrates decision points
- circle: demonstrates a break in the process

The flowchart in Figure 5–4 depicts the current orientation process for Home Health Agency X. Analyzing the flowchart, one can see that at least three staff members perform the general agency orientation process based upon the classification of the employee. Is there any value added to the orientation process if the new hire receives general orientation from his or her immediate supervisor? During the evaluation of the orientation, this organization's reengineering team elicited input from staff and found that

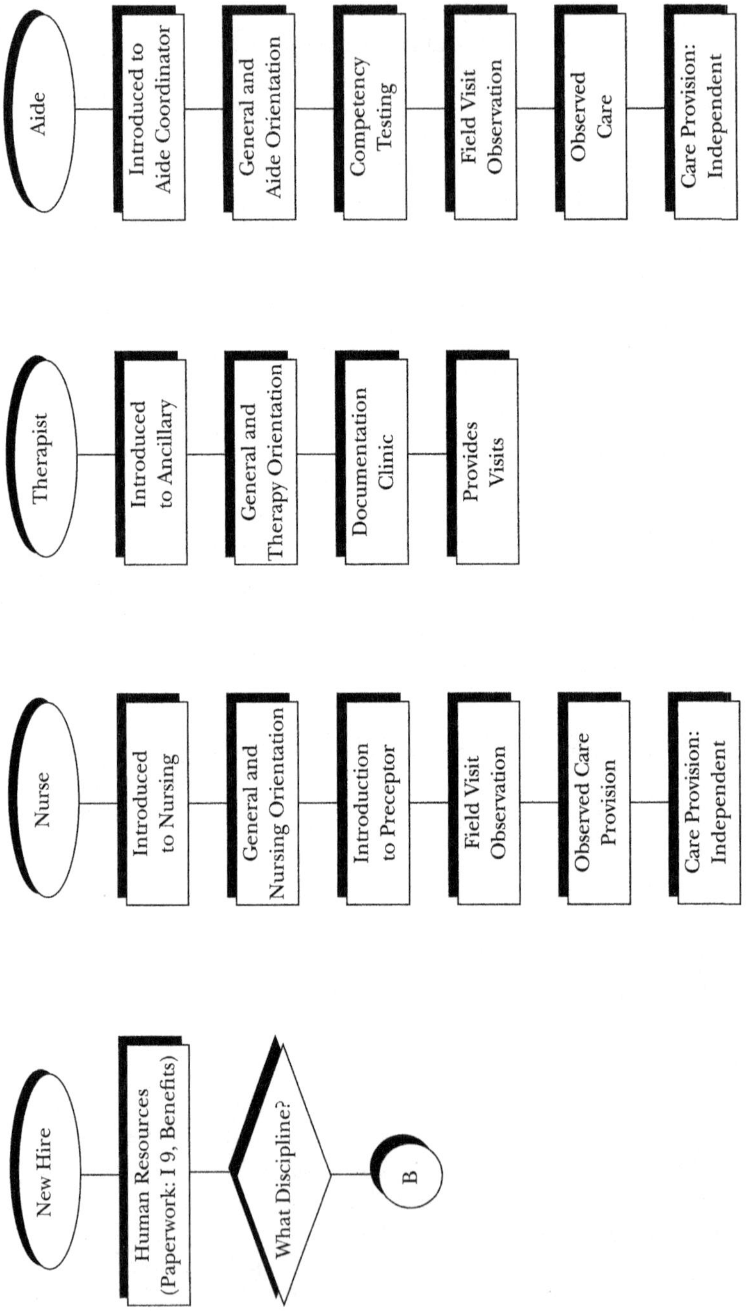

Figure 5–4 Orientation Process Flowchart Before Reengineering

no specific reason existed other than, "That's the way we always did it." In addition to the use of multiple managers for the general agency orientation, the team uncovered another area of ineffectiveness. Each manager was orienting staff with different information under the specified headings on the orientation checklist. This lack of consistency potentially can result in different rules for different people, a lack of understanding of the contents of the orientation, and ultimately, low staff morale. The team brainstormed some alternatives and reengineered the process to that delineated in Figure 5–5.

In its reengineered format, the general orientation is transferred to the human resource manager, however, the team also recommended that the orientation be placed on a videotape to streamline the process even further. Currently, this agency does not have the capability to videotape a quality general orientation but the team has placed this idea into its future planning portfolio so as to not lose sight of it. Not every idea is practical or feasible during the initial phase of reengineering so it is important to maintain a holding area for valuable processes, technical equipment, and other ideas considered by the team. To prepare the staff for this new orientation process several steps were required:

1. Staff input was obtained initially and then periodically throughout the planning phase. This established a sense of belonging and a feeling of ownership for the staff.
2. Ongoing communications were provided to the staff about the need to reengineer the orientation process.
3. The staff was informed of the tentative plan for revision and provided with an opportunity for questions and answers. Although the team had the ultimate authority to finalize the orientation process, staff questions were helpful in refining the final process.
4. The managers conducting the general orientation educated the human resource department about the contents. This cross training prepared the human resource manager for this new responsibility and also provided the organization with yet another person trained in the area of general orientation.

As the team continued to reengineer other processes, it maintained that a videotape of the general orientation would be beneficial and later added other items, such as patient education, to its list of potential areas for reengineering.

Some organizations have used the term reengineer synonymously with downsizing, which is unfortunate. Reengineering often redefines positions. Although reengineering sometimes results in a decline of FTEs due

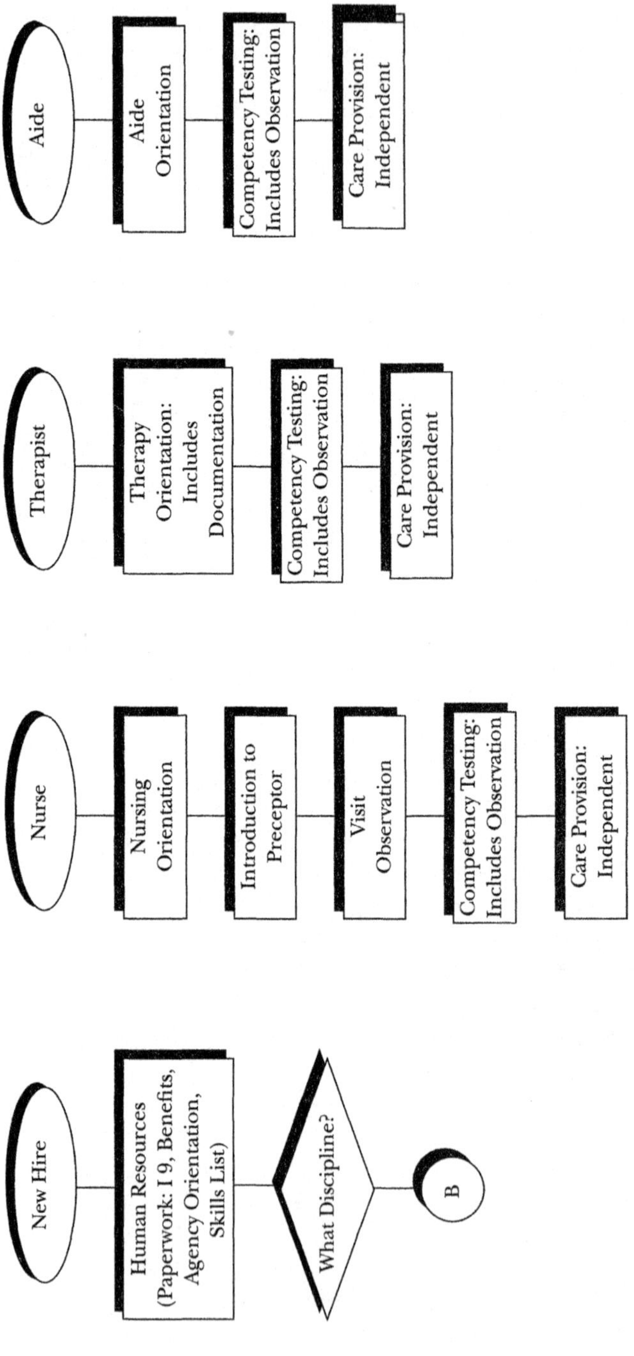

Note: new staff is introduced on an informal basis, and formally at the first monthly staff meeting.

Figure 5–5 Orientation Process Flowchart After Reengineering

to streamlined processes, the opposite can also occur. Perhaps staffing within an organization currently is not sufficient to meet the demands for the volume of work, despite streamlined and reengineered processes. At times, a new classification may need to be added for a specialty position because the position requires specific skills that cannot be taught to others. In the scenario above, for example, the organization decided that the addition of an audiovisual specialist would provide them with the in-house expertise to make not only orientation videos but also a patient education series. The team asked several important questions: Why do we need this position? Does it have to be a trained specialist or can we cross train another position familiar with audiovisual technology? What is the value of adding an expert? What is the value of adding this new capability? Ultimately, the decision to hire an audiovisual specialist might allow the agency to develop a new service line—audiovisual productions and videos.

STAFFING MIX AND PRODUCTIVITY

Home care agency leaders frequently question what is the best ratio of visits per nurse per day, average miles per staff member per day, and appropriate duration of visits per patient per day. All of this information is important in the budget development process. The National Association for Home Care (NAHC) publishes annual statistics related to these areas. Over the past few years, these statistics have remained fairly constant. Nurses make an average of 5.5 visits each per 8-hour day.[10] A random sampling of home health agencies shows that, on average, they have five employees in the billing department and two additional employees working on accounts receivable for every 100,000 visits provided annually. There is an average of one manager for every 10 employees. What do all of these numbers tell us? Not much! One cannot compare a hospital-based home care program with a free-standing agency or compare a billing department in a large, computerized organization with a small, rural Mom and Pop agency with no computer capabilities. The numbers we gather and the numbers we read are simply reported averages. Without the intrinsic knowledge of the organization's efficiency one cannot compare organization staffing mix and levels; it's like comparing apples to oranges.

Predicting and planning staffing mix and volume ratios is a vital component of any well-run organization. Determining staffing ratios and productivity expectations depends on the efficiency of the organization. Efficiency is a difficult concept to embrace. How do we know that something is efficient? The term efficiency seems to have as many definitions as letters of the alphabet. Some use the following definitions:

1. Griffith[11] defines efficiency as $\text{Efficiency} = \dfrac{\text{Output}}{\text{Input}}$
2. Webster's Dictionary defines efficiency as giving a relatively high amount of work.[12]
3. Insurers define efficiency as desired outcomes for the least expensive cost.

Regardless of the definition used, organizations need to identify a way to measure their efficiency. How do you know that the result of your resource consumption has value? Organizations need to determine a measurable way to evaluate their work processes and individual worker output. Once this is done, they can begin to compile meaningful data. Without measuring our output and looking closely at our results, we have no way of knowing if we are simply providing care or entering data or answering the phone with just speed or with quality *and* speed. The effects of reengineering help us to establish consistently good outputs with the least amount of resources, resulting in decreased costs. Using Griffiths' definition, it is conceivable that two organizations can be equally efficient yet provide care for a wide variation in cost. The answer then becomes not to increase the productivity expectation but rather to increase the technology used and streamline the processes.

Staff mix needs to change periodically. At the time of this writing, there was discussion that HCFA was planning a major social service change to the HIM 11, specifically, to reduce the qualifications for social services from a master's degree level to a bachelor's level. If this comes to fruition, it would be in the agency's best interest to hire BSWs at a lower salary than to maintain a full cadre of MSWs, unless developed programs require the special skills of the MSW. Likewise, many states have relaxed their nurse practice acts, allowing LPNs to insert intravenous access devices with the appropriate level of education. Some agencies now recognize the use of physical therapy assistants in home health care. These therapists are capable of providing physical therapy to the patient as long as they are supervised at periodic intervals by the physical therapist. BSWs, LPNs, and PTAs are just three disciplines no one anticipated in the organizational structure of the 1980s. Agencies need to consider the cost/benefit ratio of replacing some of these qualified personnel for others.

Once the organization has measured its outputs and knows that the care it is providing is efficient (good outcomes with the least amount of resources at lowered costs), it can begin to benchmark with other organizations to identify and compare productivity values and staffing needs. Only well-defined outputs provide well-defined expectations and then the expectations established can only be improved.

CONCLUSION

In summation, we have looked at a multitude of extraneous factors that must be explored as we identify staffing needs for our organizations. We have defined our services and considered the requirements of regulatory and accreditation bodies. We have considered personnel prerequisites, qualifications, and competencies. We also looked at the organizational structure and decided that there is merit to reducing the layers of personnel within an organization. We also applied reengineering principles as we streamlined the orientation process and cross trained employees to consolidated positions. All of these steps are important and need to be completed in conjunction with addressing operational issues such as documentation revisions, which will be detailed in Chapter 6.

NOTES

1. National League for Health Care, Inc. and Community Health Accreditation Program, Inc., *Standards of Excellence for Home Care Organizations* (New York, N.Y.: 1993), 57.
2. Joint Commission on Accreditation of Healthcare Organizations, *1995 AMHC Accreditation Manual* (Oakbrook Terrace, Ill.: 1994), 284.
3. HCFA, U.S. Department of Health and Human Services, *A Provider's Guide to the Home Health Certification Process,* Reg. 484.4 (Washington, D.C.: 1993).
4. National League, *Standards of Excellence,* Glossary 6.
5. Joint Commission, *1995 AMHC Accreditation Manual,* 284.
6. Ibid., 292.
7. C.R. Curran, *Developing Integrated Delivery Networks.* (Presentation at meeting of ACHE, Williamsburg, Virginia, July 27, 1995).
8. National League, *Standards of Excellence,* Glossary 6.
9. Joint Commission, *1995 AMHC Accreditation Manual,* 282.
10. Random survey conducted by authors.
11. J.R. Griffith, *The Well Managed Community Hospital,* 2nd ed. (Ann Arbor, Mich.: Health Administration Press, 1992), 664.
12. Webster's Handy College Dictionary (1981), 176.

Appendix 5–A

Tools

Tool 5–A–1 Position Activities

List the activities that comprise your workday and estimate the percentage of time you engage in each activity. Remember, the percentages must add up to 100%.

Activity	Percentage of Time	
	Total	**100%**

Tool 5–A–2 Time Study

Position ____

Please document your activities in 5-minute increments:

Time begins at 7 AM – 7 PM (circle one)

7:00	10:00	1:00	4:00
7:05	10:05	1:05	4:05
7:10	10:10	1:10	4:10
7:15	10:15	1:15	4:15
7:20	10:20	1:20	4:20
7:25	10:25	1:25	4:25
7:30	10:30	1:30	4:30
7:35	10:35	1:35	4:35
7:40	10:40	1:40	4:40
7:45	10:45	1:45	4:45
7:50	10:50	1:50	4:50
7:55	10:55	1:55	4:55
8:00	11:00	2:00	5:00
8:05	11:05	2:05	5:05
8:10	11:10	2:10	5:10
8:15	11:15	2:15	5:15
8:20	11:20	2:20	5:20
8:25	11:25	2:25	5:25
8:30	11:30	2:30	5:30
8:35	11:35	2:35	5:35
8:40	11:40	2:40	5:40
8:45	11:45	2:45	5:45
8:50	11:50	2:50	5:50
8:55	11:55	2:55	5:55
9:00	12:00	3:00	6:00
9:05	12:05	3:05	6:05
9:10	12:10	3:10	6:10
9:15	12:15	3:15	6:15
9:20	12:20	3:20	6:20
9:25	12:25	3:25	6:25
9:30	12:30	3:30	6:30
9:35	12:35	3:35	6:35
9:40	12:40	3:40	6:40
9:45	12:45	3:45	6:45
9:50	12:50	3:50	6:50
9:55	12:55	3:55	6:55

Chapter 6

Operational Considerations

The primary outcomes for reengineered organizations are demonstrated improvements in the areas of patient satisfaction, worker satisfaction, staffing, organizational and clinical outcomes, and cost savings.[1] In determining the operational considerations, each of these outcomes, along with the generation of increased revenue, must be included in the reengineering process. Flarey and Blancett list the outcomes of reengineering as simplicity, expediency, cultural transformation, increased market share, and increased viability.[2] These too are commendable outcomes.

To be successful in reengineering the organization's operations, the leaders of the organization and the reengineering team must overcome some commonly recognized barriers. Murphy identifies these barriers as top management hesitation, physician concern, staff resistance, union opposition, departmental walls, middle management paradigms, and cost of physical renovations.[3] These operational barriers to reengineering must be given serious consideration. These authors also include the expense of capital equipment, work flow, and organizational culture as additional barriers to change. How does the leader transform a reengineering plan into action and what operational issues must be considered prior to actual implementation?

Transitioning the organization into a reengineered entity requires forethought and careful planning. The organization seeking excellence and efficiency as its mission has a commendable goal. An organized learning approach to the process and task analysis was previously discussed in Chapter 1. The following chapters apply these strategies within the home care setting in the areas of staffing needs and accreditation and regulatory requirements. In this chapter, we will discuss transitioning and operational concerns that arise as we move the redesigned processes forward. Many leadership skills are required throughout all stages of a reengineering project, but at this transition stage the consolidated efforts of members from all teams are needed to continue the project's success. Redesigning and reengineering requires consideration of the interrelated operations that will be affected by the reengineered tasks and processes. They also require the availability of the necessary supplies, staff, and equipment to implement the project, without unnecessary delays and impediments to the initiation of the newly designed process.

OPERATIONAL STRATEGIES

Those strategies that demonstrated the application of the reengineering process to home care in Chapter 3 will now be discussed from the aspect of operational considerations that must be included when implementing reengineered processes. The strategies discussed here have emerged most often in the home care organization that has undergone the reengineering process. *Strategy 1,* Documentation Simplification, has historically received attention in the home health care arena due to the ever-growing burden of paperwork in home care. *Strategy 2,* Skill Mix Revision, has also taken on an increased importance in the current home health reimbursement arena in which the Medicare cost caps have seen increasingly diminished increases. The need to provide quality care with a changing mix of field staff has also been affected by the universal problem of unavailability of the physical therapist. In those states where a physical therapy assistant is permitted to practice within the home setting, home care organizations have already experienced a revision of staffing patterns and skill mix. As a response to the increased focus on customer service and responsiveness to home care's referral sources, *Strategy 3,* Admission/Referral Process Redesign, can serve to enhance customer relations and perceptions of the home care organization's services. Finally, *Strategy 4,* Hierarchy Redesign, has emerged as a consistent element of all reengineering projects. The flattening out of the organizational chart is one of the most critical elements within any reengineering project. These four strategies have been chosen for discussion because of their significant impact and importance to home care as well as their universal presence within most home care reengineering projects.

Strategy 1: Documentation Simplification

Prior to implementation of a redesigned documentation process, a number of operational considerations must be examined, such as the current status of the documentation system—is it paper or is it computerized, is the current system a narrative or checklist format? Recently, in discussing a reengineering design project, the question of computer compatibility and computer application support arose, and both of the senior management individuals readily acknowledged that the computer system in place could not support the redesigns being considered. For this organization the state of its computer systems was a critical consideration in determining the direction of its reengineered documentation system. In this case, as in most reengineering projects, enhancement of technological support in the form of a new computer system was recognized as also being integral to the overall success of the project and thus the reengineering of the documentation system need not be confined to what was presently in place in terms of computer support. The barriers of middle management paradigms and staff satisfaction are factors in this reengineering strategy.

If one of the middle management paradigms is that all nursing documentation must be made in the form of narrative charting, then the redesign of the documentation process, for example, to a streamlined checklist approach, will meet with a great deal of opposition. Within each of us exists paradigm or tunnel thinking. In order to achieve success with reengineering, each of us truly needs to step out of the box and look at the situation with new eyes and minds. Similarly the registered nurse's satisfaction or dissatisfaction with the redesigned documentation system will affect the implementation and acceptance of the new system. The identification of the barriers within each of these employee groups will assist in a smooth transition to the newly redesigned documentation system. The outcome of documentation simplification should be a cost-efficient, labor-saving approach to the paperwork accompanying each and every home care visit. The staff and the middle management must believe that the new documentation process will be better and cost-efficient without diminishing patient care and satisfaction. The barrier of organizational culture (i.e., the old way of doing things) must be overcome to implement this change successfully.

Staff Inservicing

When an organization decides to revise its documentation processes, inservice training must be planned to orient all field, support, and management staff to the revisions. Content for the inservice should include the new format itself, the flow of the chart forms throughout the organization, the coding system to use for documentation, and the implications of Medicare regulations and other accreditation standards for the new documentation. In addition to the how tos of the new documentation system, it is also important to inform staff of the whys—why the documentation process is being revised. This would include discussion of what went into the decisions and what enhancements are expected as a result of this redesigned charting system. Management should provide the staff with input prior to the actual implementation. Also, the new system should contain a mechanism for obtaining ongoing staff feedback regarding the functional use of the new system and suggested refinements.

Form Redesign

The process of redesigning forms is also an operational consideration of the reengineered documentation process. In redesigning forms, the task force on form redesign should include data entry, billing, and field personnel to ensure that new form design is functional in all areas of use. The data entry staff must be able to read and understand the new format, which must be easy to enter into the computer system. Forms must also provide all information needed for billing department employees to prepare and submit accurate bills to the payers.

Pricing and acquisition of a start-up supply of the new forms is important in the operational implementation planning of the task force. It is suggested that only a 30-day supply be purchased initially, to allow for refinement and revision based on the input of field and office staff once utilization begins. If a huge inventory is purchased too early in the process, money and resources can be wasted.

Strategy 2: Skill Mix Revision

Staff Meeting

The newly revised position responsibilities should be presented in a staff meeting, which allows an opportunity for all staff to ask questions about the changes and revisions. Management should explain the decision process used to realign staffing skill mix and responsibilities of the positions affected. Job revisions should be discussed with those affected, prior to the first full staff meeting. In this staff meeting, the whys of the decision and the expanded importance of each staff member's role in the organization should be emphasized. It should be explained that not only will the given example of LPN/RN skill level mix be implemented, but that many other positions will be similarly affected.

The staff meeting is also the time for management to communicate to the staff the expected outcomes for the organization that will result from having cross-trained and multiskilled workers. The redesigning of office, management, and care teams all contribute to the successful implementation of this reengineering strategy.

Job Description/Performance Appraisal Redesign

In order to support the redesigned multiskilled work teams, the organization needs to rewrite position descriptions and its performance appraisal system. This allows for individuals to be evaluated according to the newly defined position responsibilities. Professional development goals will also need to be revised to account for new multiskilled tasks and cross training.

When implementing the work redesign/staff skill mix revisions and developing the supporting performance appraisal/job description system, this task force should include representatives from the human resources department, as well as from clerical and field staff. Input from these individuals regarding the inservice education, skills cross training, and initiation of the new performance appraisal process are essential to the success of this process redesign.

Strategy 3: Admission/Referral Process Redesign

These operational outcomes, patient satisfaction and the barrier of physician concerns, are often those considered the primary focus in this redesign process. When redesigning this process, these considerations, in turn, become the goals—to improve the operational process of the referral and admitting of a patient, thus enhancing patient satisfaction. With enhanced patient satisfaction and improved referral/admission process, physician concerns regarding the quality of the services of the organization will be diminished.

Input from high-volume referral sources is important to streamlining the admission/referral process to meet or exceed customer expectations. It is recommended that major organizational referral sources be represented on this implementation task force. Other task force members should include a community liaison coordinator, intake and admission nurses, and support service personnel. These individuals are vital contributors to the revised forms and processes. Ask your customers what you can do better in the referral process and they will provide you with a wealth of information.

Technology

Laptop computers for the in-home field staff to input data directly at the time of admission are essential for timely and nonduplicative information gathering for newly admitted patients. These data can then be downloaded onto the hard drive of the main computer in the office. Admission data should be assigned priority for printing or on-line access in order to provide for dissemination to the entire patient care team and the billing and registration staff. The benefits of this technology far outweigh the costs, but the issue of cost must be considered and addressed in the redesign of the admission/referral process.

Customer Service Training

Staffing satisfaction, staffing outcomes, and clinical outcomes will be enhanced as a result of customer service training. This training is provided throughout the organization. Participation of support/office staff, management staff, and intake and admitting staff in a comprehensive customer service training program enhances the effectiveness of the newly redesigned admission/referral process. If time and resources allow, it is important to provide a condensed customer training program to all employees of the organization in which the emphasis on exceeding customer expectations can be presented and discussed in detail.

Job Description/Performance Appraisal System

Rewriting of the new combined roles for admission/referral staff and staff orientation to these new roles is critical for implementation of this reengineering strategy. All positions will include customer service responsibilities and expectations. These revisions can be made simultaneously with those of the skill mix and cross-training revisions.

Strategy 4: Hierarchy Redesign

Hierarchy redesign is often equated to the flattening out of an organizational chart, but it is much more than this. Hierarchy redesign includes the study of role responsibilities and relationships in order to determine not just how many levels there are to an organizational chart, but also which positions most appropriately report to which job titles and positions. It is also necessary to determine which positions are most suited for cross-training and blending. In home health care the utilization of a case manager, whose role might correlate to that of the "lead worker" in a reengineered health care organization, is already recognized and in place. But when reengineering, the typical home care positions will be expanded and combined into other examples, such as the case manager, which currently exists.

Barriers to be considered when implementing this reengineered structural design include top management hesitation, middle management paradigms, and union and staff opposition. It is the authors' belief that it is important to not only recognize these barriers, but also to take a proactive approach to these barriers.

For the organization that is unionized, the services of a highly trained expert in the field of union negotiations might be required in order that the reengineering of staff positions be accomplished. In some cases, the expert, after careful evaluation of the union's influence within the organization, might be able to achieve a "no" vote and free up the organization to proceed without the influence of the union representative.

Staff opposition must be heard, responded to, and included in the decisions being made about the reengineered positions and the redesign of the organization's structure. In order to achieve staff buy in and support, the first two barriers must be addressed and resolved. The top management must also be listened to and educated about reengineering and hierarchy redesign in order that their support be gained, and they in turn can overcome the paradigms of thinking of the middle management team.

Because all employees are aware that all positions are being examined for value and relevancy to the organization, all employees will naturally feel concerned about their future. This should be dealt with openly and honestly at this stage of the reengineering project where hierarchy redesign and position redesign are occurring. In taking a proactive approach, i.e., recognizing, addressing, and responding to these very real concerns at this stage of the project, the potential for success is greatly enhanced.

Job Descriptions/Performance Appraisals

When reengineering and redesigning the organization, as stated earlier, all positions will be affected. That means that each and every position is scrutinized for relevancy and value and that each job description is likely to undergo revisions and changes. Because, in many cases, positions are eliminated, with those remaining taking on the key functions of the eliminated positions, time must be provided for staff training and orientation to the changes. These newly redesigned position descriptions and performance appraisals require that staff be oriented to their new responsibilities and expectations. The revisions also should coincide with those examples and strategies explained above, so that only one revision of the job descriptions/performance appraisals is necessary.

Orientation/Training

If current employees do not meet the competency and proficiency expectations of the newly redesigned positions, several alternatives are available to the organization. They include requiring the application, interviewing, and rehiring process for the individuals currently on staff; external recruitment of qualified personnel; establishing professional development expectations for individuals within the organization and/or provision of planned training and inservice offerings to the personnel on staff in order that they are prepared for the competencies, skills, and expectations of these positions.

Outplacement Services

If the organization decides not to place current employees in the newly redesigned positions, then it should develop outplacement services and severance packages. These services assist the employee in the transition process and in seeking alternative employment. It is the individual organization's decision as to the extent of the services and types of packages provided. Length of time with the organization is often one factor in determining the packages provided. Management, human resource, fiscal, and board input are included in designing a suitable package that is in keeping with the organization's resources.

KEY OPERATIONAL CONSIDERATIONS

In addition to these specific operational applications of reengineering strategies, there are many operational considerations necessary for the successful reengineering of the organization. Following are some of the key considerations that must be examined in the implementation of other reengineering strategies.

Fiscal/Budgetary Priorities

Consideration must be given to the capital expenditure budget in order to prioritize the allocation of the organization's resources. One area of process reengineering involves the enhancement of computerization/information systems. Instant on-line access to data is vital to efficiency and to the elimination of rework and duplication of efforts.

Laptop and hand-held computers available to the organization can provide on-line access. This can be an expensive capital outlay and may necessitate a long-range purchasing plan, prioritizing who will receive the first computers purchased. The computer analysis tool discussed in Chapter 4 and included in Appendix 4–A can be used to evaluate and choose the computer systems best suited to meet the needs of the organization.

Another fiscal consideration involves the current retrospective Medicare reimbursement structure, which allows capital expenditure decisions to be made based upon the organization's cost relationship to its caps. If Medicare retrospective reimbursement remains in force, it is to the organization's advantage to prepare itself for prospective payment and managed care by acquiring the tools and equipment necessary to support efficiency.

A streamlined and more accurate billing and collections process is an important consideration in a redesigned organizational structure. The project team should consider the implications of all revisions in light of the organization's fiscal processes.

Human Resources

Regarding the area of human resources, we earlier discussed the rewriting of job descriptions and performance appraisals necessary to support the reengineering project. The orientation and retraining of multiskilled workers for the newly expanded job descriptions/positions is another key support element in the implementation process. Outplacement services discussed earlier are offered to support any employees who find their positions have been eliminated as a result of reengineering. When applicable, early retirement packages should also be considered to ease the transition of the employee with many years of seniority who might also be approaching retirement age.

In organizations that have union employees, union representation should be included early in the reengineering project. Union acceptance of the redesigned positions will be important to the organization's ability to move forward with the reengineering project.

Improving Organizational Performance/Quality Improvement

As part of the reengineering process, it is important to consider any redesigns in light of the quality improvement program or improving organizational performance plan. The existing quality improvement/quality assurance data provide information to the task forces upon which to make decisions regarding process redesign. The newly reengineered processes also provide projects to be considered for organizational performance improvement. Redesigned and reengineered processes should be monitored for performance improvement and variances that are tracked, trended, aggregated, benchmarked, and summarized. Properly monitored improving organizational performance projects will provide considerable opportunity for reengineering and streamlining organizational activities. This topic is vital to maintaining the reengineered organization and is detailed in Chapter 8. With the reengineering project's redesigns, outcomes and goals are established as yardsticks for measuring results. These achievements serve as verification of the effectiveness of the reengineered process redesigns. Since the continuing quality initiative is still a strong force within health care, these goals and outcomes are continuously revised to encourage ongoing streamlining and reengineering of the organization.

Public Relations and Marketing

The outcomes and achievements of the reengineering projects can form a basis for the efforts of the organization's marketing department. The ongoing streamlining of operations and resultant reduction in costs for services provide a wealth of marketing material for the organization. Marketing and public relations cover a broad spectrum of initiatives, from cost/charge reductions as a result of operational redesign to customer service initiatives undertaken. The organization should use its reengineering efforts to its advantage. Customer groups surveyed about their expectations by the reengineering task forces should be provided with the positive results affecting their areas of interest and concern. Reengineering results that are used as the focus of marketing materials and public relations releases can be correlated to the seven Cs of change management as described by Crego and Schiffen in their book *Customer Centered Reengineering: Remapping for Total Customer Value.*[4] These seven Cs and their relationship to the marketing efforts of the organization are as follows:

1. Closeness: the subject matter of present interest to the customer
2. Clarity: a clear vision, purpose, and presentation
3. Courage: the sharing of both the positive and the negative aspects of the project
4. Creativity: the presentation of the material in new and unusual ways
5. Competitiveness: the presentation of the expertise and value of the organization
6. Commitment: the organization's ability to persevere in its efforts
7. Consistency: the data released, both verbal and nonverbal, are compatible with the results provided to the public

As the marketing/public relations department shares the progress and status of the reengineering project with the community, it is also important that consideration be given to the internal information flow.

Organizational Information Flow

Communicate! Communicate! Communicate! The authors of this book believe that the three Cs to the employee's acceptance of the changes and the reengineering project are communicate, communicate, and communicate. To instill a feeling of self-worth in employees, it is vital that they be the first to receive news of the project's start-up and that they receive this news from the president or CEO of the organization. After the initial announcement, regular updates and status reports as described in Chapter 1 must be provided to employees. The timeliness and accuracy of the information can either make or break the project. Information flow is a two-way street and in the learning organization, employees contribute actively to the process and change. In the reengineered organization, it is important that the management hierarchy elicit, hear, and accept the input and the ideas of the employees. The greater the number of involved workers, the greater the level of diversity and creativity is applied to the problem-solving and task analysis process. Efforts to involve the employees can take various forms, but regardless of the method, the involvement must be there.

Change Management

At one time, the authors planned to conduct a Three Cs of Management workshop. These three Cs were communication (discussed above), change management, and conflict resolution. Today's health care leader must be the master of change management. He or she must be receptive to change and eagerly seek out and anticipate the remapped ways of accomplishing results. The change cycle is decreasing all the time, which means experiencing change in health care is like being caught in a revolving door. You find yourself going round and round, spun forward by the speed of other individuals within the compartments of the revolving door. Unlike a real revolving door, which leads you to a known destination, the health care revolving door deposits you in new and unanticipated spots. To lead the change, the administrator needs to instill the vision of the future and trust in the outcomes in employees.

In the process of managing change, it is also important to understand how change occurs. There are barriers to change and driving forces that encourage change. Some of the common barriers we can find within home care include the staff's attitude and resistance to change, fear of the unknown, comfort with the status quo, lack of time to assimilate and process the change, and fear of loss of power. To decrease the effects of this resistance to change, we can proceed in one of two ways: (1) we can encourage the effects of the driving forces, or (2) we can diminish the effects of those resisting change. Kurt Lewin, one of the most well-known change theorists, described this in 1947 as the force field analysis of change.[5] Think of this theory as an internal tug of war within the staff or an external tug of war among departments. The status quo is the line drawn in the sand that the other team must cross over in order for your team to win. How can you "pull" that team over to your side? This can be done by adding increasing strength to your team. Strengths within the organization that bring about change include enhanced benefits to employees, as a result of the change; increased understanding by the employee as to why change is needed; or perceived management strength/power on the part of the employee. The other way to win the change tug of war is to weaken the other team. This can be accomplished by explaining and responding to the fears and distrust of the employees or removing the employees' power base. Obviously, the first of these two methods is the most positive way to bring about changes. The leader who instills and uses positive examples and avoids negative examples such as those listed above, is to be commended in her or his leadership efforts. The organization's employees will embrace the reengineering efforts and move forward to prepare for prospective payment and managed care.

Conflict Resolution

The third management trait shared in the Three Cs of Management Workshop was conflict resolution. This too is an operational consideration for the leader in pursuit of a reengineered organization. Conflict between the project team and the task forces is a given. Prepare for the conflict and defuse it as quickly and efficiently as possible. To defuse the conflict, the leader needs to acknowledge and accept the conflict. This helps create an open and trusting environment. The continuous quality improvement team process of having the team establish its own meeting rules is one aspect of team interaction that can serve to decrease and defuse conflict. As professionals we must agree to disagree on some issues. Team members must also be open to compromise and negotiations.

In order to move forward at times of team conflict, the "whole" must be the primary focus, meaning the needs of the organization outweigh the opinions and interests of the individual. The organization is the focus and the source of long-term strength and support for the employee. Each individual employee is of value to the organization, but the organization provides the long-term security to the employee. For that reason, when the decisions get tough, the overriding focus must be to meet the mission and goals of the organization to provide the best outcome for the organization.

Space Assignment/Realignment

Critical to the success of the reengineered processes is the alignment of space to meet the needs of expanding program areas, as well as contracting areas. Not only should the size of the space be considered, but the placement of space as well. As it becomes clearer which programs are interrelated, these program/office space areas should be placed contiguously. This increases the ease of communication and decreases the travel time between program areas/departments, thus enhancing efficiency and interaction. Areas to be considered for close alignment would be the admission/referral areas, to the billing/business areas, and the temporary nurses to the Medicare intermittent services. An often adopted reengineering strategy for the organization is to realign staff mix and create patient-focused care teams. If this becomes one of the organization's reengineered processes (i.e., the delivery of patient care via assigned patient-focused care teams), then the team members should be provided with office or charting space within one office area. This, no doubt, will enhance team conferencing and team communications. In some redesigned teams, the reengineering of the patient-focused care team includes an addition of a shared medical records clerk/secretary that would decrease the team's professional caregiver's documentation and office processing time. In the realignment of the space, this support staff individual should also be in close proximity to the team. If team patient records are filed in this area it will decrease travel time to and from office areas and increase the time available to focus on the primary responsibilities. Clerical support assigned to the patient care teams is often another home health care reengineering strategy and when implemented, is enhanced by the above suggestions relative to space and record storage.

Space for the organization's computer and technological support, which is centralized to provide access for all users, is given consideration when total organizational operational efficiency is the goal.

Satellite offices, equipment, and staff needed to provide efficient and comprehensive services are analyzed versus the volume of patients and revenues anticipated or projected for the satellite office. If the satellite serves a public relations function and is determined to be a marketing strategy necessary to meet needs of referral sources/customer groups, then the bottom line might not be the basis of decision making regarding satellite offices. It is important to determine if these satellites are to demonstrate a profit, or are in fact marketing loss leaders.

When the organization has outgrown its existing available space and the reengineering process has determined a need to contract for or acquire additional square footage off site or off campus, careful consideration must be made of the operation of organization services placed in the off-site space. Consideration also must be given to the needed support services at the off-site location and the communications between the organization's multiple locations. An analysis of the equipment needed to support different off-site options can assist in determining the best choice for the off-site location. Comprehensive service delivery from all locations of the organization is necessary for success.

Patient-Focused Care Teams

As discussed earlier, the patient-focused care team is often a selected reengineering strategy. If this is the case within your organization, subsequent redesign of the space must provide for the team's interaction and ease of information transfer, whether in person or by technological support services. The total team should be afforded ready access to the patient caseload's records and data. The home health aide assigned to the patient care team should also have workspace in the team's office. Pagers and telephone access via mobile/cellular telephone enables team members to communicate with each other throughout the day. The ability to report the changes in the patient condition/status verbally throughout and at the end of the day is enhanced by remote access to other team members and by office space shared by all team members.

Transition Team

Just as important as the reengineering project team is the reengineering transition team. This team provides support to employees involved in the reengineering process implementation. The inclusion of a representative cross section of the employees on this team will ensure a diversity of skills, seniority, and experience. Included on the team should be both technology support personnel and a training specialist.[6] The technology support specialists can provide insight into anticipated time frames for arrival of newly purchased equipment, such as the laptop or hand-held computers. Along with the planned time for availability, the training specialist is able to plan with the technology specialist for the training programs needed for proper utilization of the equipment.

The transition team plans a time line for implementation that staggers the start-up of the reengineering strategies. This allows for a smooth and coordinated approach to the redesigned process implementation. As the reengineering project moves along, it will become obvious that certain redesigns must begin prior to others. There is often a domino effect to the redesigned processes (i.e., the redesigned processes interlock and/or interrelate so much that they affect other processes). There are derived incremental and ancillary effects from the redesigned processes and as more of the redesigned processes are transitioned into place.

In some instances, it will be determined that the most effective way for the redesigned processes to be implemented will be to transition them into place. For other redesigned processes, the best implementation will be immediate and across the entire organization at once.

The transition team will be given the final decision-making authority for starting additional redesigns and for determining whether the reengineering process should start with a pilot study. This team monitors progress toward anticipated outcomes and goals. Representation of those involved in the organization reengineering project in the membership of the transition team is essential to its understanding of the project and to the coordinated efforts between the project team and the transition team.

In this stage of reengineering, communication and employee involvement continue to be of paramount importance. The transition team plans the implementation time lines and coordinates the implementation of the changes to avoid confusion and ensure a smooth transition. This team must also be aware of the need to provide employees with timely progress reports, as well as updates on the coming implementation strategies.

Implementation

Chapter 7 details the implementation of the reengineered redesigned processes, however, the operational considerations related to implementation include some of the following suggestions.

The transition team should continue "in command" and monitor the status of the projects in relationship to the implementation time line. As the reengineering project team and task forces decide upon additional reengineered processes, these are approved and incorporated into the time line.

It is sometimes recommended that the implementation begin with simple, less involved reengineering projects, rather than organization-wide ones. As these changes become familiar, they will ease the way for more comprehensive redesigns.

When implementation occurs, there should be adequate staff available to provide patient care services and to continue meeting the many other customer group expectations. It is important to avoid disturbing patient care service delivery and the referral and admission of patients when planning for the implementation of the reengineered processes. As the scout motto says, you should "be prepared" and think ahead to anticipate problems that could potentially occur during implementation.

Assigned cycle times for completion of the process—sometimes referred to as the critical path method of implementation—are described by Roberts in *Process Reengineering, the Key to Achieving Breakthrough Success.*[7] The transition/implementation team will monitor the adherence to the critical path of implementation.

Verification/Evaluation Process

As the reengineering process redesign becomes operational, the organization should consider verification of the anticipated results. The failure of an organization to verify the projected improvements and the redesigned process undermines the success of the entire reengineering project. If anticipated improvements/results are not forthcoming, it might be necessary to rethink the design and refine or revise the reengineered process.

The use of reengineering as a management tool is intended to be a complete analysis of tasks and processes with a complete redesign implemented all at once. If the redesign is not providing the results expected, it is important not to just leave it as it was reengineered. It is important to rethink the process. It is also important not to return to the prereengineering time of the organization. Instead take more time and put on your outside of the box thinking caps. Find a creative atmosphere and experience the redesigned process with all your senses. The immersion of self into creative thinking means thinking in three dimensions. This includes sight, smell, touch, taste, and hearing. To think creatively invokes visioning in color and with pictures rather than words. So step back from the newly redesigned processes and revamp again. Get that project team together and have a reengineering "think tank" party. Reengineering is not meant to be incremental change, but rather drastic and complete change. If necessary to redo, however, it is better to redo than to settle for less than optimal results.

The reengineered organization should evaluate the anticipated outcomes. The evaluation of the results should include all the identified customer groups of the organization, including the staff. The reengineering project team and the transition and implementation team should evaluate not only the reengineering results, but also the team's interaction, participation, and contribution to the overall success of the organization's reengineering.

CONCLUSION

The implementation of the reengineering process involves more than just the doing. It involves careful planning, communicating, and coordinating. The successful organization's reengineering innovations are systematic, organized, and managed rather than sporadic, incidental, and accidental.[8] The implementation of the reengineering/redesigned processes must also follow this same systematic, organized, and managed pattern of innovation.

Milton et al. describe Roger's theoretical process of diffusion of innovation as five basic stages. These are (1) knowledge, (2) persuasion, (3) decision, (4) implementation, and (5) confirmation.[9] These authors also support an additional sixth stage, that of awareness. This awareness stage combined with persuasion and confirmation is believed to be related to the level of correctness and acceptance of decisions made. If the organization has placed both its formal and informal leaders on the project team, their very presence provides validity and credibility to the committee's actions. As spokespeople for the reengineering project, these individuals, who are respected by their peers, provide the persuasiveness necessary for organization-wide support. These project team members and the management of the organization must continually increase the staff's level of awareness by the ongoing communication of the need for and value of the reengineering project and the anticipated improvements in cost containment, quality, and process.

The long-term viability of the organization in the new and changing health care reimbursement environment is one of the many values of the reengineering project. This one outcome alone often is the overriding positive improvement that makes the project acceptable to the staff. The staff's confirmation of the value of long-term viability of the organization also confirms the value of the reengineering project and the subsequent rapid changes that will occur.

In communicating information, it is also important that a "common language" be spoken. I once read a book titled, *The Language of Goldfish.* Being a keeper of goldfish in my backyard pond, I thought it most appropriate that I "speak" their language. This is also the case in reengineering. A language that is understood by all staff is important so that the communications fall on hearing and understanding ears. A glossary of terms and their definitions form the tools to understanding and comprehension by all staff.[10]

Successful implementation of the reengineering/redesign strategies can be likened to planning and traveling within a foreign country. The maps and roadways are studied and a route chosen. The fellow travelers review the maps and confirm the decisions regarding the routes to be taken. Everyone must then pack the necessary clothing, medicines, money, and personal items (i.e., the supplies and resources necessary for the duration of the trip). Someone will take along an English guide to the languages of the countries visited in the hope that at least one of the travelers can speak and understand the languages of the countries on the itinerary. As the embarkation dates gets closer, the travelers communicate to their close friends, families, and neighbors to arrange for the necessary caretaking services at their homes while they are gone. Then at last, after much planning, the trip begins. The wise travelers have planned rest stops to regroup and reassess prior to moving onward. So too, is it necessary with reengineering for the wise manager to plan a "stop" to reevaluate and reassess prior to the next implementation. Then, after objectively surveying the project/process status, the organization is ready once again to move forward with the implementation, renewed and invigorated.

NOTES

1. R. Murphy, Work Reengineering: The Benefits and the Barriers, An Analytical Review, *Journal of the Society for Health Systems* 5, no. 1 (1994): 73.
2. D.L. Flarey and S. Smith Blancett, Reengineering: The Road Best Traveled, in *Reengineering Nursing and Health Care,* ed. S. Smith Blancett and D.L. Flarey (Gaithersburg, Md.: Aspen Publishers, Inc., 1995), 33.
3. Murphy, Work Reengineering, 81–84.
4. E.T. Crego Jr. and P.D. Schiffrin, *Customer-Centered Reengineering, Remapping for Total Customer Value* (Burr Ridge, IL: Irwin Professional Publishing, 1995), 79.
5. B.S. Gingerich and D.A. Ondeck, *Discharge Planning for the Home Health Care, A Multidisciplinary Team Approach* (Gaithersburg, Md.: Aspen Publishers, Inc., 1994), 131. 1st edition.
6. L. Roberts, *Process Reengineering: The Key To Achieving Breakthrough Success* (Milwaukee, Wis.: ASQC Press, 1994), 135.

7. Roberts, *Process Reengineering,* 148.
8. J. Manion, Chaos or Transformation? Managing Innovation, in *Reengineering Nursing and Health Care,* ed. S. Smith Blancett and D.L. Flarey (Gaithersburg, Md., Aspen Publishers, Inc., 1995), 167.
9. D. Milton et al., Tools To Evaluate Reengineering Progress, in *Reengineering Nursing and Health Care,* ed. S. Smith Blancett and D.L. Flarey (Gaithersburg, Md.: Aspen Publishers, Inc., 1995), 197.
10. K. Zander, CareMap Systems and Case Management: Creating Waves of Restructured Care, in *Reengineering Nursing and Health Care,* ed. S. Smith Blancett and D.L. Flarey (Gaithersburg, Md.: Aspen Publishers, Inc., 1995), 224.

Chapter 7

Implementing the Reengineering Process

One of the most critical aspects of a reengineering project lies within its presentation and implementation. By this time, organizational leaders have explored the concepts of reengineering, determined their potential value for the organization, and decided to commit themselves to evaluating and redesigning, where appropriate, the entire operation. It is at this point that a cautionary note for the leadership is in order. Remember the time it has taken to consider the process in relationship to your organization as it currently exists. Remember that, although you have explored this concept and understand it, some of the middle managers and staff may not be "on the same page" as you. For reengineering to be successful, the entire organization needs to have a basic understanding of it and be as supportive as possible. To create the illusion that the organization is rapidly jumping into reengineering decisions without much forethought generates fear and a lack of trust among the staff. Leaders cannot expect their staff automatically to buy into and support efforts for "radical change" when they themselves took three or six months to make this decision. Time is needed.

REENGINEERING PROCESS TIME FRAMES

Establishing realistic time lines assists the organization in implementing the reengineering process. Sometimes it is difficult to look at such a massive undertaking and know where to begin or even how to approach the task. Other times you may recognize that reengineering is the answer to your prayers and you should have done it a year ago. Fears of losing market share or of declining customer satisfaction can create a desire to rush through the process, but long-term success is built on a foundation of time, total organizational commitment, and the process. Figure 7–1 shows

Figure 7–1 Reengineering Project Implementation Time Line

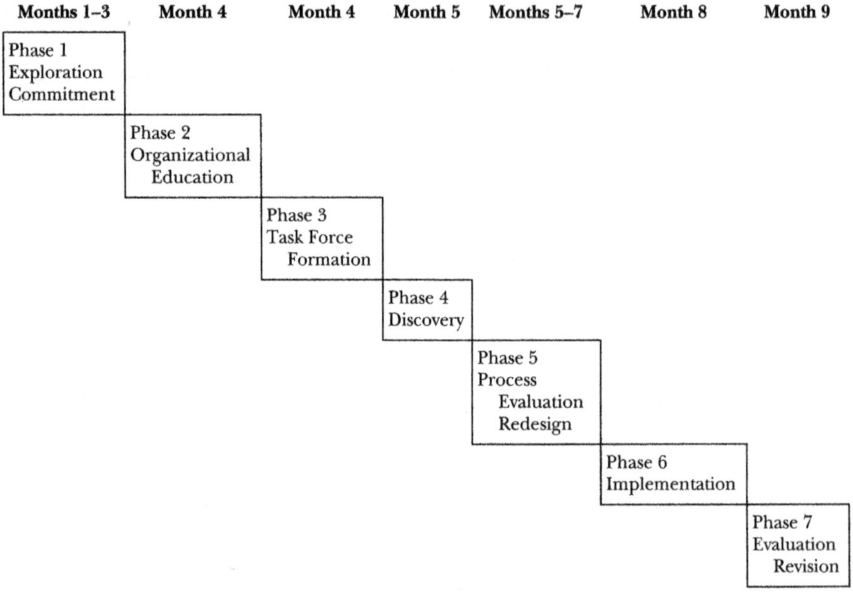

such a time line. Although this figure depicts a realistic time line for most organizations, the leaders of each organization are in the best position to determine the practicality of this time frame. For very large organizations it may be possible to speed up the process by one to two months, given the availability of more staff on the project team. On the other hand, given the large number of staff, large organizations may require more time to gather total organizational input in some of the phases.

EXPLORATION AND COMMITMENT

Exhibit 7–1 shows the phases of reengineering that will be discussed throughout the remainder of this chapter. The initial phase—Phase 1—generally requires one to three months of time depending on the past professional experiences of the leadership and their knowledge of the reengineering process. The leaders explore the reengineering process during this phase. Much can be learned through formalized educational programming in the area of professional development, operational management/development, and reengineering strategies. It is virtually impossible to miss similar topics in professional publications. To augment the education, it is suggested that a literature search be conducted in the corporate

Exhibit 7–1 Phases of Reengineering

Phase 1: Exploration and Commitment
- Educate the leaders about the reengineering principles through seminar attendance, literature review, and professional networking.
- Complete a needs assessment detailing the organization's strengths, weaknesses, opportunities, and threats.
- Evaluate the organization's culture and preparedness.
- Select a consultant to spearhead the project.

Phase 2: Organizational Education
- Educate the middle management staff.
- Educate the field and office staff.

Phase 3: Task Force Formation
- Select an organizational project coordinator.
- Select a cross-sectional project team.
- Communicate the project status to the entire organization.

Phase 4: Period of Discovery
- Map out cross-sectional organizational processes.
- Survey cross-sectional organization regarding current practices and processes.
- Communicate the project status to the entire organization.

Phase 5: Process Evaluation and Redesign
- Brainstorm process changes.
- Make decisions about process change.
- Develop an implementation plan.
- Communicate the project status to the entire organization.

Phase 6: Implementation
- Implement the newly designed or redesigned processes.
- Provide necessary support throughout the implementation.
- Communicate the project status to the entire organization.

Phase 7: Evaluation and Revision
- Survey the cross-sectional organization to determine improvement opportunities.
- Communicate the project status to the entire organization.

business section of local libraries or libraries of regional colleges with business management programs.

During this phase the leaders are expanding their knowledge base about the process and the outcomes of reengineering. They also need to evaluate whether there is a need to ensure their organization's future viability. To make that evaluation, the leaders need to conduct an organizational analysis. This analysis should list honestly the organization's strengths, weaknesses, opportunities, and threats (SWOT). The purpose of this analysis is to critically evaluate what the organization has going for it and what it has working against it. To avoid narrow-mindedness, the leaders may want to ask for assistance from a cross section of the organization to brainstorm the SWOT analysis. (See Exhibit 7–2.)

Exhibit 7–2 Organizational SWOT Analysis

List the strengths and weaknesses of the organization in relation to

- Financial status
- Mission, values, and organizational culture
- Programs:
    - traditional
    - nontraditional
    - patient population-specific
- Personnel:
    - management
    - field staff
    - office staff
    - technological support staff
    - office support staff
- Public image
- Service area
- Maturity of the organization

List the opportunities and threats in the internal and external environment, including

- Clinical expertise
- Community
- Competition
- Demographics of the service area
- Labor relations
- Patient population
- Reimbursement sources
- Regulatory bodies

Preparing the Organization for Reengineering—Organizational Education

Preparing an organization for reengineering encompasses planned interventions to develop a supportive culture, one of the basic ingredients in an efficient organization. Some common techniques used to evaluate the current culture and identify areas for improvement or change of the culture follow.

Surveys

Opinion or attitude surveys of leaders and staff help to define problem areas, which can be better stated as opportunities for improvement.

Educational Activities

Understanding human and organizational behavior allows employees a higher level of functioning in stressful situations. Educational in-services about topics such as change, communication, conflict, and team building assist the employees individually and as groups to understand differing opinions.

Coaching and Mentoring

This element balances needed assistance with autonomy, as those more experienced with reengineering processes help develop others with less experience. Coaching occurs when a facilitator builds on the strengths of the team or individual. It requires a commitment of time and ongoing support and consequently helps individuals or teams to reach their goals.[1] Although some would argue that mentoring is the same as coaching, the level of commitment is deeper. The mentor is "seasoned and filled with the drive and patience necessary to develop another person in their area of expertise."[2] Mentoring often continues for years, whereas coaching usually lasts for the duration of a project or the length of time the individuals are working side by side.

Personal and Professional Goal Establishment

This process heightens the awareness of the individual as an integral part of the organization. Recognizing the individuality of employees allows us to understand the importance and correlation between personal and professional goals. For example, a staff member needs to manage personal stresses. Establishing personal goals for this employee to incorporate stress management activities into his or her daily routine provides the organization with a healthier and happier employee. Likewise, this same individual may realize his or her value as an employee if permitted to establish a professional goal with the employer, such as completion of a training program in a new high-tech area.

Positive Praise

Sincere public and private praise demonstrate that the organization values success and fosters good will among its employees.

Third-Party Peacemaker

This is a useful technique when organizational conflict is at dangerous levels. Usually a consultant works with organizational staff to identify problems and seek resolutions. Organizational leaders who are unaware of the need for a third-party peacemaker are sometimes shocked when disgruntled employees resign or contact union representatives for support. Such events become part of the lore that unfortunately formulate the organization's culture.

Team Building

Working as a cohesive unit or team is essential to individual and organizational growth. This topic will be explored in more detail later in this chapter.

Each of these techniques to develop and improve organizational culture involves caring about employees as people. When our employees have their basic needs met they can move on to self-actualization and be pillars for our organization as it seeks to reengineer. The organization needs to be mature and prepared for the changes that occur with reengineering. Failure of leaders to take the time to develop an unprepared organization most likely would result in a dysfunctional organization.

Selection of a Consultant

Most organizations approach reengineering with the help of a consultant to guide them through the process. While treading in uncharted waters, it is soothing to have the support of someone who has already undertaken the reengineering process. Rules of logic can help the organization choose the right consultant to meet its needs. Seeking a consultant equipped with the tools needed for reengineering and prepared to help the organization reengineer into new processes specific to the organization is imperative. Some consultants boast that they will cut 50 percent off the bottom line or that they will reduce the staff by 40 percent without first evaluating the organization. This approach can result in the specified cost savings at the risk of losing the quality and uniqueness of the organization. The selected consultant or consultants must spearhead the project team—a team from within the organization—and be a resource for the organization's leaders and project team as they assist with conflict resolution.

Home health care organizations using consultants currently can take advantage of Medicare reimbursement. Consultant fees can be passed through to the cost report (assuming the organization is under Medicare caps) for retrieval at the end of the year.

The organization needs to evaluate the consulting team prior to executing a contract. Similar to any other profession there are a few bad apples that can spoil the consumer's perception of the whole barrel. In reality, there are many well-qualified and knowledgeable professionals who have chosen the consulting field to do what they do best—assist organizations to reach a higher level of functioning. Leaders should ensure that the consultant sent to complete the assignment is as competent as the consultant selling the service. The knowledge base of the consultant in the area being reengineered is essential. When the organization's leaders compare consultants, they sometimes lament the decision because they all look the same. Usually, however, they have overlooked one of the most important deciding factors—their instincts. Does the organization like this person? Are its leaders comfortable with this consultant as a person? Do they trust this consultant? Do they feel confident that this consultant is committed to their organization and dedicated to doing a quality job? What kind of support will the consultant offer outside of the on-site time? What do they charge?

Organizations should feel comfortable interviewing potential consultants and asking for references. Hiring a consultant encompasses the same hiring practices used to hire a good employee. Increasingly, organizations are seeking outside expertise to assist them through major undertakings. Reengineering the home health care organization is certainly a major undertaking.

Once this initial phase is completed, it is time to enter the organizational communication phase. Now is the time for the leaders to communicate their thoughts and decision to pursue reengineering to the rest of the organization. Given the cautionary note at the beginning of this chapter and the brief discussion of communications in Chapter 6, the leaders know they need to plan communications and carefully coordinate their timing and content. This phase begins the ongoing process of sharing information. To avoid communication, leaders would be denied valuable input from the organization's employees. Staff need ongoing communication to be assured that the sky is not falling.

TEAM FORMATION

In a previous chapter we briefly discussed communication, change, and conflict, which provide a great start for team formation and team building. So much in our world depends on good communication techniques and our willingness to understand the other party's perspective. As children we were told to play with our brothers and sisters despite the fact that we just didn't want to play with them. Our pleas to do something different yielded firm parental warnings that we were to play nice and just get along and have a good time. In our immature minds, we sure did figure out how to play nice, get along and have a good time! In fact, we did such a good job that early childhood specialists have given it some names, such as sibling rivalry, passive-aggressive behavior, and gaming. Look around your organization. We bet you'll see someone's big sister or little brother and guess what?!?!?! Some are still playing! It's a forgivable fact that our folks didn't teach us team building when we were developing; after all we wouldn't have understood or cared about the concepts at that stage of our lives. Team building is a necessary activity in the workplace today. No longer can one administrator take the organization where it needs to go. Groups of individuals with various life experiences and levels of expertise are needed to collaborate and improve upon ideas to build strong organizations and competent employees. Preparing an organization for a successful reengineering project requires careful selection and preparation of individuals to work collaboratively in a team setting.

Team Member Selection

As the organization prepares a list of potential team members, it needs to consider the potential of the individuals, not their personalities. Given that highly creative people can become poor performers when left unchallenged, there may exist some well-hidden gems within the walls of the organization. To locate potential team members, the leaders need to explain the project team concept to the entire staff and ask for any interested individuals to volunteer.

Other individuals should be targeted as potential members because of their clinical, administrative, organizational, or technical expertise. Individuals volunteering or chosen as team members for a reengineering project are committing to a large amount of work. Some may need to delegate their routine roles and responsibilities to other employees to allow time for their newly created role of redefining the organization. A possible home health care team composition might include one nurse or aide, one therapist or social worker, an information systems analyst, one supervisor/coordinator, one office support staff member, and one interested party. From this group a facilitator is selected to be the project manager.

Facilitators keep the team on target and follow through on any team-related issues. Depending on the type of task assigned to the team, nonadministrative facilitators work best as they minimize the reluctance of team members to participate "because the boss is here." Facilitators must be interested in the process, committed to the project, and eager to help and also to learn. Facilitators need to be doers when the doing needs done, and listeners when the team is working well together.

Common Team Problems

To promote the effectiveness of the teams we establish, let's consider some of the more common problems that can derail the work of a team.

Understanding these pitfalls enhances our ability to deal with them offensively, thus allowing teams to focus on the organization's problems, rather than on interpersonal issues.

Hesitancy

When first approached with the opportunity to work with a group (i.e., task force, project team, committee) individuals may hesitate out of fear of the unknown or a fear of rejection or ridicule from their peers for being selected. They may wonder whether or not they are knowledgeable and articulate enough to represent their respective programs. To counter this hesitancy, the organization's leader should approach a prospective team member when both have sufficient time to discuss the project thoroughly. The leader needs to provide as much information as possible to alleviate unnecessary fears. The best situation is to have a trusting relationship between the leader and the prospective team member so as to encourage the expression of concerns in honest dialogue.

Opinions or Facts?

Some people fail to learn that just because they have an opinion about an issue, it is not a fact. Some listeners assume that anything said by managers, fellow workers with higher degrees, or peers who are well liked must be true and factual. Group members need to be educated about opinions and facts. This helps speakers evaluate what they say prior to speaking and aids listeners to evaluate what they actually hear rather than what they think they are hearing.

Domineering Team Members

Sometimes we attend group meetings and find that one person talks incessantly. That person knows everything about everything. The team will lose its effectiveness if other members simply clam up and allow their talkative teammate to dominate. Unknown to the domineering party, the rest of the team gathers outside the task force meeting to complain to each other about their domineering peer. The group's facilitator must take charge by asking others for their opinions or collaborating with the group to establish acceptable rules of behavior for future meetings.

Digression

Sometimes, one subject leads to another and the team finds itself discussing Aunt Rosa's meatloaf recipe. Although the meatloaf recipe may be the best, such discussions do not contribute to the team's goals. Some conversations digress into conversations about other organizational issues. It is best to set such problems aside until the meeting is over. Then the facilitator can discuss the issue or delegate its discussion to another time and place. Meeting times and agendas need to be respected to demonstrate sensitivity to everyone's time and commitment.

Method of Decision Making

The group needs to determine how decisions will be made when there is a serious difference of opinions. It is detrimental for the team to use a majority rules method, since it can leave some members uncomfortable about the team's accomplishments. This method also leads to rushed work as members quickly vote to end the issue. Consensus building is best. Although it takes more time and involves give and take from all team members, everyone feels an ownership with the team's decision.

Closed Minds

Sometimes, one team member will come to the first meeting with a preconceived solution to the team problems. When this happens this answer becomes "the answer" because every action and reaction he or she has pushes the team in the direction of the preconceived answer. Team members need to be aware that there is more to the picture that what they are considering, and that they need to evaluate alternative solutions thoroughly.

Conflict among Team Members

Conflict may relate to turf issues, personality issues, or differing views. Conflicts are more severe when they arise over principles and values than over basic facts. In addition to work-related conflict, team members may have personal or internal conflicts that have nothing to do with the work setting. The conflict will affect the team member regardless of its source.

Team Building

Building an autonomous team and assisting it to be a successful team is the best method of empowering employees. Although the team members may have worked together for years they may not know one another very well. To enhance team cohesiveness, the team members need to find a common ground with each other. This can be accomplished through ice breaker types of introductions during the first meeting, which will set the tone for subsequent meetings. The team facilitator needs to act as host during this meeting and keep it rolling and light while silently observing the interactions between members. The goal of team building is to create groups of people who are capable of reaching consensus in sometimes forced relationships as they work toward an organizational achievement. Exhibit 7–3 is a credo for team members.

Once the reengineering project team has been introduced, the facilitator should discuss the reengineering project with the team, emphasizing the proposed time line and exploring concerns. The team needs to establish clear expectations for acceptable behavior as it relates to project team activities. Some rules of conduct might include the following:

1. The meetings will begin and end promptly at specified times.
2. Attendance by all team members is required.
3. No interruptions will be allowed during meeting times.
4. Every person will contribute opinions, suggestions, and facts openly and honestly.
5. No one will judge other team members' contributions as insincere.
6. Each team member will commit to the reengineering project and complete all assignments as requested.

The facilitator should identify an early accomplishment of the team and laud its success. Perhaps this early accomplishment will be the team's consensus building regarding rules of conduct. Regardless of the accomplishment, it is important that the team's successes be recognized and commended.

Exhibit 7–3 Team Credo

Credo of Team Membership

Team members give and take.
They listen and speak.
Team members recognize their similarities and their differences.
They are able to put aside their individuality in pursuit of a commonality.
Team members communicate openly and honestly.
They respect the rights of others to form differing opinions.

But above all . . .
Team members strive for solutions to their shared problem.

Exhibit 7–4 Outside the Paradigm: Nontypical Job Description for Project Facilitator

Position Title: Project facilitator
Reports to: Chief executive officer
Positions Reporting to This Position: None
Experience and Qualifications: People skills, articulate in written and verbal communications, team player
Responsibilities:

1. Seeks answers to questions posed by the project team.
2. Acts as liaison between organizational leadership and the project team.
3. Is available for coaching when needed.
4. Observes without comment when the team is functioning well.
5. Injects fuel for thought when indicated.
6. Challenges the thoughts and ideas the team has created.
7. Provides feedback from other organizational staff.
8. Schedules meeting rooms as necessary.
9. Coordinates the total organizational communication process.
10. Assists with problem solving and personality issues.

Note: This position description is temporary, to be used in lieu of the employee's regular position description.

The facilitator needs to be all things to all members of the project team. Exhibit 7–4 is a nontypical sample job description for the project facilitator's position. This may be used on a temporary basis only for this project while the facilitator delegates his or her regular responsibilities to others. Team members should be recognized informally and formally on their performance appraisals for their *team* accomplishments. As we reengineer our thinking outside normal comfort zones, we need to give serious consideration to team performance appraisals. These can be completed in addition to individual performance appraisals that would elevate the value of team performance. Exhibit 7–5 is a nontraditional position description for a team member, which can be used in addition to the team members' routine position description. To satisfy the Joint Commission, the organization would develop performance appraisals that mimic the job description's responsibility section and then apply a measurement technique to each responsibility. As we learned in Chapter 5, the HIM 11 and CHAP do not regulate this aspect of the employee performance appraisal.

Spending much time together is another effective technique for team building. The more the team members are together the more they will understand each other, trust each other, and feel comfortable sharing their thoughts and ideas without fear of reprisal. Finally, use positive feedback as often as possible. When providing positive feedback, be genuine! Otherwise, it shows.

Exhibit 7–5 Outside the Paradigm: Nontypical Job Description for Team Member

Position Title: Team member
Reports to: ______________________________
Positions Reporting to This Position: ______________________
Experience and Qualifications: People skills, articulate in written and verbal communications, team player, flexible thinking, creative nature, open-minded
Responsibilities:

1. Participates actively in committee activities.
2. Communicates openly and honestly.
3. Participates in brainstorming activities.
4. Analyzes alternatives critically.
5. Represents ________________ position(s).
6. Acts as liaison between workplace peers and the team, when necessary.
7. Completes assignments as requested.
8. Maintains self-esteem of others in all interactions.
9. Works collaboratively to meet the goals of the team.

Note: This position description is in addition to the employee's regular responsibilities.

All of these tactics for team building eventually will create the organizational culture leaders seek for efficiency and effectiveness. As each team learns firsthand, it will become a role model for the rest of the organization. Receiving positive praise makes one want to give positive praise in return. It feels good. As teams spread goodwill, the organization's employees begin to mesh and it is that bond that creates a strong and committed organizational family—the ultimate team!

DISCOVERY

Now that the project team has been established, it needs to consider thoughts, concerns, and suggestions from the entire organization. In communicating to the organizational staff, it needs to emphasize the importance of sharing information. The team should explain its plan for communication and then conduct an employee survey. What are their opinions? What organizational changes do they want to make? Do they have suggestions for improvement? What do they think is working well? Do they feel their opinions are valued? Do they trust that they will receive open and honest communication during the process? This feedback can be used by the project team, organizational leadership, and consultant as they plan future communications and evaluate their organization's operations.

This fourth phase of reengineering—discovery—also requires the team to look systematically at all processes. It must consider all steps in each organizational process to find areas of duplication (rework) or areas of unnecessary delay. The project team needs to consider the flow of the patient through the organization, starting with the point of entry and concluding with the discontinuation of services. Then the team examines specific functional processes, such as the assessment of the patient, the intake process, the scheduling process, the documentation process, and so on.

The use of flowcharts provides the project team and other interested groups with a picture diagram of each operational process. Flowcharts capture all of the steps in the process and magnify the complexity of what we do in our daily operations. Even though our current process may be working, the project team analyzes it to identify opportunities for streamlining and eliminating unnecessary work. When you think about it, some processes may have been created to correct performance problems of a particular employee who no longer works for the organization. Steps may have been added to other processes that create additional elements incorporated into our daily routine. The rationales for current processes at the time of their inception most likely were sound, but as we reengineer for operational efficiency for today we need to weed the path to make room for a smooth and open highway. As we consider all steps in our process, we encapsulate them with meaningful shapes, using the flowchart principle outlined in Chapter 4.

Figure 7–2 is an example of a flowchart depicting the initial phase of the patient scheduling process. An important step in patient scheduling for this organization involves referral process. The collection of vital patient and reimbursement information provides the intake coordinator with the facts needed to forward the referral to the appropriate area for scheduling since this agency is divided into Medicare, insurance, and managed care divisions. In this particular process, there are six points of information exchange and an equal number of actions with that information. This initial phase of the scheduling process leads to four other processes, two of which are needed to complete the scheduling of the patient's caregivers. Figures 7–3 and 7–4 show a continuation of the scheduling process in the areas of aide and therapy scheduling.

During this discovery period, the project team also considers processes that cut across the entire organization such as the communication or the staff scheduling process. This phase of reengineering requires input from the entire organization.

PROJECT EVALUATION AND REDESIGN

During the next phase—project evaluation and redesign—the project team considers alternatives to the processes as they currently exist through

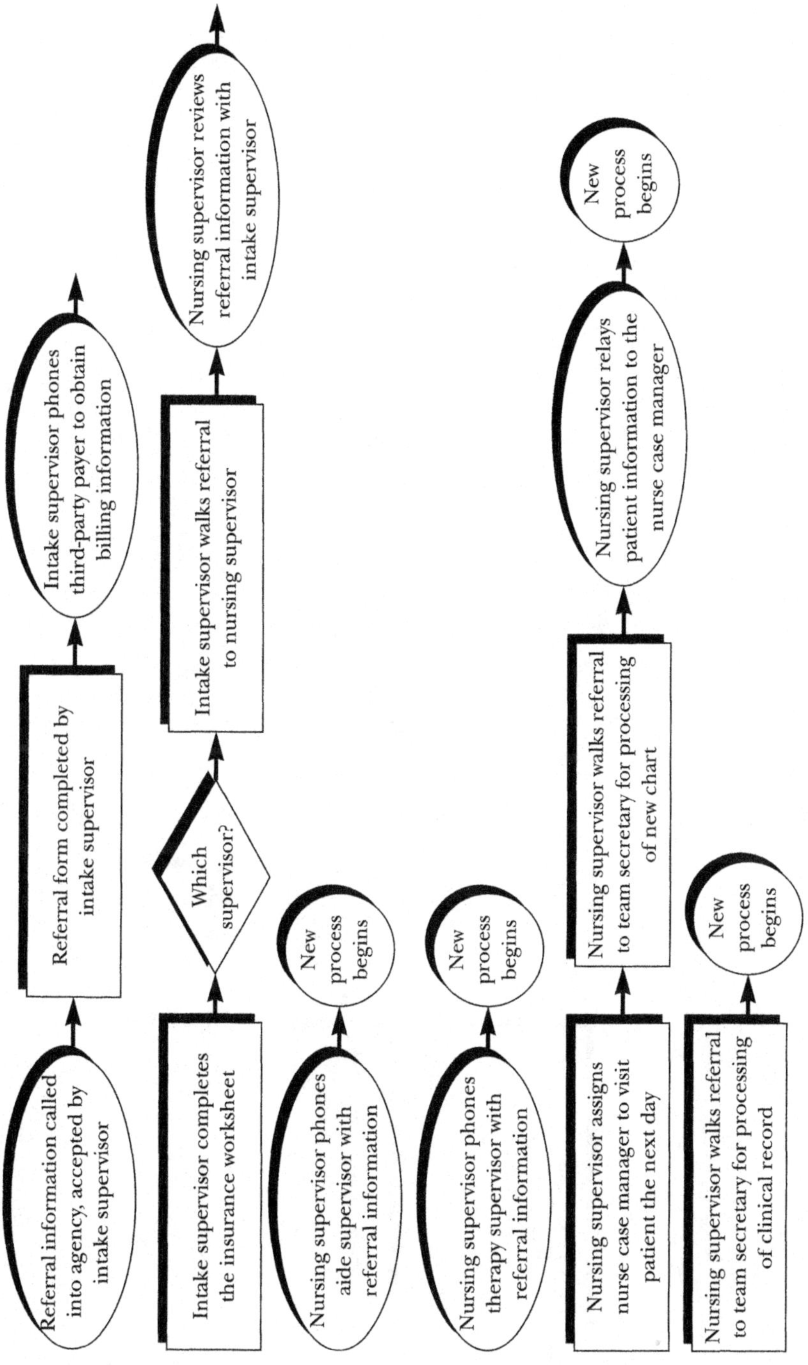

Figure 7–2 Initial Phase of Patient Scheduling Process

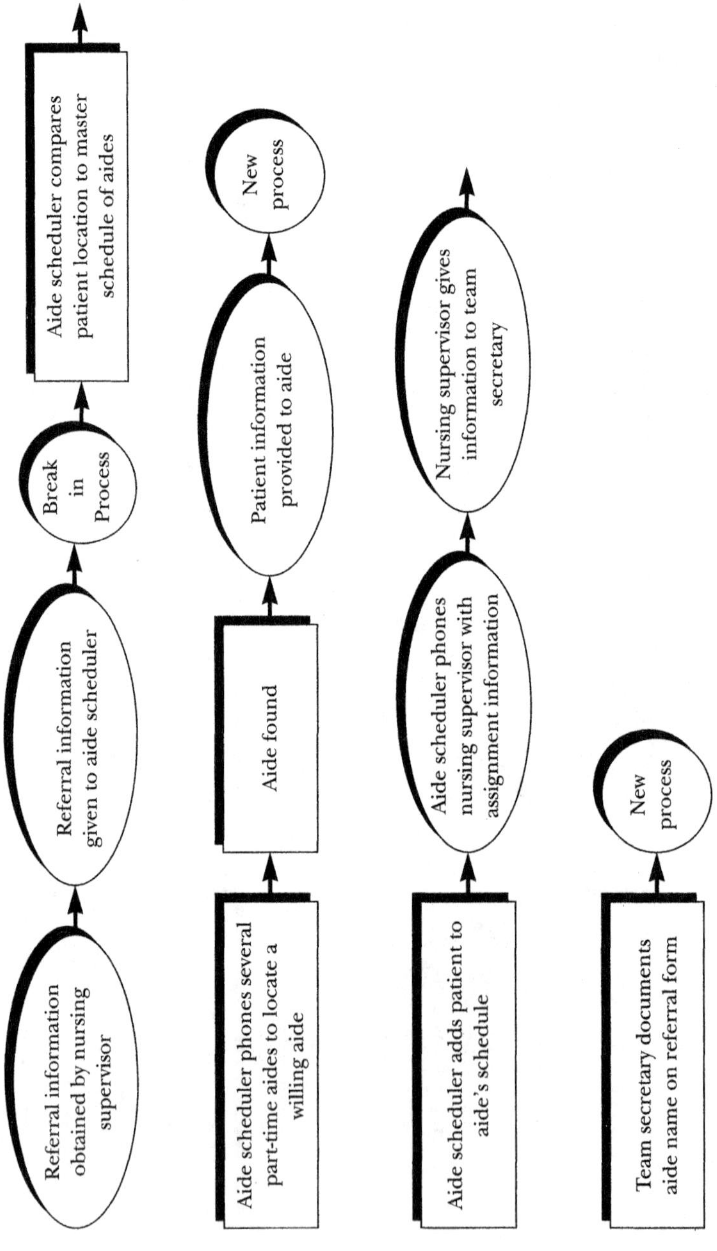

Figure 7–3 Patient Scheduling Process: Aide Scheduling

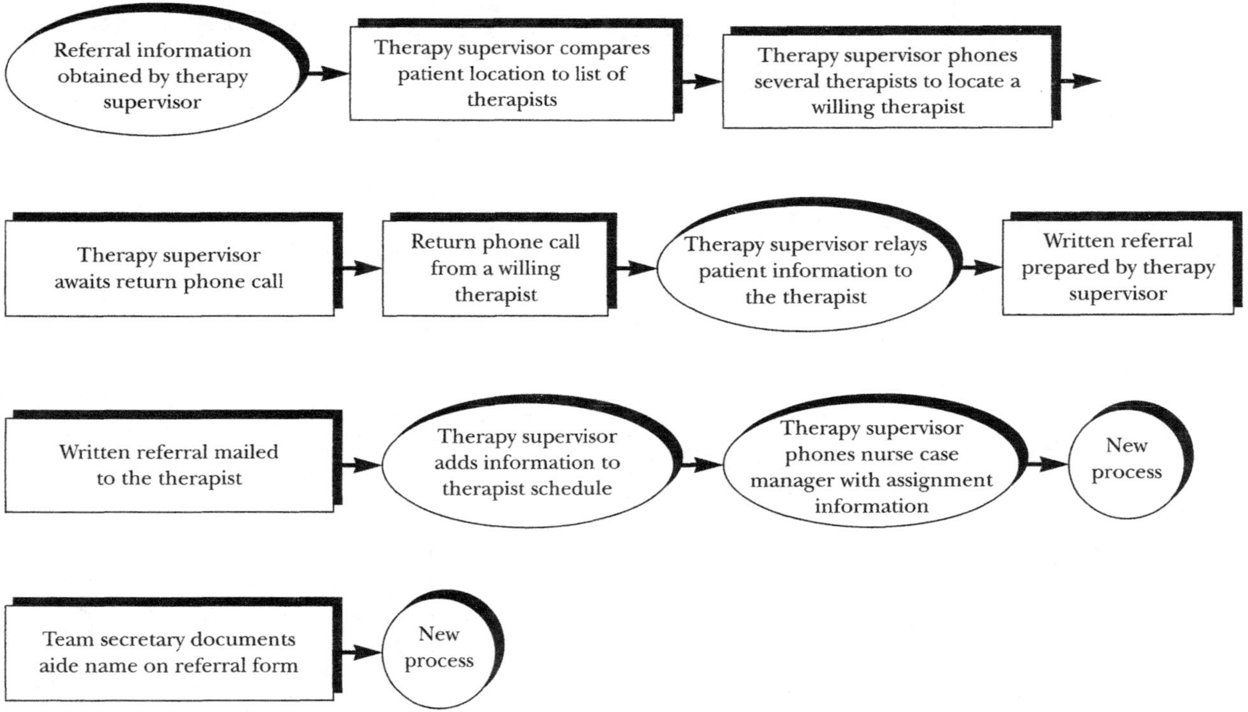

Figure 7–4 Patient Scheduling Process: Therapy Scheduling

brainstorming sessions. During this phase the team needs to have immediate access to pens, paper, or the like, and be uninterrupted as it escapes from the world of "what is" to the world of "what could be." Some organizational processes will be so cumbersome or opinions may vary so greatly that the team will need to revisit these at a later time. This is exhaustive work but the results are well worth the energy.

Following through with our scheduling process example, we see that until a patient is scheduled to be visited by a nurse, aide, and therapist 32 steps are required. A quick evaluation of the 32 steps reveals much redundancy and several possible solutions. Assuming no changes in this organization's staffing level or structure, the project team may want to consider a computer network linking the intake coordinator, nursing supervisor, therapy supervisor, and aide scheduler. Each position has access to patient information and can update the data from their desks. This process change alone eliminates at least 12 steps in the process.

The project team may also conclude that the aide scheduler position should be realigned into a general scheduler position to handle the scheduling of therapists and nurses as well. Without using a flowchart, however, the project team may have overlooked some of the steps and potential opportunities to reduce duplication.

Another choice for the project team at this point is to allow the process to remain unchanged, as long as it has a justifiable rationale for doing so. Any rationale or decision will be acceptable for the organization as long as the team considers the process, options, reasoning, and needs of the organization.

To ensure that the organization is involved with the reengineering process, the team needs to provide feedback to the staff. When the team is evaluating a particular area, it is helpful if the team then channels its questions to the leaders or staff in that area. Although the leaders and staff are not the decision makers for the reengineering process, their input is valuable and they may have some practical solutions or even justification for keeping the process the same. They may ultimately support a change they had never considered in the past. The project team members are not experts in all areas. Although it may sound reasonable to expand the admission policy to include nonhomebound Medicare patients, this decision would result in nonreimbursable care. The project team needs to clarify with others that its decisions do not conflict with any regulations.

IMPLEMENTATION

Once the team has considered all of the suggestions provided in the staff survey and evaluated all operational processes, it proceeds to the next phase—implementation of process changes in the organization. Staff, meanwhile, become more anxious. Will they still have their current jobs? Will they have any job? Will they like the changes or find they no longer enjoy their jobs? This is usually a time of apprehension, not only for staff and management, but also for the project team. Did the project team members overlook anything? Will their decisions be accepted? How will the organization respond to them when they return to their full-time positions? Anxieties are even higher when everyone knows that some positions will be eliminated. What positions?

The project team, organization, leadership, and consultant complete an implementation plan for the reengineered organization. This implementation may be phased in over a six-month or three-year period. The planning of many changes must be well coordinated. Appendix 7–A contains an action plan worksheet for implementation of the process changes. Completion of an action plan is necessary at many levels. The project team may plan for the overall implementation schedule, leaving the fine details to each department in the organization.

During the implementation phase, each area of the organization must adhere to its deadlines because a delay in one area can throw the entire organization's schedule off track. An implementation team from each area should be selected. This team will develop and oversee the implementation of its specific plan, ensuring that they remain on schedule and keep up with the master implementation plan. All staff should be apprised of the overall schedule and its part in the process. It is a time when everyone needs to work together for the good of the organization. Leaders should be cognizant of the normal apprehensions experienced by their staff at this time and should make themselves readily available to provide support and listen. Leaders themselves need a support system, be it each other or external to the organization. This is a time when everyone should be aware of the need for stress management. Somewhere in this phase, the staff and leaders recognize that the brunt of the process is over, they have survived, and they now know the direction the organization will take.

EVALUATION AND REVISION

As a follow-up to the implementation phase, the organization's leaders and staff should be surveyed to determine their response to changes. Opinion surveys at this point assist the leaders in knowing how to proceed with their interactions. Have they been effective up to this point? Do the staff members feel that they are valued? How do they perceive the reengineering process? Were the changes effective? Was the transition smooth?

What more could the leaders have done to make the process work better? Do they have any suggestions for revision or improvement?

The project team needs to meet weekly at first, at least monthly during the implementation phase, and then three months after total implementation to discuss the process changes and revisions. Analyzing staff's comments and suggestions provides valuable input for the team, leaders, and consultant to address. Process revisions are made in a similar fashion as the original work except more emphasis will be placed on staff input. The team will discuss the problems and suggestions, brainstorm alternative solutions, if appropriate, and make revision decisions.

CONCLUSION

Throughout the process of reengineering, we have discussed the empowerment of the staff and the decision-making capacity of the project team. Prior to implementation, the administrative management and board of directors must give final approval to the planned revisions, since both retain ultimate authority and responsibility for the management of the organization.

NOTES

1. *Coaching for Success* (Pittsburgh, Penn.: Development Dimensions International, 1987), 2A.
2. D.A. Ondeck and B.S. Gingerich, The Mentoring Relationship, *Journal of Home Health Care Practice* 6, no. 4 (1994): 1.

Appendix 7–A

Tools

Tool 7–A1 Implementation Action Plan Worksheet

Process: Implementation Team Facilitator:

Activity	Person Responsible	Date Due	✔ When Done	Comments

Chapter 8

Improving the Organization's Performance

Looking objectively at our organization is sometimes next to impossible because we often are too close to the situation. We make assumptions about the status of other organizations and convince ourselves that all organizations have similar problems, ergo there is nothing more that can be done to eliminate a particular issue. For example, the unavailability of physical therapists is something that plagues home health care organizations throughout the United States. This *nationwide* problem leads us to believe that there is nothing anyone can do about a problem of this scope. At the heart, organization performance improvement is the loss of cost-effectiveness that results from inefficient processes and the costly effects of high turnover due to dissatisfied staff. This, in and of itself, negatively affects the financial picture of the organization. But even more ominous for home health care is the congressional movement toward prospective payment legislation for home health care. Organizations operating at lower costs in a managed care environment are positioning themselves for survival. Contracts are granted based on the outcomes of care and the cost efficiency of that care. Organizational improvement strives to improve many processes within the organization. Recognizing that nothing is ever perfect, virtually everything can be evaluated for operational efficiency and improvement. Prior to digging our heels in, we need to determine the "process to use to evaluate processes."

Organizations seeking improvement can sometimes identify solutions by comparing themselves with others. Throughout our lives, we have become accustomed to making comparisons. During our school years, the school measured out performance and provided us with a grade point average, often listing the class range and averages. These averages were then used for comparison purposes. Few are unable to recall a time when we were internally, if not externally, competing with another. We compared our accomplishments with theirs and found a deep level of motivation and commitment erupting from within. Our objective was to do better than the other person. One of the benefits of comparison is the stimulation of our competitive nature. But the most essential benefit is the collaboration that occurs between two individuals or two organizations being compared. We can learn from others' successes and mistakes.

BENCHMARKING

Over the past several years comparison, referred to as benchmarking, has increasingly been used in the health care industry. A benchmark is a point of reference or standard by which something can be measured or judged. Benchmarking is a means to compare one organization to another according to specific measurements and standards.[1] Benchmarking can occur between two organizations or multiple organizations. It can also occur within branch offices of regional or national home care companies. Companies have emerged, specific to home health care, to provide benchmarking services to these agencies. Each organization is categorized by size, type, services, and location to ensure that apples to apples comparisons are being made. The services of such companies are exceptionally helpful to the smaller home health care organization.

Benchmarking requires that our organizations collect and aggregate patient outcomes data. These outcomes are the result of our care and services and allow us to identify measurements to convey to other health care organizations as well as those to whom we market our services. In looking at outcomes we find that there is always some level of variation. Eighty five percent of the variation is inherent to the process. Thus there is something that we can change with our process to affect our outcomes of care.[2]

Organizations can conduct benchmarking through local networking and mutual association memberships. One such example is the Florida Hospital Association. Its home care division asked for interested hospital-based agencies to unite in the development, collection of data, and reporting of the following benchmarks:

- visit, documentation, and administrative task time for field staff
- office staff productivity
- hospital utilization of home care[3]

This approach allows for a statistically significant and rapid accumulation of data for comparison that can be used by other interested agencies. The collected information then can be used to evaluate the organizations with higher productivity levels. The keys to benchmarking are to make certain that the same types of organizations are being compared and then to evaluate and select the processes used by the most efficient organization to improve the performance of your organization. What allows them to be better? How does their staff compare with your staff? What form of documentation do they utilize? What are their hours of operation? To what do they attribute their efficiencies?

Some home health agencies have united locally to share data collection for areas such as infection rates, incidents, and medication errors. This can occur only in a mature market where the organizations recognize the value of uniting for the common good of their community. For example, the organizations with a lower patient infection ratio may have valuable information to share with the organizations with higher ratios. Perhaps there is an infection control practice they have identified or a particular brand of disinfectant they used to reduce their infection rate. Benchmarking allows organizations not only to engage in friendly competition but to target opportunities for improvement as they strive to reach the best and then outperform the best.

MODELS FOR PROCESS IMPROVEMENT

Much has been published regarding basic concepts of quality improvement. It doesn't require a large time commitment to locate articles about CQI, TQM, and employee empowerment. Undoubtedly, either consciously or subconsciously, many managers have adopted principles and philosophies from these quality management methods. Although many organizations report more frequent inclusion of their staff in decision making and problem solving, leaders are sometimes uncertain as to how to proceed when faced with developing an improvement plan. Depending upon the method of quality improvement plan utilized, the organization may find that it can formulate the foundation for tackling any problem, even the organization's reengineering project.

There is a variety of models used to improve total organizational quality on a continuous basis. They all share common elements and each organization can utilize one of the established methods or create its own variation. The following three processes have been utilized with success:

1. The ***FOCUS PDCA*** Model[4]
    - ***F***ind an improvement process
    - ***O***rganize a team interested in improving the process
    - ***C***larify the current process and organizational understanding of the process
    - ***U***nderstand causes of process variation

- *S*elect the process improvement
- *P*lan the improvement
- *D*o the improvement
- *C*heck the outcome
- *A*ct to maintain the success

2. The ***FADE*** model:[5]
   - *F*ocus on the problem
   - *A*nalyze the process
   - *D*evelop an alternative process
   - *E*xecute the alternative process
3. The basic scientific approach:[6]
   - Identify the problem
   - Collect information
   - Suggest a hypothesis
   - Design and experiment to test the hypothesis
   - Carry out the experiment
   - Analyze the data
   - Draw conclusions

Application of the scientific method to home health care process improvement is similar to that used in the nursing process. Exhibit 8–1 provides an example of such an application.

Exhibit 8–1 Application of Scientific Method in Nursing

Process: Advance directives
Goal: 100 percent of clinical records will contain documentation that the nurse discussed advance directives with the patient prior to or at the time of the initial home visit.
Measurement: Random sampling of 10 percent of the clinical records
Frequency: Monthly
Responsibility: Nursing supervisor
Method: The nursing supervisor will coordinate the random pulling of 10 percent of the clinical records in the Medicare, insurance, and managed care divisions no later than the 25th of each month. The records will be reviewed for inclusion of the above documentation by the supervisor or designee. The admitting nurse will be notified of noncompliant records and the report will be forwarded to the quality improvement director no later than the 30th of the month.
Follow-up: The quality improvement director is responsible for the aggregation of data on a monthly basis. The information is discussed with the quality committee and follow-up action is defined and assigned. Reports of follow-up action will appear in subsequent quality committee meeting minutes.

Different from the documentation problems discussed in this example, it also is appropriate at times to experiment. Experiments are done in the form of pilot projects. Pilot projects provide the organization with an opportunity to try a solution without fully committing to it. It is a way to iron the wrinkles out without disrupting the entire organization. Pilot projects are highly effective for routine performance improvement plans but have created problems for organizations implementing reengineering decisions.

During pilot studies, the organizational staff has time to sabotage the decisions of the project team. Needless to say, the changes that take place with reengineering are vast and the natural human instinct is to revert back to a comfort zone. Also, staff does not always receive the message that the reengineering project is serious and that decisions—which may need to be slightly revised—are final and not to be undermined.

EVOLUTION OF QUALITY IMPROVEMENT PROCESSES

Learning about the evolution of the process for improving the organization's performance allows us to understand each of its components. During the initial quality assurance phase, plans addressing the minute details of documentation were perfectly acceptable. Health care leaders found that evaluating the completion of patient record documentation led to the identification of problem areas and offered an opportunity to develop individual staff members further in the quality of their documentation. Action plans, therefore, addressing the results of *quality assurance* activity, led to individual counseling about the finest of details in documentation. The field staff soon equated *quality assurance* with counseling and regarded it as solely negative feedback. Attempts to include field staff in *quality assurance* activities sometimes led to defensive or protective behaviors to avoid the negativism associated with the process.

Recognizing that quality cannot be assured, a major shift in thinking and process occurred. Parameters for quality measurement were developed and the intent of quality activities shifted to improving aspects of all services provided. During this phase, more involvement from staff became essential. Data collection became everyone's job and patient outcome indicators were developed. Leaders continued to audit records for reimbursement and legal purposes but the addition of patient care outcomes data collection left the field staff cautiously optimistic and somewhat more willing to participate.

The next phase in the evolution of improving organizational performances is essential to reengineering. Health care organizations throughout the United States have experienced the positive outcomes of organization-wide process improvements. Improving organizational performance is the first regulated quality process that demands total organization involvement—leaders and staff. Initially, many organizations comment that the process seems cumbersome and confusing. They cite resistance among staff until the first project team works through the process and experiences success. Volunteer participants come forward once they observe the value of new or improved processes that develop through total organizational commitment.

REGULATORY REQUIREMENTS

As discussed in Chapter 3, the HIM 11 has no requirements for organizational improvement. The CHAP requires a written plan including goals, standards, time frames, responsibilities, and follow-up actions. It can be accomplished through identification of various aspects of care, a coordinated plan for data collection, and an organized method of evaluating the data and developing and implementing an action plan. Exhibit 8–2 shows one possible format, as an example for organizing this type of quality improvement process. For this particular method to be effective there needs to be

1. education of the entire organization regarding the overall plan, process, and aspects of care to be tracked
2. development and an understanding of the use of forms by all staff members
3. a defined process for aggregating and evaluating the data
4. responsibility assigned to various organizational employees for each phase of the process (data collection, reporting, aggregation, evaluation, action planning, implementation of changes, and reevaluation)
5. a plan for periodic evaluation of the effectiveness of the quality improvement plan

The organization needs to establish which areas it considers to be priority opportunities for improvement and develop similar forms for all areas it chooses to examine.

The Joint Commission on Accreditation of Healthcare Organizations brings a different dimension to the quality improvement process by requiring a broader scope—organization-wide perspective. Using some of the Joint Commission's key concepts allows the organization to incorporate a common set of rules to improve a process. Reengineering then evolves

Exhibit 8–2 Format for Process Improvement Using CHAP Guidelines

Documentation: Aide Notes

1. **Identify the problem.** Only 48 percent of aide notes document care provision as required by the aide care plan.
2. **Collect information.** 23 aides who were surveyed gave the following reasons for the documentation problem:
   - 2–unaware of the need to be "exact"
   - 2–limited education; difficulty writing
   - 23–nurses unavailable to make needed changes in care plan
   - 3–forgot
3. **Suggest a hypothesis.** Given the reasons, the quality team's brainstorming session resulted in the following plan:

   Voice mail was installed. Aides were asked to call the nurses' voice mail the same day the need for a care plan is identified. Nurses will return a voice mail message to the aide within 24 hours indicating whether a change in the care plan was made.
4. **Develop a plan/Design an experiment.** The quality team educated the staff on the use of voice mail over the next month and implemented the plan immediately thereafter. This particular process did not require an experiment.
5. **Implement the plan/Carry out the experiment.** The plan was implemented over the following two months.
6. **Analyze the data.** A resurvey of the aide notes showed that 86 percent of the aide notes documented care provision as required by the aide care plan.
7. **Draw conclusions.** The team decided that, although it had made progress, it needed to go back to the planning stage to develop a plan to continue to improve the aide documentation. The goal was to reach 95 percent compliance.

into improving multiple processes following an organized plan. Some key concepts that would allow for the improvement of organizational processes based upon the Joint Commission standards include

1. Focus on the performance of the organization, not the individual.
2. The process is continuous and systematic and utilizes the scientific method.
3. Improvement activities cross all disciplines and programs within the organization.
4. Project selection is prioritized by the entire staff.
5. Both leadership and staff must make a time commitment for involvement.
6. Patient and organizational functions are addressed continuously.
7. Operations can always be improved.
8. The ultimate goal of the performance improvement plan is to improve patient outcomes.

Organizational improvement places the focus on the organization's operations rather than on the individual. Instead of asking why the nurse didn't document the discussion about advance directives, ask broader questions, such as: Why would the documentation be missing? Could it be because we didn't explain the process or orient the staff appropriately? Is it because all of our documentation forms prompt staff response and we do not include a prompt statement for advance directives? Is it because it wasn't discussed and if so, why not? Perhaps the answer lies within the efficiency of the intake process. Rather than individualize the problem, the organization is challenged to think broad and evaluate its processes. Similar to working with teams, the performance improvement process requires the organization to avoid knowing the answer before it studies the issue. Is there a way the organization can improve the documentation system to permit thorough documentation? Can the documentation system be streamlined? Should we consider collaborating with other health care facilities along the continuum of care to develop a congruent and coordinated system within our locale? This variation in thinking avoids a negative focus on individual performance and encourages a focus on the positive impact of working together for a common vision.

TOOLS FOR THE PERFORMANCE IMPROVEMENT PROCESS

Statistical tools are very helpful to any improvement project because they help people to visualize portions of the process. Project teams are encouraged to use statistical tools as they consider the reasons, outcomes, or results of actions, and the total dimensions of the problem. Sometimes what cannot be articulated with words can be easily understood with a graph or a chart. The thought of composing statistical tools can be intimidating to some, but need not be. A quick review of the more common statistical tools follows.

Figure 8–1 shows a traditional bar graph or histogram. This tool is used to compare data. In this case it is comparing the reasons why the aide documentation is incongruent with the aide care plan directive.

Figure 8–2 is a Pareto chart that provides the same information but with a twist. Unlike the histogram, the Pareto chart demonstrates the values from the highest to lowest measurement. When evaluating some processes, the team may find that it has 10 or more answers to those why questions. Placing these reasons (elements) within a Pareto chart provides a visualization of the major elements. This assists the team in prioritizing the ele-

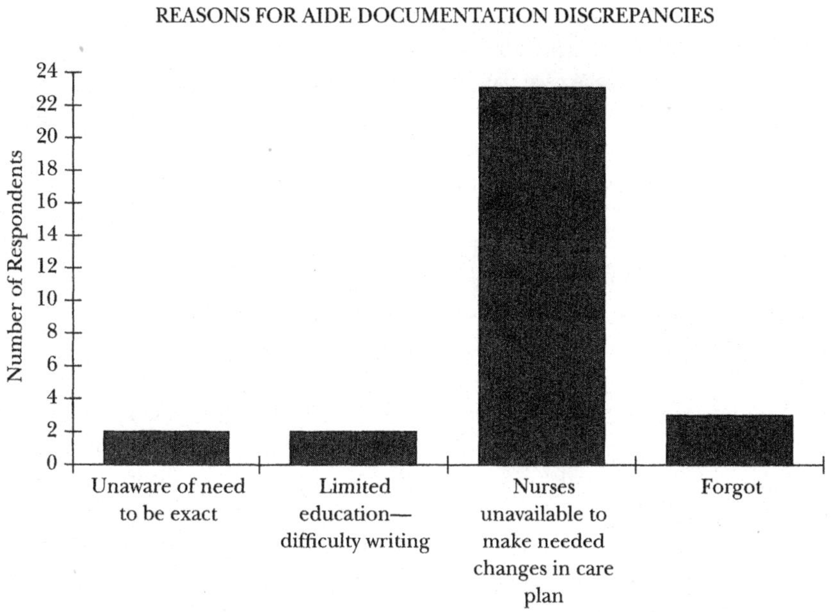

Figure 8–1 Histogram (Bar Graph)

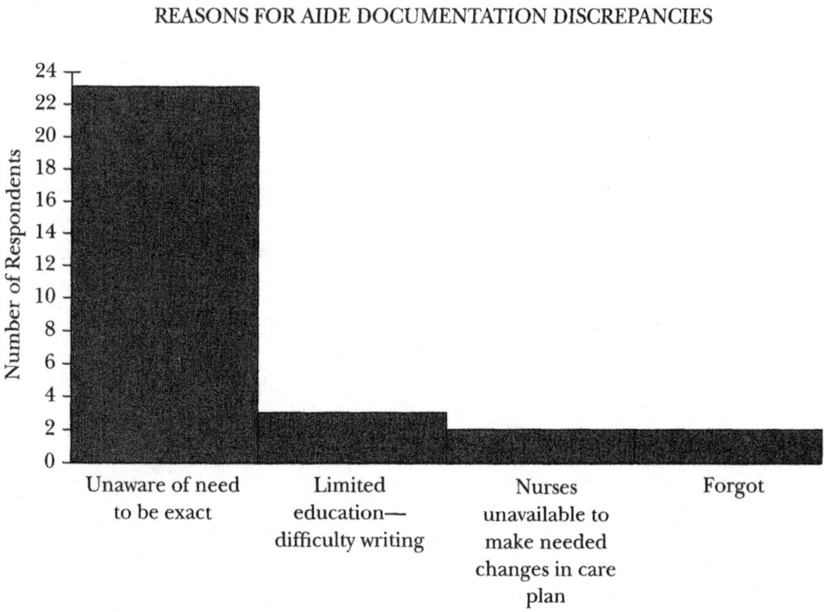

Figure 8–2 Pareto Chart

ments, so it can choose to address only the most critical factors. In this example, the nurses' unavailability towers above the other reasons and would be the priority. As we saw, the team proceeded from the perspective that addressing the largest contributor to the aide documentation problem would correct it. Once the team corrected the major problem it could then address the other issues, such as the aides' lack of knowledge and inability to read the form.

Figure 8–3 maps the same information in a line graph format, and Figure 8–4 plots the information in a pie chart format. Sometimes a portion of the pie is cut away to emphasize a particular point. Figure 8–5 is a scatter diagram and is used to plot individual points over repetitive time frames. This type of diagram is one of the most useful tools for those situations where the organization determines that no rhyme or reason exists for the problem. For example, this organization plotted the complaints it received over a one-week period from customers that the phone lines were ringing busy. Complaints received on Monday were noted in one color; Tuesday's complaints were noted in another color, and so forth. By the end of the week, this organization realized that although it received some complaints throughout the day, a majority of the complaints came between 8 A.M. and 9 A.M. and 3 P.M. and 4 P.M. The quality committee

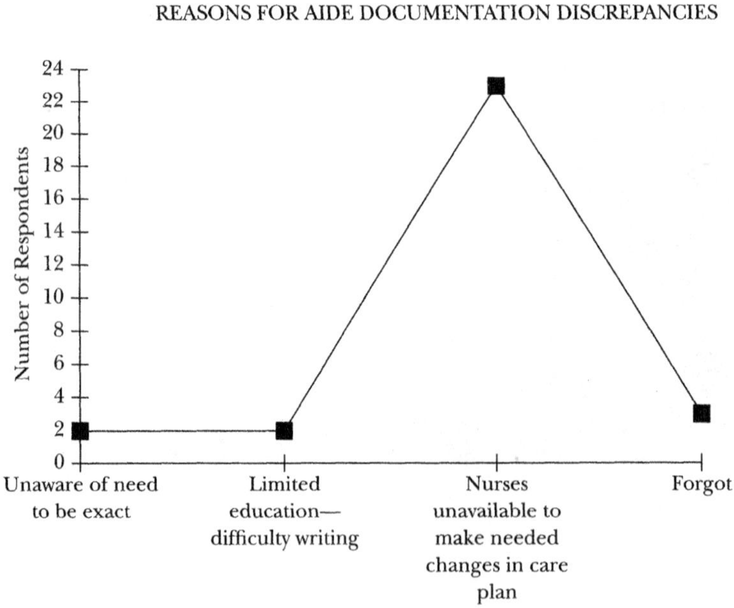

Figure 8–3 Line Graph

REASONS FOR AIDE DOCUMENTATION DISCREPANCIES

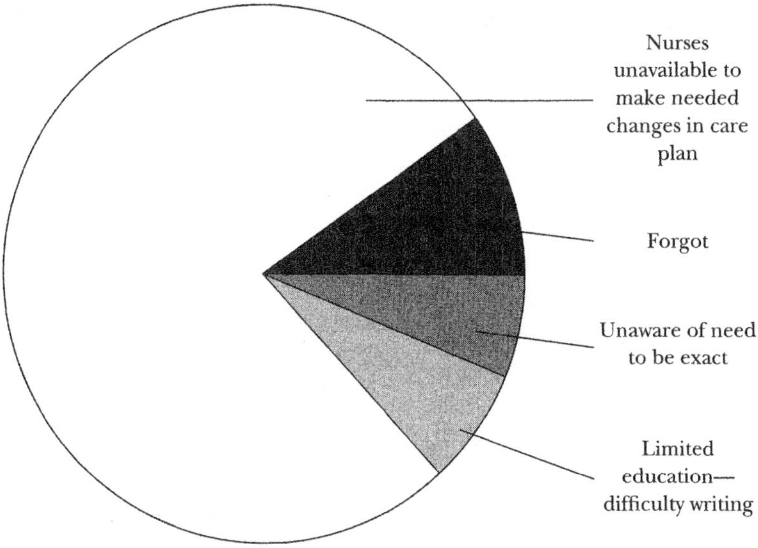

Figure 8–4 Pie Chart

PHONE LINE COMPLAINTS

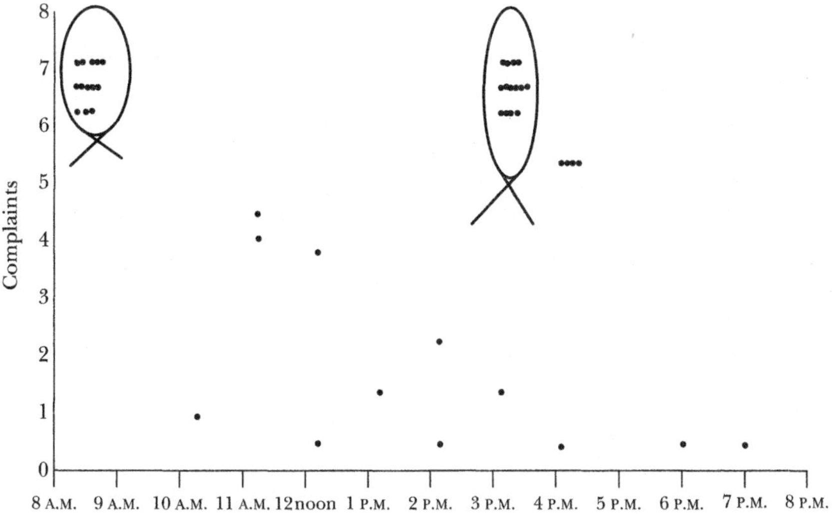

Figure 8–5 Scatter Diagram

found this data helpful and attacked the problem by addressing what was happening on the phones during these particular hours.

Tool 8–A-1 is a blank process flowchart containing an explanation of the key shapes to delineate information exchange, tasks, decision points, and breaks in processes. This tool is especially helpful and offers a visual of the steps involved in every process. Once the project team identifies each and every step within the process being analyzed, they are noted consecutively and each notation is placed within the most appropriate key shape. A completed flowchart example is shown in Exhibit 8–A-2 in the Appendix.

Tool 8–A-3 is a blank fishbone diagram. The problem is placed within the rectangle at the right (or the head of the fish). The main source categories are then placed at the end of the small bones.

KEY POINTS TO CONSIDER

To ensure that its quality improvement process is organization-wide, an organization needs to consider all of the players. Who is involved with the process? This could include individuals from within the organization as well as those external to the organization. Consider the team working with the referral process. The organization may want to invite a liaison social worker from the local nursing home to participate since the agency receives many referrals from the nursing home. Contracting and clerical staff and volunteers should not be forgotten. Input from all of these groups can be accomplished in a number of ways, including active improvement project participation, surveys, or special guest status.

Organizations also need to ensure that they've examined all of the parameters. Every possible cause needs to be explored. The team must be aware of its intuitive nature that makes it rush to judgment. Figure 8–6 demonstrates another tool to assist in the performance improvement process. Fishbone diagrams consider all reasons why the organization is having a particular problem. In this example, the problem is poor communication. Extending off the main fishbones are the major operational categories: people, machinery, office supplies, and politics. The details of the major headings are placed at the smaller bones within the diagram. Completing this diagram as part of a brainstorming session is recommended to assure that as many as possible of the factors contributing to the problem are documented.

Organizations must also not underestimate the value of input from sources external to the process. Inclusion of the volunteer or data entry secretary can provide an added dimension to the brainstorming process.

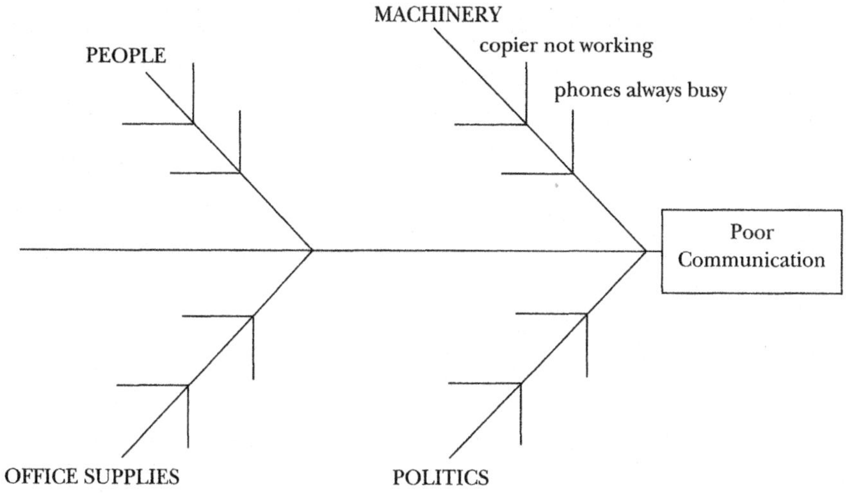

Figure 8–6 Fishbone Diagram

Performance improvement activities must be never ending. Organizations, like people, are forever growing and changing and what worked this year may not work next year. The organization is encouraged to revisit some past improvement initiatives.

The organization's plan must be committed in writing. It should be systematic, following a particular method. This written plan guides all teams through the improvement process as they evaluate and strive to improve what currently exists. The plan itself may include the method for identifying and prioritizing problems, the selection of the project team, the organization and documentation activities, the staff communication process, the statistical quality control methods to be used, the benchmarking process (internal and external), the selected method for improvement activities, and a graph showing the projects in place.

The organization's leaders are responsible for educating their staff and contractors about organizational performance improvement concepts and the organization's specific plan. This education is a precursor to total organizational involvement. It is no longer acceptable to delegate quality improvement activities to one person. The quality improvement director may coordinate or facilitate but not be *the* coordinator, *the* project team, and *the* decision maker for the projects.

As much as we would like to have a perfect world without problems, we must admit that regardless of the quality of services we provide, some dissatisfaction exists within our organization. It may be a significant amount of dissatisfaction or it may be a little amount. Our world is not perfect! Expressed frustration or dissatisfaction is a good start to a potential organizational performance projects list. Everyone within the agency should be involved in identifying projects worth studying. The facilitator may want to conduct a brainstorming session in conjunction with a monthly staff meeting. Everyone contributes ideas for projects. No ideas are worthless or too dumb to consider. Once this list is developed, everyone in the organization (staff, volunteers, contractors) is given 10 points to place wherever he or she deems high priority. The staff member may decide to divide his or her 10 points between projects or to place all 10 points on one project. Each person votes and the number of points are added up for each project to determine which project the *organization* has prioritized. The project with the most points becomes the first project addressed.

Organizational performance improvement is not a leader-run function. It also does not take the place of management projects and decision making. The managers may decide that preparing for accreditation should be top priority, but if the organization decides that looking into retention issues is top priority, the retention issue project becomes the official process project for the quality improvement team. Then, outside of the quality improvement, the leaders can conduct preparation activities for their upcoming accreditation survey.

Process improvement requires time for meetings, data collection, data tabulation, and communication. The leaders of the organization need to accommodate the needs for the participants to assure that adequate time is allocated for a thorough evaluation and solution of the problem. Likewise, staff must commit to the project at hand. Improving organizational performance can be fun. It empowers the multidisciplinary staff and promotes buy-in to organizational processes. The value of a congruent and committed staff is well worth the expense of the "nonproductive time" spent in improvement activities. Needless to say, some parameters must exist to continue day-to-day agency operations while improving processes. There needs to be an acceptable balance.

Regardless of the processes within the organization, applying process improvement concepts in a structured manner with the help of the entire organization creates a more efficient workflow, which in turn improves the service delivery. This team approach to organizational improvement fosters interest in the organization by the staff members and as such is valuable in empowerment. Implementing this process may be a drastic change for the staff members. It is recommended that the process be introduced on a small scale to allow the time to coach the team successfully. Once a team accomplishes a positive change through a group process, volunteers from the organization are readily available for future projects.

IMPLEMENTATION HURDLES

In order to make organizational performance improvement succeed within the agency, the leaders and staff need to be aware of some of the pitfalls. As discussed in Chapter 7, the most common pitfall is *having the solution before defining the problem.* This problem cannot be overemphasized. For example, a well-intentioned leader notes that the weekend visit volume is increasing. The leader knows that the nursing staff will need to increase its weekend rotations because that solved the problem in the past. The leader discussed her solution informally with several staff members. Given the leader's status in the agency, the staff began to accept this as the only solution. The project team developed to address this issue obtained suggestions, but they merely led to that predetermined solution.

The next pitfall involves *too many leaders on the project teams.* Leaders can facilitate teams but the work should not be based upon the thoughts and desires of the leaders. It is a fact that subordinates will be influenced by the presence of leaders, regardless of the openness and flexibility of the leader. Until staff feels empowered, it tends to allow the leader to lead whenever present. The presence of no more than one leader per team is a good idea. The team should be provided with the names of potential leader facilitators and should choose its own facilitator.

Another pitfall is with *management picked or staff picked teams.* The teams should be multidisciplinary and a combination of different personalities. Some of the quieter members of the staff may have very valuable input into a solution when charged with a problem. No one group of friends or colleagues should be advantaged by the group composition. This mixture avoids the same suppression of ideas that result when too many managers are on one team.

The final pitfall is *giving in to the complaints that the staff is too busy to participate* in organizational improvement. It is the leader's responsibility to allocate staff time for participation in improvement activities. Fear of the unknown may contribute to this excuse. Once the hurdle of the first project is jumped and the outcomes are noted, staff will be thrilled to participate.

CONCLUSION

Developing an all-encompassing organizational performance plan can seem overwhelming at first. Applying the guidelines and thoughts presented have assisted organizations to empower their employees into process to get started. The best way to start is to begin!

NOTES

1. The Joint Commission on Accreditation of Healthcare Organizations, *The Measurement Mandate* (Oakbrook Terrace, Ill.: 1993), 27.
2. R. Shaffer, Educational Session of the Joint Commission of Healthcare Organizations, (Oakbrook Terrace, Ill., July 1994).
3. Florida Hospital Association, *Innovative Benchmarking: A Practical Approach to Improving Productivity* (Orlando, Fla.: May 1994), 27.
4. The Joint Commission on Accreditation of Healthcare Organizations, *Process Improvement Models: Case Studies in Health Care* (Oakbrook Terrace, Ill.: 1993), 68.
5. Joint Commission, *Process Improvement Models,* 69.
6. *Life Science* (Westerville, Ohio: Glencoe/McGraw-Hill, 1995), 14.

Appendix 8–A

Tools

Tool 8–A-1 Process Flow Chart

PROCESS FLOW CHART

Map out every step of the ______________________ process utilizing the key.

Key

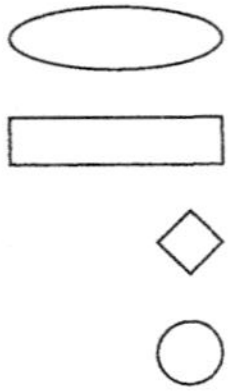

information

a task or activity

decision points

a break in the process

Tool 8-A-2 Completed Flowchart

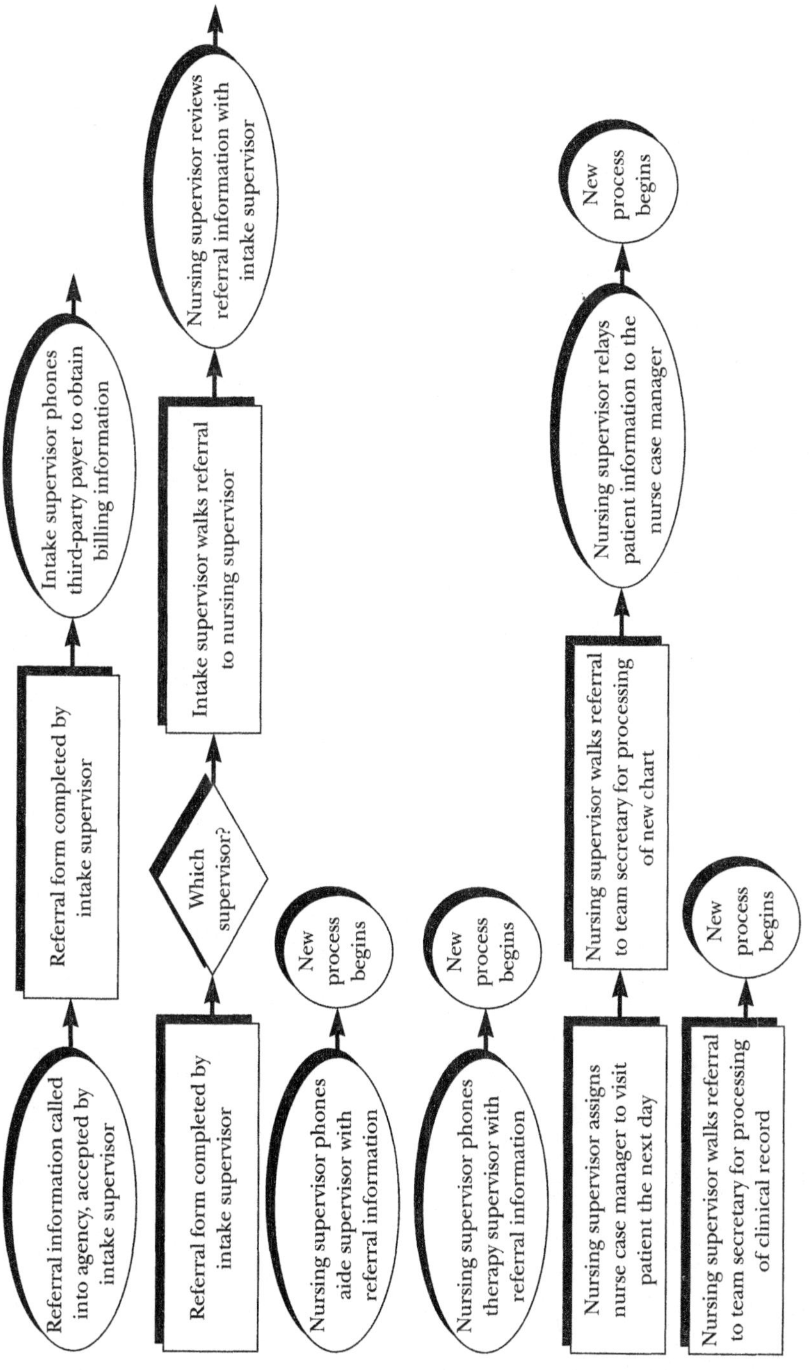

Tool 8–A-3 Fishbone Diagram

List the contributing elements leading to our ________ problem.

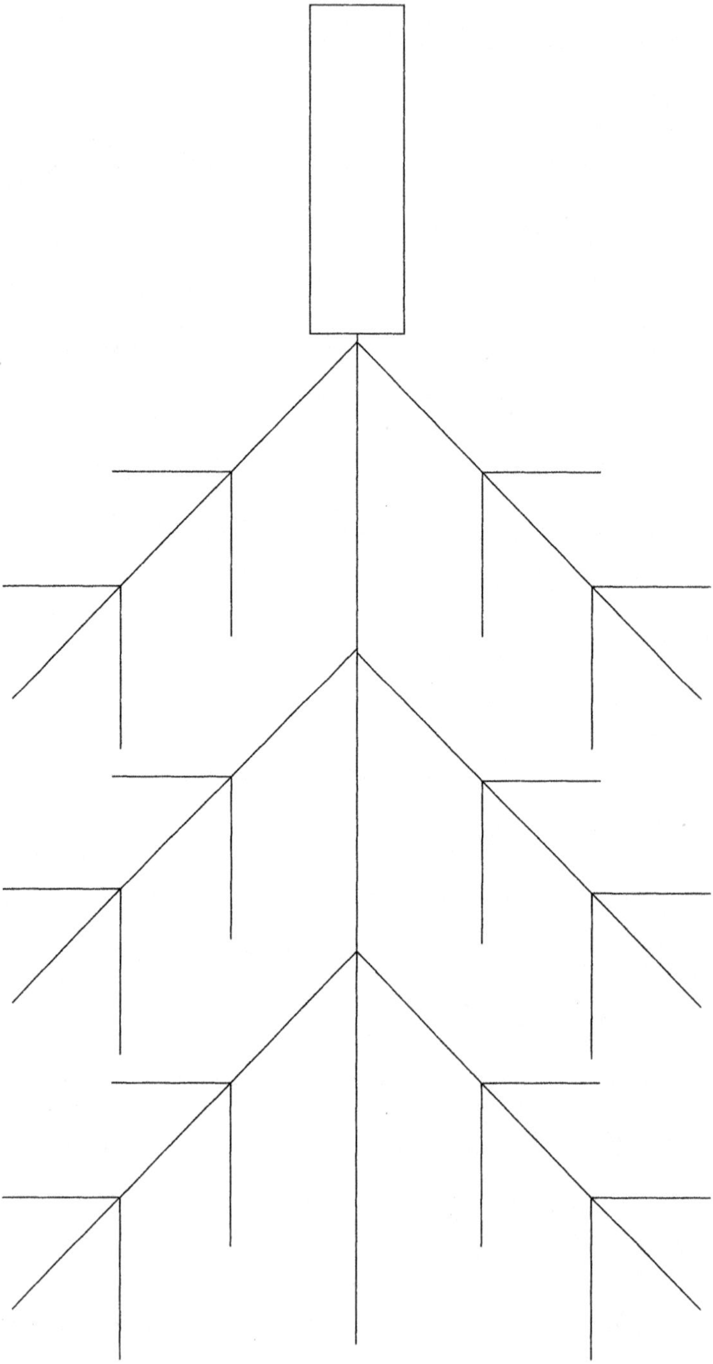

Chapter 9

Maintaining the Restructured/ Reengineered Organization

When we reflect upon the last decade in health care and view what has been occurring, we see ongoing turmoil and restructuring. In that time period, we know one hospital system that has downsized three times. Another has simply whittled away at the staffing levels and positions over the last 10 years. One set of two sister hospitals decided to build and combine staffs from the two hospitals into one hospital. How does all of this restructuring/reengineering affect the staff? Is any one way better than another? The proponents of reengineering support its approach as a once and done project.

Today's health care organizations' staffs appear to be in a constant fear of losing their positions and their incomes. They live with a "who do you think will be next" stance and constantly look over their shoulders. We have heard it said by many health care professionals throughout the United States that within their practice settings and within the hospital setting "the good ones are all leaving." They relate that the biggest topic of the times is who one thinks will be the next to leave the organization and the field.

This constant realignment of loyalties and movement among positions and organizations is not unique to health care in the twentieth century. It is commonplace in business and industry, and in all career fields. The days of 40 years at the same job within the local industry are gone, replaced by dreams of upward mobility and advancement. Perhaps the American Dream is becoming an American Nightmare. The ever-changing nature of the top echelon of an organization has created a role model for the middle management. The ever-changing middle management has created role models for its divisions and no one seems to remain long and truly care about the life of the organization and its impact on the community. This is becoming increasingly true in all work settings, not just in health care and certainly not just in home care. The professionals who came to home care in its infancy often came for the very reason of wanting stability and ongoing relationships with the patient and co-workers. As a result of the reengineering of acute health care and health care systems, displaced workers are gravitating to home health care—the health care growth field of the twenty-first century.

Now home care itself is reengineering, as a result of or in preparation for the many external impacts upon us. These external impacts are bombarding home health care professionals from all sides. They include those within the reimbursement arena such as the ever-present managed care, the at-risk contracts, and the capitation contracts. As their penetration increases throughout the country, there are also increased numbers of physician hospital organizations and health maintenance organizations, whose influence reenergizes the field of public health and preventive medicine. Home care is also influenced by the availability of qualified applicants for the positions available and by the increased regulations of government agencies such as OSHA on this practice setting. The need to effectively market the home health care organization's value and presence within this increasingly competitive field was not something that needed the organization's attention or resources in the past. But today these external influences, combined with the anticipation of prospective payment, bring the impacts made by diagnosis-related groups to acute care and ambulatory patients groups to ambulatory care seem more real to the field of community/home health. Gingerich and Ondeck describe these impacts in detail within Chapter 1 of their publication, *Clinical Pathways for the Multidisciplinary Home Care Team.* With the reengineering of health care and home care, we must reflect upon the results and plan for the sustenance of these results over the long haul. These reengineered efforts must demonstrate their longevity to our audience of disbelievers—our employees. It is time for us to examine our organizations, complete the restructuring with a dramatic reengineering effort, and work diligently to maintain what we have created. If we do not maintain the results achieved from the reengineering project, we allow a devaluation of the resources of time, effort, and money that have contributed to the reengineering project itself. This is a true disservice to the concept of reengineering.

RESOURCE REVIEWS

In preparation for this chapter, we reviewed not only the literature, but we also reviewed the doers. It was important to talk with the health care leaders who had reengineered their organizations and were still there, maintaining the integrity of the reengineering project. This review was conducted by telephone and through personal interviews. Among the leaders we interviewed were senior vice presidents of large health care systems, chief executive officers of hospitals within regional and rehabilitation health care systems, leaders within the acute and community rehabilitation fields, and middle and entry level managers within each of these practice settings. Also interviewed were the leaders at all levels within community health/home health organizations. Interviews were conducted in both informal and formal settings and occurred with leaders across the Eastern, Midwestern, and Southern regions of the country. The openness of those individuals with whom we spoke is deeply appreciated by the authors.

Most interviewees related that even though the initial work is done and processes are streamlined, the organization cannot rest on its laurels, nor relax its guard. Well, perhaps one can take a moment to rest, but there must be an ongoing drive and commitment to maintaining, monitoring, and ongoing reengineering of the organization. Reengineered processes might need further revision as a result of future changes in the health care environment.

LEADERSHIP TRAITS

In our discussions, we reflected on the individuals who had successfully persevered in reengineering projects within their organization. In this reflection, the leadership qualities as described by Stephen Covey in his book, *The Seven Habits of Highly Effective People,* came to mind. This new generation of health care leaders was demonstrating many of these qualities. These and similar qualities will assist the organization to succeed in maintaining its reengineered efforts.

Stephen Covey described the maturity continuum as the incremental, sequential, highly integrated approach to the development of personal and interpersonal effectiveness.[1] In the reengineering process, the concept of team and the empowerment of the team is a keystone to its success. Maintaining the reengineered organization cannot be left up to one individual; rather the empowered team must carry the effort forward. It is our belief that with the maturing of the individual along the maturity continuum, the individual becomes more comfortable with team empowerment and transfer of power and responsibility.

Covey's habits go from an internal/self focus to a public/organizational focus that can be likened to Maslow's[2] self actualization hierarchy. The seven habits as described by Covey are

1. Be proactive
2. Begin with the end in mind
3. Put first things first
4. Think win/win
5. Seek first to understand, then to be understood
6. Synergism
7. Sharpen the saw[3]

It is not the recognition of these habits that makes them unique nor is it these habits in themselves that make them unique. Rather it is the combination of these long-recognized qualities and traits as a paradigm that was created by Covey that lends a uniqueness to these qualities. Do you see many of the habits in Covey's list in those leaders whom you admire and respect? Which of this list are your individual strengths? Which, if any, are your weaknesses? We need to evaluate ourselves and our management team realistically and prepare ourselves for the ongoing work of maintaining the reengineered structure.

All of these traits are important to the success of a reengineering project. In order for the project to have been successful, the project team must possess these qualities either through combination of the individual traits of the team members or by the individual project team members. It is the last of the seven habits, the "sharpen the saw" habit, that we believe is most often neglected by our leaders. This is the habit that provides relaxation and refreshment of self. Reenergizing oneself is necessary to prevent burnout and to maintain the intensity of energy needed to sustain the reengineering movement.

While interviewing health care leaders regarding their reengineering efforts, their personal philosophies of leadership emerged, as well as their beliefs regarding the future trends in health care. The traits identified by Covey were apparent and visualized many times over. In meeting with health care organizations' management teams, it was apparent that although all these traits might not be present in any one individual, they were present collectively among the team of leaders. The levels or degrees of specific individual traits varied from leader to leader, lending a balance to the team.

All of these traits necessary for the executive to maintain the reengineered/restructured organization are present within the leaders of health care, but other traits also lend value to the individual's efforts. Other traits identified by these authors in their work include those in the discussion that follows.

Dynamos of Energy

These leaders appear to be eternal dynamos of energy, never faltering in their pursuits on behalf of the organization. They are ceaseless in their abilities to listen to their staff and reflect upon what they have heard. It is in this reflection that they are able to translate what they have heard into action plans. Disorganized fragments of reality seem to be formed easily into a meaningful whole by these individuals. The energy is sustained through meeting after meeting, through survey after survey, through the day into the evening meetings at ever-increasing levels of interest and enthusiasm. These leaders appear to have an internal intensity and focus that propels them forward in their work.

Caring, Charisma, Competence, Confidence, and Courage

The caring aspects of these leaders' personalities is apparent to the staff of the organization. These leaders appear to have an endless memory for the names and interests of their staffs and take a personal interest in them. Is this the charisma that has been described in the past? Perhaps, but in addition to these personal interrelationship qualities, there is conveyed an air of competence and confidence. It is not necessary, in today's high-tech world, that the leader "know it all," rather it is more important that the leader "know where to go for the information." The generalist is becoming increasingly marketable in today's health care arena and the leader who leads the organization through the reengineering project and beyond is no exception to this.

The leader, as a person, must be able to relate to many diverse groups of individuals—the physician referral group, the hospital executives, the community at large, the organization's board, the management team, the staff, the third-party payer groups, and the patients. Leaders must also be able to feel at ease within small or large groups and in individual one-on-one meetings.

Without courage, the leader of the reengineered organization will not lead through the process. It takes courage to undertake and initiate this project, but it takes even more courage to maintain the streamlined structure. Goldsmith predicts that, without courage, the following will occur in the stages of reengineering as he describes them. In the stage of initiation, the right problems will not be identified without courage. In the second stage—assessment—the numbers will not be accurate, but will be "soft pedaled." In the stage of redesign, the leader without courage is too careful of who might be offended, and in the stage of deployment, or maintenance, departments and managers of the organization will be allowed to slide. But it is in the final stage, the stage of evaluation, where the leader without courage allows the organization to suffer most. It is in this stage that the leader without courage is unable to evaluate the results and the current status of the organization.[4]

Team Concept

The leader who is successful in maintaining the reengineered/restructured organization is acutely aware that this is the result not of one individual's efforts, but of the team's efforts. In recruitment and hiring of the management team, the leader must perceive the interviewee's abilities as well as personality traits. In choosing or developing the team in the reengineered/restructured organization, it is vital that leaders share information and mentor the team in whatever areas are necessary for the organization's continued success. This can be likened to the interdependence point of Covey's maturity continuum in that the team and the leader become interdependent. This is not to infer that managers must become carbon copies of the leaders, but rather that their skills, experiences, and expertise should complement and enhance the remainder of the team. Like a chain, the strength of the whole is stronger than any one of its links. Individual personalities and interests of the managers are important, as well as a diversity of backgrounds, because these attributes expand the horizons of the visioning processes and break down existing paradigms.

Commitment

The leader displays commitment to the process and to the long-term strategic plan. It takes time to realize the full potential of the changes made in the reengineering project, but the ongoing faith and support in the decisions made can prevent premature abortion of the plan. It is important in the maintenance of the reengineered organization that the leaders persevere in their support of the reengineering project team's decisions.

Like an irritating pebble in your shoe, some dissatisfaction with the reengineered/restructured processes creates a constant reminder that maintaining the reengineered/restructured organization requires a continued reexamination of revised processes and a search for new reengineering opportunities in all processes and structures. For example, when new regulations emerge, our habitual response is to add another layer to our existing work in order to meet our interpretation of the regulation. We often develop a new form to capture the information required or add another step in the process to respond to the new regulation. In the reengineered organization, it is important for the team or the work unit to ask whether it really needs to develop this form or take another step. Is the information already being captured somewhere else? Could we simply add a question on an existing form and accomplish what we need to? Sometimes it seems easier to add a new form than to get everyone to agree to changes on existing forms. But to maintain the positive effects of the reengineering, it might be necessary to do just that.

This same examination process must apply to all requests, including requests for additional facility space for expanding programs. Look carefully at the space requirements and the current needs of the expanding department as well as the needs of the surrounding departments. Continual analysis of where space needs can be decreased, what departments are best aligned together, and which truly need the room to grow, is necessary in order to maintain the benefits derived from the reengineering project.

Don't overreact and respond to pressured requests, but look at the whole picture. On the other hand, however, don't paralyze the organization with delays—empower the managers to make these tough decisions. As the employees and managers are more comfortable with the new organization, these requests will become more founded in true need.

Entrepreneurial Spirit

The entrepreneur is defined as "one who organizes and directs industrial enterprises."[5] In the past, the entrepreneurs were considered the leaders in the business field—competitive, futuristic thinkers who were dynamic and ever forward moving. In the health care setting, the entrepreneur was often faced with frustration and aggravation as he or she pushed to move the organization forward as a business and compete for the patient population. The bureaucratic slowness that characterizes the large health care system is one of the problems that both Hallmark and AT&T recognized and utilized the principles of reengineering to eliminate within their newly restructured processes and organizations.

To maintain the reengineered/restructured organization, it is important that this entrepreneurial quality be developed in the executive director/

chief executive officer, as well as in the management team of the organization. The entrepreneurial leader seeks new opportunities in the health care and related fields so that the organization will increase its revenue producing services and succeed in the ever-changing health care arena. The entrepreneurial leader evaluates services and revises or eliminates those that are not profitable.

The external health care environment—the climate of cost cutting and efficiency, competitiveness and quality care, customer responsiveness and focus, and business-mindedness—must be internalized in order for the reengineered/restructured organization to be maintained.[6] Employees need to be given the opportunity to understand business thinking and to be able to identify all internal and external customers. One of the best ways to convey how to treat the external customer is to treat the employees as you would like them to treat the organization's customers. The good business person has learned the art of diplomacy and courtesy early in his or her personal and professional development. This art stands the organization in good stead in its ongoing ability to maintain the reengineered structure and respond to changing external health care needs.

CULTURE CHANGE PROCESS

Key to the success of the reengineering project is the culture change. Many estimate that truly to change the culture takes three to five years from beginning to end. All four levels of culture should have been addressed during the reengineering project, but it is during the maintenance of the effects that these changes will really occur. All levels of culture—macro, enterprise, sublevel, and micro—have been addressed and it is all these levels that must accept the reengineering results.[7] Acceptance of these redesigned processes by all cultures of the organization requires that a balance be maintained between implementing and managing the new organizational transactions and leading the transformation. To succeed in the maintaining of the restructured organization, it is necessary that transformational leadership emerges and is sustained in its efforts to continue the reengineering process.[8]

CONSTANT VIGILANCE AND MONITORING

In a speech, Michael Vance[9] credits Walt Disney with making a statement to the effect that the secret of Disney World and the world of imagination is that it is a world of "no chipped paint."[10] How do we maintain a world of "no chipped paint" in the reengineered home care organization? This entails constant vigilance and caretaking. It requires constant monitoring of the reengineered processes and the reengineered organization. It is easy to allow unplanned and uncontrolled growth to occur. It is also easy for duplication of efforts and unnecessary steps in a process to re-emerge. As each new piece of technology, treatment modality, accreditation criteria, or changing federal regulation arrives on the scene, the organization must carefully analyze the data to determine their true value to the organization. It is important not to overreact; rather investigate and determine the relevance to the organization. It is at these points in the progress of the organization that staff involvement is crucial. The inclusion of staff in the decision-making process when the decisions relate to the future of the organization makes them owners of the process.

INNOVATIVE/CREATIVE THINKING

To be free of the paradigms and the conditioning of our experiences allows us to use our creative natures. As children, our imaginations allowed us to explore far away lands and to experience the unknown. As we entered a structured learning environment, the creativity and freedom to explore was controlled. We were directed to color within the lines and were questioned if we used "unusual" color choices. We were rewarded for being part of the expected group behavior and were frowned at when we did not want to follow the leader, but rather wanted to lead. We grew and learned and we began to lose our imagination.

It is within this new home care environment that innovation is encouraged and rewarded, and in fact, the real work of the home care organization comes to include innovative thinking and action.[11] Efforts must now be made to regain our imaginations and to free our minds to explore outside our existing paradigms. The ongoing emphasis and continual focusing on creative opportunities assist us in maintaining the reengineered/restructured organization.

Acceptance of ideas and exploration of ideas that are unusual encourages creative thinking. When one of these authors participated in a "coaching for storytelling success" workshop, the first activity of the weekend was to pair off and share in creative imagining. The participants were instructed to describe a scene for the other to see. Imagine my chagrin when I was paired off for this initial exercise with Jay O'Callahan, a nationally known professional storyteller, who in my eyes is one of the best storytellers and creators of imagery. The scene was described, color was added, then smell, then touch, and so on in increasing detail. One of these descriptive exercise examples was chosen for presentation to the whole group. This example was expanded upon further with other creative elements until it took on form and substance and appeared to come to life before our eyes. This same example was recreated with a different emphasis and its meaning changed entirely. The leaders of this weekend storytelling workshop, Jay O'Callahan and Doug Lipman, are two of this author's favorite storytellers. Doug Lipman provides numerous workshops for professional storytellers and is also a frequent presenter of stories throughout the United States. The combination of Jay and Doug coaching and mentoring the participants in tandem was truly one of the highpoints of personal development experienced by this author. Participation in this weekend workshop assisted me in regaining my imagination and I like to think as a result of this experience I am better prepared to tackle the reengineering and maintaining of the organization.

This same imagining process applied to your staff's creative suggestions and solutions can give substance and credence to their ideas. As new ideas float to the surface in team meetings, it is important to explore them for viability and application. Try these ideas with descriptions of the settings in which they might work and try them with emphasis on different parts. My motto today is "Explore them or record them, but never ignore them." If sufficient time is available, explore them at once. If time is not available for exploration, then record them and keep an ongoing list of ideas for future exploration. This can be likened to utilizing a short-term storage shed of ideas. Keep that list of ideas visible and at every meeting provide an opportunity to take at least one idea from the shed and try it out. Treat these ideas like treasures and explore their nooks and crannies.

When seeking to create and imagine, again think in all senses—the smell, taste, sight, sound, and the touch of the idea. One of my favorite creating spots is in my backyard by a small pond and waterfall. There in the spring when the blue periwinkle and deep purple lilac trees begin to bloom, I can smell the sweet smell of lavender. As the sun grows warm after the winter cold, I can sit and listen to the water running down over the pebbles making a small waterfall into the pond. In that pond abound brilliant orange goldfish, frogs, and a red slider turtle. This peaceful setting, where fish swim amidst the pond plants, the breeze flows through the trees, and the sounds of the birds abound with their songs of spring, brings a freeing of the mind from day-to-day issues and allows creative thoughts to emerge, often bringing solutions to unanswered questions of the day. Could you see and smell this spot? Could you hear and feel the solitude? As you read this paragraph you probably began to visualize this spot. Is the temperature of the water warm or cool today? Is the turtle out on his limb warming his body in the sun? Or is it too cool, too early in the year? Each of you will have different answers to these questions. You might have seen a country setting amidst much land, but in reality this is a backyard in the suburbs of York, Pennsylvania where I live and write. Better yet, maybe you didn't visualize the spot described, but began to experience and recall a setting that is special to you. Bring that setting to life and enjoy that setting in your mind through all the seasons of the year. Even in the deep of winter when the snow fills the pond and the aquatic life is nestled in the bottom, safe until spring, my mind allows me to see that pond in all its summer splendor. The butterflies in the surrounding garden sparkle like jewels in the sunlight even in the darkest day of winter because of my ability to once again create and enjoy that special spot in my mind.

When each of us is able to find our creative settings, we can choose to visit them in our minds or on location. This setting will provide the reenergizing and recreating necessary to help us maintain the reengineering/restructuring of the organization. As leaders, we must assist our management teams and our staff to regain their creative natures. The stories of the world often have provided my staff with the message needed to tackle the next step in a project. We do not have to be storytellers to be creative, we just need to give our imaginations a chance to come to life once again.

CARE DELIVERY MAINTENANCE

All of the leaders interviewed emphasized their concern for the quality of the services delivered and the need to maintain the direct care staff at an acceptable level for safe and consistent care delivery. Some individuals indicated that they believed the direct service staff cuts had gone as deep as they could go and that the continuing reengineering efforts must focus on other avenues of expense reduction. Always an alternative to expense reduction, revenue production was also at the top of their lists of things to do. These leaders are looking to expand profitable services and replace unprofitable ones. They know they can no longer look to the organization's usual and customary revenue production services, but must use the creative energy of the staff to find new services and to refashion the existing ones into profitable services sought by the surrounding community.

Standing out in the minds of the health care leaders and the staff of the reengineered organizations was the need for excellence in service delivery and patient care. This was considered by everyone interviewed and every organization visited to be of major importance to the long-term success of the reengineering project. These individuals believed, further, that patient and organizational outcomes measurement must be part of any care delivery model adopted by the organization.

UTILIZATION/VARIANCE TRACKING

As part of the maintenance of the reengineered/restructured organization, the utilization audits and variance tracking reports assume increasing importance. Utilization audits provide data and input into the actual service volumes versus the projected/anticipated volumes. Realignment of staffing structures based on service volumes continues to be made as trends in volumes are objectively measured. Decisions to adjust staffing levels can be based on predetermined utilization targets. This eliminates the emotional aspect of staffing reductions and provides rational measurable data for increasing staffing within the needed home care service delivery areas.

Utilization audits of inventory and supply levels also can provide supply volume and usage levels as they correlate to service volumes. Pre-established utilization supply ratios provide predetermined amounts of needed supplies based on patient/visit volumes. Fluctuations outside of the ratio and an established acceptable range are investigated and corrected. Pre-established ratios allow for volume fluctuations; such decreases or increases can occur without a rework of the established system. These pre-established targets allow for business growth—increased volumes and subsequent increased supply inventories—without a total relook at the process. These predetermined fluctuations allow for the maintaining of the integrity of the reengineered/restructured processes.

Tracking of care delivery variances provides empirical data related to patient care. These tracking mechanisms provide concurrent and retrospective information regarding patient outcomes and variations in caregivers, referral sources, and patients.

The leaders who were interviewed supported the development and implementation of the clinical pathway care delivery models as one avenue for establishing and evaluating care delivery standards. Variance tracking is part of any of the available clinical pathway models. The clinical pathway model of care delivery is a relatively new concept in home care and as such, will continue to be refined based upon utilization statistics, variance trends, and caregiver and patient variances. While these aforementioned impacts are internal, there will also be many external impacts on these pathways. External impacts will include the changing reimbursement models of both Medicare and third-party payer groups. It has been the authors' experience that patterns of care delivery reflect the reimbursement trends of the geographic region. For example, while presenting a clinical pathway workshop the topic of visit numbers emerged. There is great variation between allowable visits among the Medicare fiscal intermediaries. This has been especially noticeable in the discipline of social work. When prospective payment comes to home care the variations in

Medicare fiscal intermediaries will diminish in importance and impact to the home care organization.

The reengineered/restructured organization must keep a watchful eye on what is occurring internally with care delivery and what external influences are occurring that will affect practice patterns. In maintaining a watchful vigilance, ongoing refinements to the reengineered care delivery structure can occur concurrently. Thus there will be a maintenance of the effectiveness of the reengineered care delivery process.

VALUES ANALYSIS

Values analysis, the looking at the results and the outcomes in relationship to the amount of organizational resources used in obtaining this end result or outcome, is key to the ability to verbalize the success of the reengineering project in measurable terms. The breaking down and analyzing of processes is the first step of resource analysis. The creation of the perfect end solution is the end result or outcome desired. When combined in the reengineering project, true value analysis occurs. This aspect of the reengineering project can produce dramatic results, yielding an enhanced bottom line and better allocation of resources. While the ongoing analysis of outcomes in relationship to resource consumption of tasks and processes might not provide dramatic results, we believe that ongoing vigilance in this area will provide slow, incremental gains and prevent backsliding. These incremental gains ensure the ongoing viability of the reengineered structure and processes of the organization. For it is through the slow insidious "loss of ground" in the battle against the inefficient use of resources that the organization in turn, unleashes the effect of the reengineering project.

CUSTOMER SURVEYS

It is not enough to reengineer dramatically and say, "Okay, we've gotten the customers' input, now let's move on to the next project." The organization that maintains its reengineering effectiveness will be the organization that routinely and regularly seeks input from all its customer groups. This does not imply that this process is allowed to interfere with the organization's operation. Rather this implies that the need for customer input is recognized and a plan developed for ongoing solicitation of this information. Staff, patients, physicians, referral sources, community agencies, and business leaders all make up important customer groups. It is through ongoing community interactions and activities that we can maintain our organization in step with customer needs.

Focusing on the customer groups, one at a time, and seeking functional integration is the goal of customer service in the reengineered organization.[12] With the initiation of customer service processes one at a time, it is important not to lose sight of the total picture. Returning to these groups time and again is one way of validating the ongoing results.

As customer groups emerge and change, it is increasingly important to gain their perspective of our services and our purpose. As managed care's impact is felt increasingly throughout geographic areas of the country, this customer group will provide input to the organization of its desires and expectations. The impact of this newly emerging customer group will take on increasing importance. Earlier in this book we described the stages of managed care market penetration as a four-stage process. It now appears that the managed care market penetration is proceeding to a fifth stage, making it a five-stage process. These stages are described as follows:

1. Unstructured: Little managed care exists.
2. Loose framework: Managed care discounting is occurring and physicians are organizing into groups.
3. Consolidation: There is heavy managed care infiltration with the emergence of capitation in the primary care setting.
4. Managed competition: Fee-for-service payment structures are greatly reduced and there is greater than 50 percent HMO penetration.
5. End game: Health care provider networks and integrated care systems have emerged.[13]

Where is your marketplace as you read this book? Do you know? If not, it is imperative that you find out quickly. Have you prepared wisely? How can the maintenance of your reengineered structure contribute to your success within this type of marketplace?

INTEGRATED CARE DELIVERY/NETWORKING

Repeatedly we have heard that the reengineered organization's maintenance strategies should include the development of networks for care delivery. Although it is not necessary to control every facet of health care delivery within the continuum of care, it is important to provide access to your organization's catchment area and patient population to all facets of health care delivery.

What does this mean? It means allowing "niche" providers to emerge and excel if they are able to provide quality, efficient services. The health care leaders recognize that one entity can be all things to all people and in this recognition acquiesce to the need for partners in care delivery. As stated by one health care executive, "There is not a need to duplicate services if there are others that are already providing them efficiently, and with a focus on quality, competition in some areas is healthy because it will mean higher quality, more cost effective care."[14] In his opinion, there will always be some competition in health care, but that organizations will begin to consider outsourcing, networking, and joint venturing for some services (i.e., those that **are** available and **meet** established quality standards).

This belief assists the organization in maintaining its reengineered structure, because it allows the organization to take the time to evaluate new programs and services in relationship to resource allocation and expenditures, not only for start-up operations, but also for the long haul. This long haul includes the start-up, growth, and expansion phases of services. A complete review of any proposed new service is essential to the maintaining of the reengineered/restructured organization.

The recognition that outsourcing of services and networks in care delivery are acceptable practices allows for ongoing evaluation and analysis of new projects in relationship to the principles of reengineering. This in turn serves to stem the insidious growth and excess layering of structures and programs. The emphasis can continue to be on the "real work" of the organization, the "value added" work identified in the reengineering/restructuring process.

MAINTENANCE THROUGH PILOT PROJECTS

Although this is not the recommended method for reengineering/restructuring the organization, we have seen value gleaned from this approach when the process has been utilized appropriately.

In the large home care organization or large health care system where constant growth and expansion are occurring, it is sometimes necessary to adapt the reengineering process to the situation. The organization might know from experience and historical data that there is strong physician group resistance to projects that encompass the entire organization. This resistance could be anticipated when initiating a total organizational reengineering. Physicians might express concerns, justifiably, regarding the project's potential to interfere with care delivery. In such cases, it might be both pragmatic and diplomatic to pilot some of the proven concepts of reengineering within receptive patient care units. For example, the positive results and aspects of the clinical pathway care delivery model or the development of patient-focused care units might be the right way to approach the reengineering project. The enhanced job satisfaction of the staff members involved in patient-focused care will transfuse the organization with enthusiasm for the total reengineering project. The staff will also verbally support the project, and the physicians, whose patients have benefited from the patient-focused care and clinical pathway models of care delivery, can also become advocates for the reengineering/restructuring process. All of these individuals, as a result of their positive experience with reengineering, will become believers and supporters of the cause and their support will serve to move the project forward. With acceptance and support from the physician referral groups, the way has been prepared for a total reengineering/restructuring of the health care organization.

With the success of these pilot projects and the ongoing infiltration of the reengineering concepts among other patient care teams and ancillary service providers, this approach will help to maintain the effects of the reengineering project. As additional patient care teams adopt the clinical pathway method of care delivery and enhance the team approach to patient care, there will be continued positive results and continued enthusiasm for reengineering by the individuals involved. Enthusiasm is contagious! So keep those reengineered processes flowing and keep the enthusiasm growing.

This growth of the project and growth of the enthusiasm for the reengineering project utilizes the pilot study as a wedge theory approach to reengineering. In a financially solvent organization with ample resources, this approach is possible. The financially solvent organization with good service volumes and a healthy bottom line has the luxury of time—the time to take a modified approach to reengineering such as discussed above. In the organization with limited resources, it is usually best to approach the reengineering project in its totality at its inception since this approach will give the most dramatic results in efficiency and care delivery.

STAFF EDUCATION

As a former teacher, I truly believe that if we provide the learner and the staff with the tools necessary to perform their jobs, they will do their jobs well. As individuals start out they all want to do a good job and to meet or exceed the expectations of their positions. It is our job to provide employees with the opportunity to continue to develop their skills. It is also our job to ensure that the expectations of their positions are clearly understood. If we want something to be accomplished, then provide employees with a measurable, clearly stated goal, and then measure their performance against this goal consistently.

To maintain the effect of reengineering, there must be an ongoing emphasis on staff education regarding empowerment, self-governance, and reengineering itself. Staff turnover is ongoing and with new staff unfamiliar with these concepts entering into the home care organization, we find in some cases, these staff members are uncomfortable and unsure of the dimensions of empowerment. In the organization's orientation, some time should be allocated for the inclusion of this content. Practice applications of decision making and reengineering activities made available to new staff in the form of case studies can provide reinforcement of this content.

Learning is a lifelong task and as such must be given lifelong attention. The reengineered organization must continually reeducate staff in the concepts and principles of reengineering and its expectations of its staff as they relate to reengineering. It is through these educational sessions that the effects of the reengineered processes will be maintained.

COMMUNICATION AND CHANGE

One of the most common threads on our loom is the thread of communication and change. All the leaders interviewed for this chapter stated that they saw ongoing communication and acceptance of change as keys to the successful maintenance of the results of the restructuring/reengineering project. They all also emphasized that the communication didn't end with the project and that the change **never** ends!

Communication by the leaders of the progress and the results of the reengineering/restructuring serves as the avenue for communicating the ongoing activities to maintain the new cost-efficient structure. The communication of any newly created regulations and accreditation criteria and the organization's analysis and resultant strategy for meeting these expectations will provide the staff with confidence in the ability of their leaders and in the organization itself. A continued use of a newsletter and on-line question and answer access to staff regarding the continued reengineering/restructuring efforts will maintain the staff's interest and enthusiasm for the project. This also provides them with the opportunity to input their suggestions and ideas to the project team on a regular basis.

The leader/CEO must excel in his or her ability to communicate his or her vision and the vision of the organization. The staff who feel a personal connection with the individual at the top is the staff who will respond to the needs of the organization and accept changes, even if they are unpleasant.

As leaders, we must be able to recognize, accept, and communicate to our staff that the one unchanging aspect about change is that it is inevitable and that it is a constant presence in the world in which we work. It is important to communicate that change is positive and moves us forward, whereas failure to change causes us to lose ground in the health care service arena. Change must be seen as a desirable component of our day-to-day work environment and staff must be encouraged to seek new solutions to problems encountered. The level of confidence of the CEO/leader of the organization in communicating with all levels of staff and community leaders and his or her comfort level with handling change and the accompanying uncertainty are vital to the maintenance and long-term viability of the reengineered/restructured organization.

PSYCHOLOGICAL PLAN

The psychological plan of the organization requires at least 30 percent of the leaders' time. It is the development of a well-thought-out psychological plan that allows the organization to maintain the effects derived by the project. This involves efforts to get inside the minds of the survivors, after the effects of reengineering are felt. It also involves designing programs to assist them in dealing with their sense of loss, grief, and guilt. Support to the employees should include coaching and mentoring for success and career growth.[15] Recommitment to the organization accompanies the empowerment that flows throughout the organization. Shared profits through an employee profit-sharing plan also can provide an ongoing employee commitment to maintaining the streamlined processes.

CONCLUSION

Some would-be reengineering projects seem to get aborted prematurely. Why? The combination of the amount of time needed to support the project, the amount of organizational resources necessary to commit to the project, the expense of the project and/or the consultants, and perhaps even the magnitude of the change itself are all reasons that might lead to a short-term success or aborted reengineering project.

It is important that future leaders display the attributes of those leaders who brought about the transformation and that the constant monitoring and long-range vision be ever-present, like a beacon of light shining throughout the entire organization.

What are the long-term success rates for the reengineered health care organization? As of this writing, there are no significant data available relative to hospital systems, let alone home care organizations. Future editions of this book will include data as they become available.

Home health care site visits to reengineered organizations have tended to reemphasize the newness of this application of the concepts and principles of reengineering to home health care. These organizations have successfully demonstrated the short-term effectiveness of their reengineering/restructuring efforts. The results have been appreciable and measurable, however, the literature search fails to yield significant data relative to the long-term effectiveness of the reengineering projects within the home care setting.

The authors believe that the proactive approach of reengineering and ongoing maintenance of the streamlined processes will prove to generate positive long-term benefits to the organization. The very nature of the principles of reengineering enhances the value of the process to home care. As with the "halo effect" in research studies, the halo effect in the reengineered organization of values analysis, streamlining of service delivery, process simplification, and focus on customer service all enhance the organization's operations. All of these concepts, individually and collectively, enhance the short- and long-term viability of the organization.

NOTES

1. S. Covey, *The Seven Habits of Highly Effective People* (New York, N.Y.: Simon & Schuster, Inc., 1990), 48.
2. Maslow identified and named this theory of self actualization as a result of his work, which is referred to universally within the field of psychology. He himself described and wrote of this theory throughout his many books, including *Motivation and Personality* published in 1954 by Harper.
3. S. Covey, *The Seven Habits of Highly Effective People,* 53.
4. N. Goldsmith, *Downsizing Is Not Reengineering,* Report No. 1097-94-CH (The Conference Board, 1994), 23.
5. *Webster's New Twentieth Century Unabridged Dictionary* (Cleveland, Ohio: World Publishing Company, 1951), 581.
6. J. Manion, Chaos or Transformation, in *Reengineering Nursing and Health Care,* ed. S. Blancett and D.L. Flarey (Gaithersburg, Md.: Aspen Publishers, 1995), 167.
7. H. Brite, *Reengineering the Hierarchy,* Report No. 1097-94-CH (The Conference Board, 1994), 15.
8. Brite, *Reengineering the Hierarchy,* 16.
9. Michael Vance is widely regarded as the dean of creative thinking and was named by *USA Today* as one of the most requested speakers in this country. He and his associates provide leaders with the resources and tools for innovative out of the box thinking. A former

dean of Disney University, for seven years he had the responsibility for management development and training for Disneyland, Disney World, and Disney Studios.

10. M. Vance, Speech presented at meeting of National Association of Home Care Annual Meeting, September 1995.
11. J. Manion, Chaos or Transformation, 167.
12. G. Bennett, *Aim, Discover, Deploy, Plan,* Report No. 1097-94-CH (The Conference Board, 1994), 13.
13. How Markets Evolve, *Hospital and Health Networks* 69, no. 9 (1995): 48.
14. A. Walsh, "Tolmie Follows Prescription for St. Joseph's Success," *Intelligencer Journal* (Lancaster, Pa.: 11 December 1995), p. 9.
15. J. Clark and R. Koonce, Engaging Organizational Survivors, *Training and Development* (August 1995): 25.

Chapter 10

Envisioning the Future of Home Care

The crystal ball of health care's future is what everyone would like to have sitting on the corner of their desk. Over time, when a decision needed to be made, they could pick it up, give it a shake, and have the perfect answer for the future health care arena. As the home care organization finds itself within this new world of health care, the crystal ball would become a significantly great advantage.

This health care world is becoming a highly competitive environment, one in which resources are limited and only the fittest survive. The efficient, cost-effective, customer/user friendly, quality provider will be central to health care delivery. The multiservice provider or coordinator of services will be sought after by the physicians and referral sources so that their time can be spent as efficiently as possible. The "no hassles" guarantee might just become the motto of home care in the twenty-first century.

The owners of that crystal ball will be there first with the services to meet the changing health care needs within their geographic region and catchment area. So how do we get our hands on that crystal ball? That seems to be the question that needs answering here! Well, we all know that there really isn't any health care crystal ball. If there was we would be out there shaking that ball and planning our next health care business instead of reading this book.

When we reflect upon the future of home care and the future of health care in general, we see a fast-moving rollercoaster that whizzes up the climbs and down the chutes, depending on the ever-changing reimbursement track. We have included some of the future trends in both home care and health care in this chapter because we believe they are intertwined. Some of these trends are being realized now; some will be realized within the near future; yet others may occur in a more distant future.

OUTSOURCING GROWTH

With the evolving health care reimbursement arena and the reengineering/restructuring of health care systems, CEOs and boards of health care systems will be analyzing and evaluating current proposed services more closely. As the information/computerization systems of health care systems can more accurately allocate resource consumption and expenses to the service areas, a truer bottom-line picture per services can be determined. With this determination, health care systems will come to realize which services are best provided directly by the health care system and which are better to be outsourced.

Outsourcing of services can be accomplished by the formal establishment of network and preferred provider relationships or by the informal establishment of patterns of referral lines for the delivery of services to patients. The key to these formal and informal relationships is the ability of the participants to accept not maintaining total control of service delivery and to collaborate with other health care providers in the delivery of care to patients.

STAFF HIRING VERSUS CONTRACTING

In addition to determining the fiscal viability of new and current services, these more sophisticated capabilities of the organization's fiscal information systems provides CEOs and the boards of directors with additional in-depth data to evaluate the cost of directly hiring staff. These data can evaluate the total cost of directly hiring employees for service delivery versus the cost of procuring staff through staffing or management operation's agreements. As the costs associated with providing benefit packages to employees continue to increase astronomically there will be increased utilization of independent contractors or procurement of staff through staffing agencies.

With the increased utilization of outside employees versus the direct hiring of employees, there is a related need for increased assurance of the quality of care provision that meets the organization's standards. We believe that the employees of the organization are the best public relations agents an organization can have and with the procurement of staff through contracting agreements, we foresee that the organization will need to increase its marketing and public relations efforts as a whole. Loyalty and commitment to the organization will decrease and the prime motivator for the contracted staff will be their individual financial reimbursement.

In the cases where management contracts are awarded, it will be important for the organization to negotiate for consistency in the individual appointed to fulfill the term of the contract. This consistency would be based upon satisfactory performance of the individual and his or her ability to meet the goals established by the organization.

Nurses within the acute care field will seek additional education to prepare themselves for available positions. Programs such as those developed in Massachusetts by a consortium of home care providers and hospitals will catch on in other parts of the country. This program is designed to provide the enrollee with 12 credits over two semesters. Courses and clinical practicums are required in each of the two semesters, however this curriculum has been planned with the working nurse in mind and is offered in the evening and on weekends.[1] Associate and baccalaureate degree curriculums also should look to the future and be redesigned so their courses provide the graduates with the skills necessary to function in future health care settings. These changes will once again provide a pool of qualified nurses for the home health care field of practice.

NICHE BUSINESS GROWTH

The above two trends in health care delivery lead us to the next example—niche businesses. The outsourcing of services and the utilization of contract staffing will provide opportunities for entrepreneurs to develop and succeed in business. Staying aware of what services the health care organizations within your community will be outsourcing provides the entrepreneur a heads up on business development.

When developing a new niche service, it is important to emphasize the quality and cost-effectiveness of the service. As a home care entrepreneur, it is important to maintain the streamlined processes developed as part of the reengineered/restructured project. It will also be important to anticipate and exceed your customers' (the health care system) expectations.

It is in the niche business growth area that we see home care's role emerging. Many of today's health care entrepreneurs are in home care and these individuals will lead their organizations in the development of complementing niche services. We would foresee several types of complementary niche services that could be developed by entrepreneurial home care organization.

One example of niche business growth might be the care center concept adopted by Bellin Memorial Hospital in Green Bay, Wisconsin. In order to combat decreasing inpatient statistics, Bellin Memorial developed clinical care centers and from these centers is now bringing its services to the patients within the care center.[2] Will the home care entrepreneur go one step further and collaborate with the care center in taking the care to communities where patients reside? This could be one niche business opportunity available to home care organizations in the near future.

CUSTOMER GROUP EXPECTATIONS

The Patient Group

As population demographics continue to change, we will continue to find increases in older individuals living alone, increases in the female proportion of the total elderly population, increases in geographic disbursement of the elderly, and decreases in family support systems.[3]

The current Medicare home care benefit does not provide the services necessary to allow the elderly to meet their own expectations of remaining in their own homes and to receive home delivery of health care services. As a home care entrepreneur, a complementary niche business includes the development of an adult day care program that can meet and exceed this customer group's expectations. This service should include transportation between the home and the day care setting. In addition to the usual adult day care services, the transportation allows the patient to get safely to and from the day care program and the day care center itself would provide breakfast, lunch, and dinner to the participants, thus freeing them from the necessity of grocery shopping.

We propose that the truly entrepreneurial home health care organization go even further in its creative development of services for the twenty-first century. If the current private duty services offered by the organization are expanded to include overnight companion services at a reasonable rate, the companion could get the patient ready in the morning and assist in the transfer of the patient onto the transport bus.

This form of combined services (i.e., adult day care, transportation, meals, and overnight companion) can be offered as a creative package and thus not only meet but truly exceed the expectations of this home care customer group.

The Physician Referral Group

What are this customer group's expectations? How can we exceed this group's expectations? Physicians desire quality care for their patients with minimal interruptions to their work day. One entrepreneurial approach to this expectation might be patterned after that of the Access Center of the VNA of Omaha, Nebraska. This center was established to provide a centralized access unit that responds to physician referrals and contacts.

The authors perceive several refinements to the access center in the future of home care. These refinements include an intake nurse availability within the access center from 7:00 A.M. until 10:00 P.M. on a daily basis. This nurse would record the referral data into the information system and, in the event of multiple referrals and admissions to schedule, triage the patients for admission to the home care services. The nurse is responsible for the scheduling of the admission visit, assignment of an admission nurse, and a patient-focused care team based on geographic, skill-mix distribution, and staff qualifications. This intake nurse completes and verifies the insurance/payer information and the referring physician and primary physician of the patient. At this point the name of the admitting physician and the physician credentials are verified by the access center staff according to established policy.

The physician liaison nurse assigned to the home care access center serves as the liaison between the field caregiver staff and the physician offices. Direct e-mail access by the field staff to these nurses provides instantaneous on-line patient status reports and information regarding the physician contacts initiated for orders or status report updates. The liaison nurses are also available from 7:00 A.M. until 10:00 P.M., Monday through Saturday. The intake nurse and physician nurse liaison are crosstrained to enable the organization to provide consistent, high-quality staff to this aspect of the access center. The evening on-call nurses are also assigned to this center and after-hour visits are scheduled and made out of the access center.

The Third-Party Payer Group

This group will have increasingly larger percentages of managed care organizations determining the providers utilized for services. In order to meet its expectations (i.e., the lowest cost for the highest quality care), the upgraded computer on-line availability with the home health agency and between the home health agency and physician or referral sources will also be made available to the third-party payer groups. Instead of calling with periodic updates, these updates will be sent by e-mail. With increasing amounts of capitation, these reports will not be for the purpose of obtaining additional visit approvals, but rather will be true patient status report updates. The e-mail approach to these updates will prove to be a more efficient and less costly method for the organization.

The third-party payer group is requesting the organization to seek accreditation and those organizations who achieve accreditation with commendation ensure their acceptance into the ranks of the best health care providers within the country.[4]

TECHNOLOGY SUPPORT

Today we have access to a wide world of data, made possible by technology that is present in most homes and offices. How we utilize these data and design our technological support is up to us. If we want on-line access with our physician and other referral sources it is possible.

Organizational communications to the central access center will either be through the field staff's laptop, on-line, e-mail capability or by a telemedicine/telemetry approach. The use of telemetry is described in more detail later in this chapter.

All field staff will have cellular phones with voice mail access and laptop computers equipped with modems for sending and receiving e-mail. Referrals will come into the central access center via direct telephone contact, voice mail, e-mail, or on-line interoffice telemetry capabilities. Organizations within a health care system or network of care will interface through a local area information system network. The receiving organizations can download the referral information regarding the patient into their information systems, providing both efficiency and accuracy to the referral process. The utilization of a central access center provides the admitting organization with more comprehensive, complete, accurate, and current information than presently exists between organizations.

Physician offices will also have the opportunity to participate in this local area information network. This will allow the home health agency to fax directly from its computers to these offices through the use of modems.

The issue of confidentiality of patient information takes on ever-increasing importance in this new world of electronic information exchange and will be the subject of many risk management and liability discussions.

REGIONALIZING SERVICE OFFERINGS

With increasing amounts of managed care infiltration within our communities and negotiated preferred provider contracts, the independent home health agency will form home health coalitions for the express purpose of maintaining a competitive advantage in the managed care reimbursement arena.

State home health associations are currently in the best position to encourage collaboration of their members in negotiation of managed care contracts within the state. Regions, as currently delineated by the National Association of Home Care, can lead the way in the development of regional collaborative groups of home care providers.

These collaborative groups of home care providers will need to develop significant internal commonalties in order to provide consistent services to the managed care company's enrollees. Examples of areas in which commonalties of process will need to be developed include

1. definition of service parameters covered by the contract
2. establishment of fees for each service defined and included
3. skill level, competence, and proficiency of staff
4. utilization patterns
5. standards of care
6. variance tracking systems
7. customer satisfaction surveys
8. intake and referral process
9. interagency communication exchange
10. others, as designated by the managed care contract

EXPANSION OF IN-HOME SERVICES

In the world of capitation, maintenance of the level of wellness of the insured group takes on an increasing importance. This means that a renewed emphasis will be placed on patient and caregiver education and compliance with care. Verification of understanding and reinforcement of positive behaviors will become a routine part of service delivery. Prenatal care, well-baby care, and immunizations also take on increasing importance in this new reimbursement world of capitation.

The 80/20 rule (i.e., that 80 percent of the profits are derived from 20 percent of the efforts), might well apply here.[5] It is important that the new programs initiated begin to provide some of the 80 percent of the profits intended above. In the total day-to-day of home care many of the activities will not generate large profits, so choose those new services wisely and develop realistic operational budgets so that they can be successful. Blood pressure and laboratory screenings will be made available to the "healthy" enrollees covered by the capitation agreements so they maintain or improve their level of health and their level of independence. In addition to laboratory and blood pressure screenings and radiology testing, self examinations (such as breast and testicular) will be taught and screened for on a regular basis.

The wise regional coalition that is successful in the negotiations for managed care contracts will not only negotiate on a per enrollee fixed fee for provision of in-home intermittent care services, but in the vein of entrepreneurial thinking, will negotiate rates for related services. These aforementioned preventive and wellness services can be negotiated for coverage, as well as companion and homemaker services if in fact the total cost to remain within the home is less than in a skilled nursing facility or personal care home. The managed care insurer seeks to decrease the overall expenses for health care provision and these types of services can create a healthier individual and a healthier and safer environment, thus decreasing the rate of utilization among the enrollee group. This in turn decreases the utilization of the more traditional in-home skilled health care services. As these services decrease, the new service areas can draw upon the existing available staff within the organization rather than hiring or contracting for additional staff.

ADVANCEMENTS IN TREATMENT TECHNOLOGY

Advances in treatment technology will be many and will have far-reaching effects on the home care business. One example of new standards of practice emerging today that will drastically affect home care's future is transcutaneous phlebotomy. In today's home health care world, many visits are made for phlebotomy services for the procurement of blood specimens. These specimens are then transported by the nurses to a laboratory for analysis. Reports are provided to the home care agency and the physician with orders revised appropriately.

The ability for phlebotomy procedures to be performed transcutaneously rather than by venous puncture access will affect not only the procedure, but potentially the level of employee necessary to obtain the blood specimens. This change in technology and procedure will have far-reaching effects on home care. The transcutaneous access to the venous circulation will also affect the manner in which home infusion therapy services will be provided. Many of the current procedures for access and infusion into the venous system will become antiquated and obsolete. It will be important to be aware of these and other changes in treatment technology in order to redesign proactively and lead the way in new treatment technology.

This is but one example of advancement in clinical practice and technology that will be affecting home care practice in the near future. Will home care be ready for this change? How will the reporting of laboratory results be handled when robots are performing the testing within the laboratory setting? Perhaps we will be provided with identification codes to access the robot's memory banks and procure the results for ourselves. The possibilities are endless.

Will home care be ready for the multitude of changes that are right around the bend? Only the leaders of home care today can assure home care's readiness tomorrow.

TELEMETRY SCREENING AND ASSESSMENT

What will the future role of home care be in the utilization of telemetry systems? This author's experiences with telemonitoring date back as far as the mid-1980s when home care clients were provided a response system monitored by a control center within the emergency department of the hospital. These were sometimes called a "lifeline." This device, which stayed on the individual, sent a signal to the control center when activated. A telephone call was made and/or an ambulance was sent. Today, 10 prisons in Wisconsin are linked to the University of Wisconsin via a video camera and monitoring system. This project has been funded by a grant in order to decrease the costs of transportation, security, and health care for more than 450 inmates who need treatment monthly. The level of care varied from physical exams to radiology transmissions. With the use of telephone lines for transmission, the cost of the system is more economical. Plans are underway to test ophthalmolic and otoscopic transmissions in the near future.[6]

Today monitoring devices are also available to monitor vital signs, check blood pressure readings, record the pulse or temperature, time and monitor uterine contractions, and check blood glucose levels. Transmission of these monitored and recorded data can be made by either telephone line or by direct satellite transmission.[7]

How will these capabilities be enhanced and expanded in future years? As a student at West Virginia University, I had the opportunity to participate in satellite closed conferences and classroom lectures while remaining at my own work site approximately 60 miles away. Today my co-author has the opportunity to enroll in classes across the Worldwide Web of communications via the Internet. Tomorrow, perhaps holographs of the professors will appear right in our own front room. If we can provide these types of transmissions (i.e., video conferences, classroom lectures over satellite services), is there any reason why we cannot offer these same video transmission capabilities to our patients? This would allow the home health agency to provide group transmission of patient and caregiver education sessions to a group of selected patients via this satellite transmission.

The session could be offered at times convenient to the caregivers and families with a call-in time for questions and answers. This would certainly enhance the productivity of the professional staff. This too will become the accepted manner of providing home health aide inservices and professional staff continuing education.

Crampton et al., of Health Tech Services Corporation, outline and describe in their article "Home Telemedicine, Home Health Agency Strategy for Maximizing Resources," the availability of the following information transmission types. There are five types of information, three types that are patient-specific data and two types of information transmission described that address the capability to transmit audio and video images via home telemonitoring systems.[8] These three types of patient data include vital sign monitoring, personal emergency status, and a monitoring of a single physical indicator, such as blood glucose. The two other related uses of information transmission, besides video conferencing, are medication reminding and voice-activated computer aids to assist the individuals within the home setting to lead a more independent life style.[9]

In addition to the use of the telephone lines and satellite transmission, Crampton et al. list several alternative transmission services. These include an integrated services digital network transmission, cellular transmission, and fiber optic network transmissions.[10] These transmission and monitoring capabilities are only the "tip of the iceberg." As with computers, once the breakthrough technology becomes readily available at an affordable cost, the capabilities and the applications will grow by leaps and bounds. This, too, will be the case with the field of electronic transmission and monitoring. As the usage becomes more commonplace, the technology will progress rapidly along paths we can only imagine today.

The central access control center recommended earlier in the chapter becomes the natural choice for the location of the home health agency's central monitoring control rooms. This central access room will be staffed 24 hours a day, 7 days a week by trained technicians adept at recognizing data variations being received via electronic transmission.

The home care organization must evaluate the expense of acquiring the capital equipment necessary for both the in-home transmission and access control center's reception of data transmission. Staffing expenses in the form of recruitment, training, salary, and benefits also contribute to the total cost versus benefit analysis of the initiation of home telemonitoring capability.

While retrospective home care reimbursement remains in effect, the visionary home care agency will be actively investigating these opportunities. During this time some of the expense incurred can potentially be allocated to the Medicare costs through the cost reporting process.

SHELTERED/SECURED COMMUNITIES

Recently in Pennsylvania, a planned community development was marketed to potential residents on the basis of security and service availability. Within these walled cities, which are of artistic and European design, the plans are to restrict access and in so doing keep out criminal elements, providing peace of mind and a sense of security to their residents. In addition, this planned community will also feature service amenities, such as a fitness center and hair salons and handicraft, fine art, and antique and collectable shops. Also planned are some basic amenities, such as a small drug store and convenience center. There will be controlled delivery access to the community by outside pharmacies, grocery stores, and meal delivery services.

The community residents, as a group, will have the opportunity to determine what additional services will be developed within the community and what, if any, additional delivery access will be granted. The community will recruit and hire employees for its own security staff to patrol and limit access to the community. Will there also be a visitor registration center for admittance of visitors? If so, this would need to be open 24 hours a day, seven days a week with anticipated listing of visitors provided to the center by the community residents.

A self-governance resident council will be elected to preside at meetings with all of the residents having the opportunity to contribute items to the meeting agendas and the responsibility to take an active part in the decision-making process.

In keeping with security concern of this planned self-contained community, will visionary home care leaders approach the community themselves to negotiate for the opportunity to be selected as the community's preferred home care provider for intermittent and private duty services?

Farther along in the development process, as the residents age and encounter declining health, the entrepreneurial home health care leader can further negotiate for a management contract for an adult day care center and/or the provision of in-home hospice services.

Look around you. Are the community developers planning such facilities near you? Are business opportunities for your home health agency being developed "right next door?"

CONCLUSION

Many believe that future reengineering projects will be focused on computer-based clinical information transmission across the technology superhighway, community building, and health care integration and access across the continuum of care.[11] Has the reengineering of your organization better prepared you for your place in this future? And what is in your home health agency's future? Is it a central access center to provide intake, referral, and physician liaison coordination? Is it a 24-hour-a-day telemetry central access center? Will your adult day care center become the hub of your home health agency? What new services will your home health agency provide in the year 2000?

We propose that the crystal ball will show that home care becomes the center, the hub for all health care services. Home care will be involved in the integrated care delivery networks at both ends of the acute care process (i.e., pre- and post-admission). In the future, home care will become the cost-effective clinical alternative to inpatient care days. In so doing, home care will be given a more active role in preadmission assessments and preoperative teaching for purpose of decreasing inpatient acute care costs. Home care will be welcomed into the collaborative care networks and with the welcome will come requests for ever-increasing high-tech support and intensive/acute care provision within the home environment. Can we still remember that not too long ago, ventilator supported care was only provided in an inpatient setting? Now ventilator-dependent individuals are routinely cared for within the home. What year do you, as a home care leader, predict will be the year that open heart surgery is done in an ambulatory care surgi-center with the patient returning home with monitoring and follow-up care?

As we reengineer/restructure our home health care organizations, we must always keep an eye looking outward to the community, the region, and the country. The reengineering changes made must be those that will support our organization's internal needs, as well as the changing external environment and health care delivery itself.

As visionaries and entrepreneurs, we would suggest that we adopt as our motto not only to "seize the day," but also to "secure the future!" By doing so we are able to see beyond the day-to-day operational needs and the crises encountered through the tunnel of today into the world beyond. Do not lose your creativity nor your curiosity, but rather nurture and encourage these qualities. It will be these qualities in combination with constant vigilance for potential opportunities that will allow us to lead our organizations through today's home health care into tomorrow's expanded home care arena. This arena will provide challenges and opportunities to each of us, if we have readied our organizations and ourselves.

NOTES

1. J.R. Smith and P. Shiner, Transforming Nursing Practice: Acute Care to Community. *Home Health Care Management and Practice* 8, no. 6 (August 1996).

2. Crafting Care Centers, *Hospitals and Health Networks* 69, no. 22 (1995): 88.
3. H. Deets, Home Care in the 21st Century, *Caring Magazine* 14, no. 9 (1995): 50.
4. L. Campbell, Revolutionary Leadership, *Outreach* 16, no. 6 (1995): p. 1.
5. Campbell, Revolutionary Leadership, 4.
6. A Prison Plugs In, *Hospitals and Health Networks* 69, no. 21 (1995): 56.
7. K. Crampton, et al. Home Telemedicine, Home Health Agency Strategy for Maximizing Resources, *Home Health Care Management and Practice* 8, no. 4 (June 1996): 1–9.
8. K. Crampton et al., Home Telemedicine, p. 2.
9. K. Crampton et al, Home Telemedicine, p. 2.
10. K. Crampton et al., Home Telemedicine, p. 3
11. T. O'Grady, Creating a New System of Health Care, in Reengineering Nursing and Health Care, ed. S. Blancett and D.L. Flarey (Gaithersburg, Md.: Aspen Publishers, Inc., 1995), 412.

Appendix A

Abbreviations

ABC—Activity Based Costing
APG—Ambulatory Patient Group
APTA—American Physical Therapy Association
AT&T—American Telephone and Telegraph

CEO—Chief Executive Officer
CHAP—Community Health Accreditation Program
COR—Comprehensive Outpatient Rehabilitation
CPI—Consumer Price Index
CPM—Continuous Passive Motion
CQI—Continuous Quality Improvement

DOH—Department of Health
DRG—Diagnosis-Related Group

FADE—Focus, Analyze, Develop, and Execute
FOCUS PDCA—Find, Organize, Clarify, Understand, Select, Plan, Do, Check, and Act
FTE—Full-Time Equivalents

HCFA—Health Care Financing Administration
HEDIS—Healthplan Employer Data and Information Set
HHA—Home Health Agency
HHCAA—Hospital Home Care Association of America
HIM 11—Health Insurance Manual—Section 11
HMO—Health Maintenance Organization
HR—Human Resource

IDN—Integrated Delivery Network

JCAHO—Joint Commission on Accreditation of Healthcare Organizations (usually referred to as the Joint Commission, formerly known as JCAH—Joint Commission on Accreditation of Hospitals)

LPN—Licensed Practical Nurse

MIS—Management Information System
MSW—Medical Social Worker

NAHC—National Association of Home Care
NCQA—National Committee for Quality Assurance
NLN—National League of Nursing

OSHA—Occupational Safety and Health Administration
OT—Occupational Therapist

PAB—Professional Advisory Board
PAC—Professional Advisory Committee
PCG—Personal Communications Group
PHO—Physician-Hospital Organization
POS—Point of Service
PPO—Preferred Provider Organization
PPS—Prospective Payment System
PT—Physical Therapist

RN—Registered Nurse

SCORE—Senior Council of Retired Executives
ST—Speech Therapist
SLP—Speech Language Pathologist
SWOT—Strengths, Weaknesses, Opportunities, and Threats

TENS—Transcutaneous Electrical Nerve Stimulation
TQM—Total Quality Management

VNA—Visiting Nurse Association

Bibliography

A Prison Plugs In. 1995 (5 November). *Hospitals and Health Networks* 69(21):56–57.

American Hospital Association. 1995. *Restructuring Health Care Delivery—Legal and Common Terms* (AHA: Chicago, IL).

Allen, R. Divide and Prosper. *AT&T Shareowners Report, 3rd quarter* (New York, NY: AT&T).

Araoz, D. and W. Sutton. 1994. *Reengineering Yourself* (Holbrook, MA: Bob Adams Inc.).

Basset, L.C. and N. Metzger. 1986. *Achieving Excellence* (Gaithersburg, MD: Aspen Publishers).

Belasco, J. 1991. *Teaching the Elephant to Dance, A Manager's Guide to Empowering Change* (New York, NY: Crown Publishers).

Bennett, G. 1994. Aim, Discover, Deploy, Plan. Corporate Reengineering: Strategies for Growth. *The Conference Board.* Report no. 1097-94-CH: 13–14.

Bittel, L.R. 1989. *The McGraw-Hill 36-Hour Management Course* (New York, NY: McGraw-Hill Publishers).

Black, H. 1979. *Black's Law Dictionary.* 5th edition. St. Paul: MN West Publishing Co.

Blancett, S. and D.L. Flarey. 1995. *Reengineering Nursing and Health Care* (Gaithersburg, MD: Aspen Publishers).

Bolman, L.G. and T.E. Deal. 1991. *Reframing Organizations: Artistry, Choice and Leadership* (San Francisco: Jossey-Bass Inc. Publishers).

Bower, J. 1986. *When Markets Quake. The Management Challenge of Restructuring Industry* (Boston, MA: Harvard Business School Press).

Brassard, M. and D. Ritter. 1994. *The Memory Jogger II.* (Methuen, MA: Goal/QPC).

Brite, H. 1994. Reengineering the Hierarchy. Corporate Reengineering: Strategies for Growth. *The Conference Board.* Report no. 1097-94-CH: 15-16.

Campbell, L. 1995. Initiating Change to Achieve Vision. *Outreach* 16(6) 1–4.

Champy, J. 1995. *Reengineering Management* (New York, NY: HarperCollins).

Clark, J. and R. Koonce. 1995, August. Engaging Organizational Survivors. *Training and Development*: 23-30.

Clarkson, I. Beyond Hospital Walls: Restructuring for the Future. *Leadership* 2(6) 12–14.

Coddington, D., et al. 1994, March/April. In Pursuit of Integration. *Healthcare Forum Journal:* 53–59.

Covey, S. 1990. *The Seven Habits of Highly Effective People* (New York, NY: Simon and Schuster).

Crafting Care Centers. 1995. *Hospital and Health Networks* 20(22): 88–90.

Crampton, K., et al. 1996. Home Telemedicine, Home Health Agency Strategy for Maximizing Resources. *Home Health Care Management And Practice* 8(4).

Crego, E.T. Jr. and P.D. Schiffrin. 1995. *Customer-Centered Reengineering* (Burr Ridge, IL: Irwin Professional Publishing).

Curren, C. 1995, August. Developing Integrated Delivery Networks. Presented at The American College of Healthcare Executives. Williamsburg, VA.

Deets, H. 1995, September. Home Care in the 21st Century. *Caring Magazine* XIV(9): 50–52.

Dent, H. 1994. Beyond Survival. Corporate Reengineering: Strategies for Growth. *The Conference Board.* Report no. 1097-94-CH: 11–12.

Donovan, R. 1995. Manufacturers Question Reengineering Need. *Central Penn Business Journal* 11(31): 16–17.

Florida Hospital Association. 1994, May. *Innovative Benchmarking: A Practical Approach to Improving Productivity* (Orlando, FL: Florida Hospital Association Task Force).

Furrey, T. 1994. Finding the Right Reengineering Process. Corporate Reengineering: Strategies for Growth. *The Conference Board.* Report no. 1097-94-CH: 19–20.

Gingerich, B.S. 1996. Home Health Care Reengineered. *Home Health Care Management and Practice* 8(2): 1–5.

Gingerich, B.S and D. Ondeck. 1995. *Clinical Pathways for the Multidisciplinary Home Health Care Team* (Gaithersburg, MD: Aspen Publishers, Inc.).

Gingerich, B.S. and D. Ondeck. 1995. *Home Health Job Descriptions and Performance Appraisals* (York, PA: ADVANTAGE Health Care Management Resources Press).

Goldsmith, N. 1994. Downsizing Is Not Reengineering. Corporate Reengineering: Strategies for Growth. *The Conference Board.* Report no.1097-94-CH: 22–24.

Gouillart, F. 1994. What Ails Reengineering Efforts. Corporate Reengineering: Strategies for Growth. *The Conference Board.* Report no. 1097-94-CH: 21–22.

Green, R. 1990, July/August. Medical Joint Venturing—An Ethical Perspective. *Hastings Center Report.*

Gregory. C. 1995. Creating a Vision for a Nursing Unit. *Nursing Management* 26(1): 38–42.

Griffith, J.R. 1992. *The Well Managed Community Hospital,* 2nd ed. (Ann Arbor, MI: Health Administration Press).

Group Health Association of America. 1994. *National Directory of HMOs Database.*

Hammer, M. and J. Champy. 1993. *Reengineering the Corporation.* (New York, NY: HarperCollins).

Hayden, C. 1986. *The Handbook of Strategic Expertise.* (New York, NY: The Free Press).

Health Care Finance Administration. 1988. *Medicare Home Health Agency HIM-11* (Washington DC: Government Printing Office).

Hospital Home Care Association of America. 1995, July. *Efforts to Block Bundling in the House Meet with Success.* Special Bulletin, No. 2: 1–7.

How Markets Evolve. 1995. *Hospital and Health Networks* 69(9): 48.

Hudson, T. 1994. Serious Sleuthing. *Hospital and Health Networks* 69(23): 40–44.

Islom, G. 1994. Creating Vision at CIGNA. Corporate Reengineering: Strategies for Growth. *The Conference Board.* Report no. 1097-94-CH: 9–10.

Is There Life After Acute Care? 1995. *Hospital and Health Networks* 69(24): 88.

Jennings, M. and S. O'Leary. 1994. The role of managed care in integrated delivery networks. *Journal of Ambulatory Care Management* 17(1): 39–47.

Jick, T. 1995. Accelerating Change for Competitive Advantage. *Organizational Dynamics* 24(1): 77–82.

Joint Commission on Accreditation of Healthcare Organizations. 1995. *1995 Accreditation Manual for Home Care. Volume II. Scoring Guidelines.* Joint Commission on Accreditation of Healthcare Organizations: Oakbrook Terrace, IL.

Joint Commission on Accreditation of Healthcare Organizations. 1993. *Process Improvement Models: Case Studies in Health Care* (Oakbrook Terrace, IL: The Joint Commission on Accreditation of Healthcare Organizations).

Joint Commission on Accreditation of Healthcare Organizations. 1993. *The Measurement Mandate* (Oakbrook Terrace, IL: The Joint Commission on Accreditation of Healthcare Organizations).

Karst, P. 1994, January-February. Is Integrated Delivery Healthcare's Breakpoint? *Health Progress:* 7–9.

Katzenbach, J.R. and D.K. Smith. 1993. *The Wisdom of Teams* (New York, NY: Harper Business Publishers).

Lifescience. 1995. (Westerville, OH: Glencoe/McGraw Hill).

Lumsdon, K. 1995. Mean Streets. *Hospital and Health Networks* 69(19) 44–52.

Lumsdon, K. 1995. Piecing The Puzzle Together. *Hospital and Health Networks* 69(23) 52.

Marsh, G., et al. 1995. Operations improvement and reengineering at Ohio State University Medical Center. *Topics in Health Information Management* 16(1): 41–46.

Maturen, V. and K. Zander. 1993, June. Outcomes Management in a Prospective Pay System. *Caring Magazine:* 46–52.

McKeon, T. 1995. *Home Health Fiscal Management* (Gaithersburg, MD: Aspen Publishers).

McKeon, T. 1995. Activity Based Cost Management: A Tool for Survival. *Journal of Home Health Care Practice* 7(4): 69–75.

Metzger, M., et al. 1995. *Business Law and the Regulatory Environment, Concepts and Cases.* 9th ed. (Homewood, IL: Richard D. Irwin, Inc.).

Moran, J.W. Jr. 1995, September. Breakthrough Thinking. *Journal for Quality and Participation:* 46–51.

Murphy, R. 1994. Work Reengineering: The Benefits and the Barriers, An Analytical Review. *Journal of the Society of Health Systems* 5(1): 73–84.

Nackel, J. 1994. Breakthrough Delivery Systems: Applying Business Process Innovation. *Journal of the Society of Health Systems* 5(1): 11–21.

NAHC Report. August 18,1995. II. *Prospective Payment.* No. 625b: 4–7.

National Committee for Quality Assurance. 1995. HEDIS Executive Summary (Washington, DC).

National League for Health Care, Inc., and Nursing. Community Health Accreditation Program, Inc., 1993. *Standards of Excellence for Home Care Organizations;* New York, NY.

New NCQA Survey Has Health Status Data. 1995. *Accountability News for Health Care Managers* 2(14): 1–2.

Noone, C., et al. 1995. Computerized Documentation in Home Health. *Journal of Nursing Administration* 25(1): 67–69.

Ondeck, D. 1996. Improving Organizational Performance. Credentialling Corner. *Home Health Care Management and Practice* 8(3): 91–95.

Presner, L. 1991. *The International Business Dictionary and Reference* (New York, NY: John Wiley and Sons, Inc.).

Roberts, L. 1994. *Process Reengineering: The Key to Achieving Breakthrough Success* (Milwaukee, WI: ASQC Press).

Scholtes, P., et al. 1991.*The Team Handbook—How To Use Teams To Improve Quality* (Madison, WI: Joiner Associates, Inc.).

Senge, P. 1990 *The Fifth Discipline: The Art and Practice of the Learning Organization* (New York, NY: Doubleday).

Shaffer, R. 1993, July. *Communications and Group Dynamics.* Educational session at the Joint Commission on Accreditation of Healthcare Organizations.

Shaughnessy, P., et al. 1994. *Medicare's Oasis: Standardized Outcome and Assessment Information Set for Home Health Care* (Denver, CO: National Association for Home Care, Center for Health Policy and Research).

Simione, W. 1995. Capitation. *Caring Magazine* XIV(6): 24–34.

Simpson, R. 1995. Reengineering: Embracing Technology To Improve Patient Care. *Nursing Management* 26(1): 33–34.

Smith, J.R. and P. Shiner. 1996, October. Transforming Nursing Practice: Acute Care to Community. *Home Health Care Management and Practice.*

Society of Ambulatory Care Professionals. 1995, October. *Trendlines.* No. C-079100. Chicago, IL.

Suh, Y. 1994, January. Genesys Health System—A Study in Integrated Delivery. *Health Care Strategic Management.*

Swendsen, K. and A. Barnett. 1994. Light at the End of the Tunnel—Corporate Reengineering: Strategies for Growth. *The Conference Board.* Report no. 1097-94-CH: 17–18.

Technology Targets Health Care. 1995. *Hospitals and Health Networks* 69(21): 56.

The Advisory Board Company. 1992. *Re-Engineering the Hospital. CEO Primer and Bottlenecks, Excess Cost, and Lost Revenue,* Washington, DC.

U.S. Department of Health and Human Services. 1993. *A Providers Guide to the Home Health Certification Process* (Rockville, MD: Government Printing Office).

Vance, M. and D. Deacon. 1995. *Think Out of the Box* (Franklin Lakes, NJ: Career Press).

Walsh, A. 1995, December 11. *Tolmie Follows Prescription for St. Joseph's Success.* Intelligence: 8–9.

Webster's New Twentieth Century Unabridged Dictionary. 1951. (Cleveland, Ohio: World Publishing Company).

What Managed Care Companies Want and Expect from Home Care. 1995, October. Presentation at National Association for Home Care. Northampton, MA: Fazzi Associates.

Youngblood, M. 1994. What You Still Need To Know. Corporate Reengineering: Strategies for Growth. *The Conference Board.* Report no. 1097-94-CH: 25–26.

Index

Note: Page numbers in *Italics* represent material found in tables, exhibits, and figures.

O

9 780834 207813

Printed in Dunstable, United Kingdom

88190708R00159